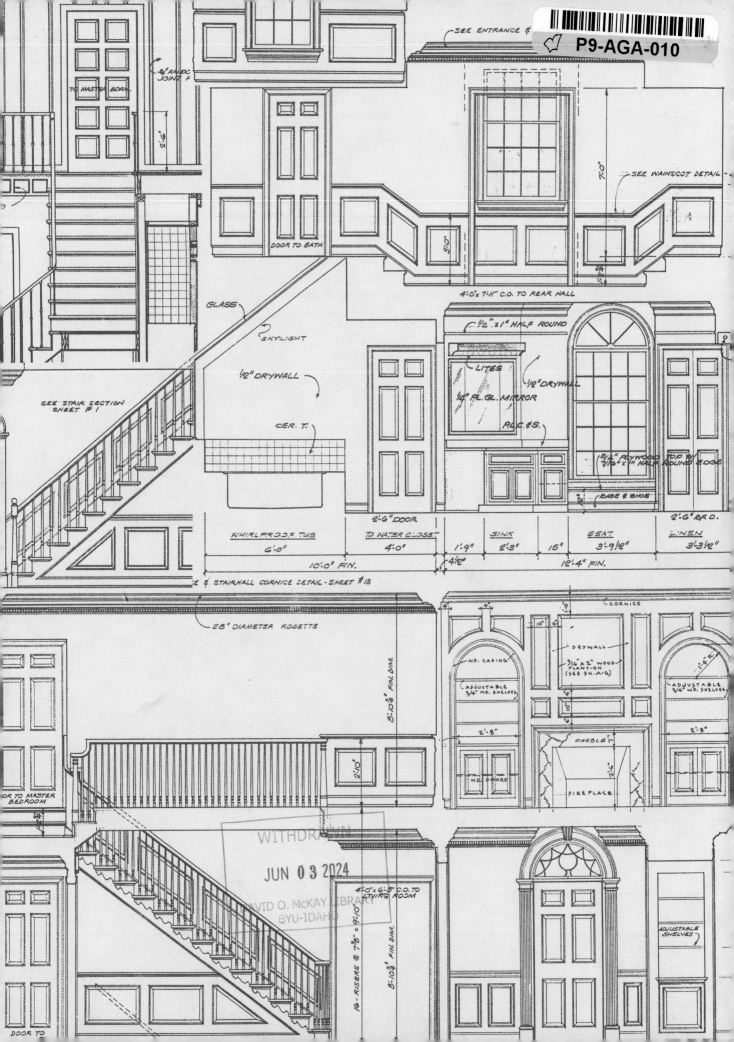

P9-AGA-010

WITHDRAWN

JUN 0 3 2024

DAVID O. McKAY LIBRARY
BYU-IDAHO

New England SAMPLER

A Treasury of Home Plans & Decorating Ideas from Colonial America

264 Plans • 200 Interiors

HOME PLANNERS, INC.

DESIGNED AND PRODUCED BY HOME PLANNERS, INC.
Charles W. Talcott, Executive Editor
Beth Nickey, Copy Editor
Paul Fitzgerald, Book Designer

Published by Home Planners, Inc.
Editorial and Corporate Offices:
3275 W. Ina Road, Suite 110
Tucson, Arizona 85741

Distribution Center:
29333 Lorie Lane
Wixom, Michigan 48393

Charles W. Talcott, Chairman
Rickard D. Bailey, President and Publisher
Cindy J. Coatsworth, Publications Manager

First Printing, September 1993
10   9   8   7   6   5   4   3   2   1

All text, designs and illustrative material copyright © 1993 by
Home Planners, Inc., Tucson, Arizona 85741. All rights reserved. No
part of this publication may be reproduced in any form or by any
means—electronic, mechanical, photomechanical, recorded or
otherwise—without the written permission of the publisher.

Printed in the United States of America

Library of Congress Catalog Card Number 93-78539

Softcover ISBN: 1-881955-08-7
Hardcover ISBN: 1-881955-09-5

On the Cover:
Our interpretation of the cover home, Design Y2188, can be found on page 195.
Back Cover
Top: An adaptation of Design Y2399, shown on page 90.
Bottom Right: A Colonial home similar to our Design Y1900, shown on page 78.

Photo Credits
Front: Michael Philip Manheim/Photo Network.
Back: E.J. Cyr/Cyr Agency.
Pages 22-23: Carolyn Ross
Pages 76-77: E.J. Cyr/Cyr Agency
Pages 118-119: © 1993 John Blake/Picture Perfect USA
Pages 172-173: Kenneth Cyr/Cyr Agency
Pages 212-213: © 1993 Allan Montaine/Picture Perfect USA
Pages 294-295: Donna Cyr/Cyr Agency

TABLE OF CONTENTS

A Chronology of Colonial Architecture

The chart below represents regions of early America (vertical divisions) and the predominant styles that were found in these regions (horizontal divisions). This period of American architecture clearly reflects climate variables, available building materials and building technologies of the various regions. However, the inherent charm of these houses is evident in their tendency to echo the ethnic traditions of those who built and lived in them.

It should be noted that while definitive terms are applied to styles and periods, architecture knows no stringent boundaries of time or form. Characteristics of certain styles overlap and repeat in thousands of variations and often adaptations occur, taking the finest points of earlier styles. Many cherished styles can also appear in several time periods. For instance, it is not unusual to find Georgian-style homes that were built during what is generally referred to as the Federal period.

A fine modern collection of historic and heritage adaptations can be found in the style sections beginning on page 22.

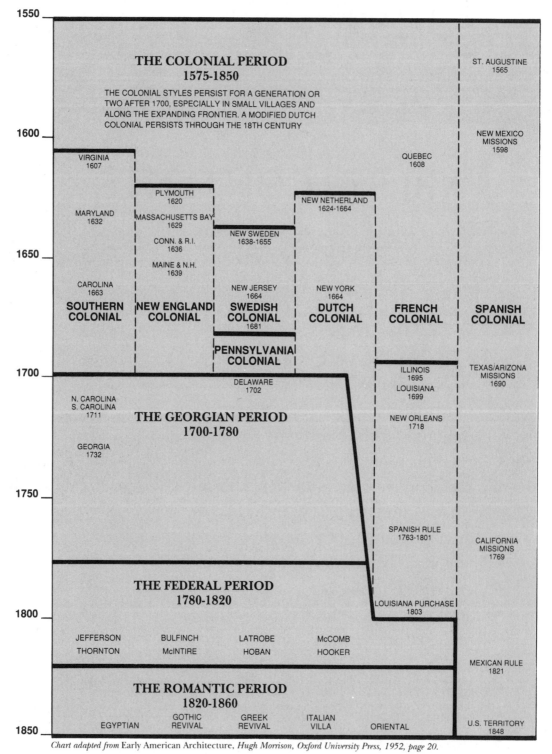

Chart adapted from Early American Architecture, *Hugh Morrison, Oxford University Press, 1952, page 20.*

17th-Century Houses

The Colonial houses of the 17th Century are noted for an unpretentious simplicity of design. Evolving from Medieval roots, these houses combine clean vertical lines, simple fenestration (often with dormer windows), steeply pitched or gambrel roofs, massive chimneys and sometimes an overhung second story.

1640—Micum McIntyre House
Scotland, ME page 88

1645—John Clark House
Farmington, CT page 80

1652—Thomas Rolfe House
Jamestown, VA page 232

1660—George Hyland House
Guilford, CT page 89

1663—John Quincy Adams House
Quincy, MA page 90

1675—Jonathan Corwin House
Salem, MA page 85

1676—Paul Revere House
Boston, MA page 87

1682—Parson Capen House
Topsfield, MA page 84

1690—Shield House
Yorktown, VA page 271

The Cape Cod House

can be found in three recognizable types: The half house with two windows to one side of the front door; the three-quarter Cape with two windows to one side of the door and one to the other side; the full Cape with a center door flanked by two windows on each side.

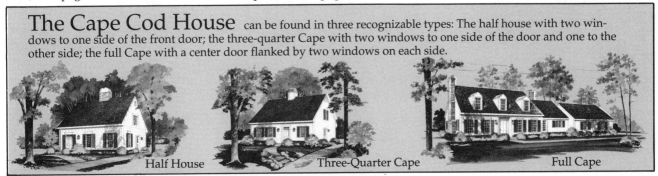

Half House   Three-Quarter Cape   Full Cape

18th-Century Houses

Georgian homes, which characterize the 18th Century, are representations of a newly emerging wealth in American society. Perfect symmetry and ornate details are joined by such features as hipped and gambrel roofs, central porticos with elaborate columns, Palladian windows, huge chimneys (often in flanking pairs) and decorative items such as dentils and quoins.

1706—West House
Yorktown, VA page 235

1715—Anne Bradstreet House
Andover, MA page 192

1717—Brush-Everard House
Williamsburg, VA page 231

18th-Century Houses (continued)

1730—John Paul Jones House
Portsmouth, NH page 181

1730—Phillip Lightfoot House
Williamsburg, VA

1739—Mission House
Stockbridge, MA page 174

1743—Mount Vernon
Mount Vernon, VA page 240

1745—Tulip Hill
Anne Arundel County, MD page 214

1748—Thomas Bannister House
Podunk, MA page 78

1750—Nathaniel Hawthorne House
Salem, MA page 82

1750—Single House
Charleston, SC page 261

1750—Robert Nicolson House
Williamsburg, VA

1752—Pottsgrove
Pottstown, PA page 140

1752—Joseph Atwood House
Chatham, MA page 45

1752—Joseph Webb House
Wethersfield, CT page 193

1755—Gunston Hall
Lorton, VA page 234

1755—Old Poole Cottage
Rockport, MA page 28

1758—Valley Forge
Valley Forge, PA page 142

1760—Lady Pepperrell House
Kittery Pointe, ME page 189

1763—John Allen House
Nantucket, MA page 42

1765—Whitehall
Anne Arundel County, MD page 257

18th-Century Houses (continued)

1770—Nathaniel Greene House
Anthony, RI page 178

1776—Pieter Lefferts House
Brooklyn, NY page 132

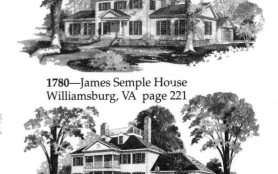

1780—James Semple House
Williamsburg, VA page 221

1781—Solomon Cowles House
Farmington, CT page 183

1790—Roberts-Vaughan House
Murfreesboro, NC page 244

1790—Julia Wood House
Falmouth, MA page 191

1791—George Read II House
New Castle, DE page 226

1794—Alexander Field House
Longmeadow, MA page 190

1799—William Gibbes House
Charleston, SC page 238

19th-Century Houses

By the late 1770s, new architectural styles began to emerge. The Federals were the essence of sophistication and dignity, borrowing much from the detailing of Georgian styles. One important introduction was the "Federal doorway"—featuring sidelights and a fanlight. The Romantic styles were highlighted by large porticos and usually featured a classic temple form with stately columns.

1800—Rose Hill
Lexington, KY page 249

1800—John Jay House
Katonah, NY page 120

1805—Jacob Martin House
Lancaster, PA page 124

1807—Dean Barstow House
Massachusetts page 177

1810—Shotgun House
New Orleans, LA page 274

1818—Richard Vreeland House
Nordhoff, NJ page 130

1820—Belle Mina
Belle Mina, AL

1820—Alexander Bunker House
Nantucket, MA page 43

1835—Asphodel
Jackson, LA page 269

GUIDE TO NEW ENGLAND ARCHITECTURE

Design Y2101 p. 84

1. English Medieval House with Overhang

This design recalls the Medieval manse built by the Rev. Joseph Capen, who became the minister of the church in Topsfield, Massachusetts in 1682. It is typical of houses of 17th-Century English colonists. Snug Garrison-style dwellings commonly featured a prominent second-floor overhang, a feature of English houses in the Middle Ages. The overhang provided rain protection to the wattling and timbers on the floor and customers of Elizabethan townhouse shops. The Parson Capen manse featured second-floor bracketed overhangs on the front elevation, third-floor overhang on gable end, heavy carved pendant drops at corners, a huge, pilastered center chimney and a cedar-shake roof.

Our English Roots

Immigrants brought their European home-building ideas with them to the new world, where the accent of their architecture stayed with them. Most early settlers emigrated from England, France and the Germanic states. Consequently, most early New England homes resemble building styles from these mother countries.

English styles today vary from the simple Cotswold cottage to the lavish Elizabethan. These sub-styles, plus multi-gabled Tudors and classic box-form Georgians, actually have much in common. Most English homes have high-pitch roofs, large chimneys, light leaded windows and masonry siding.

Early English settlers here built familiar, simple houses of saddle-notched, whole logs laid horizontally. (That's true also of many German, Finnish and Scandinavian settlers.) The typical English house was half-timbered with wooden exposed framework and wall spaces filled with brick nogging or a mixture of mud, clay and plaster.

Soon new kilns enabled brickmaking in Jamestown and Plymouth. Brick was used mainly in fireplaces and chimneys. Softer brick was used as nogging behind clapboard or outside walls. Brick was used for entire construction only when plentiful. It was also used as a new filler in timber frames or else set in decorative patterns.

The Tudor style (born during the House of Tudor reign) became popular in this country in the late 1880s. The

Elizabethan style, with its half-timbered, overhanging second floor, is only slightly less formal.

Of all English styles brought to this country, the Georgian style (born during the reign of four kings named George) became the most copied by the early 1770s. Houses based on this style later evolved into the Williamsburg and Southern Colonial styles.

Late Georgian (often called Early Federal) was the predominant style in America just after 1790.

The Clapboard House, popular in early Virginia, derives its name from the timber-frame structure that encases the building. The hall was the main living area of Medieval English cottages. Commonly, rooms flank a central chimney and a staircase that rises into two upstairs chambers.

In typical English construction, large stone buildings became the haven of wealthy landed gentry, while wooden homes became the lot of lesser personages. Today, stately English churches and some elegant stone homes remind Americans of this early class distinction.

Whether built of wood, brick or stone, most Early American dwellings reflect a common English heritage. Distinguishing characteristics include a single file of rooms, sharply angled gables, steep (sometimes thatched) roofs, tiny casement windows, lean-to additions and asymmetrical quaintness.

Most of the first settlers in New England were thrifty, hard-working English immigrants from middle-class backgrounds. Most came to the new world in quest of religious freedom more

Design Y2191 p. 85

2. A Tudor Translation

This version of a 1675 gabled Saltbox house in New England combines Medieval and Tudor styling. It is categorized as a Medieval Saltbox design because the roof line of the main house is carried low in the rear to cover an added lean-to. Tudor styling is apparent in the multiple-gabled roof lines. Cross gables are stepped out in a series of projecting over-hangs, common in early English houses. Double-leaded and triple-leaded casements are proportioned to set under overhangs. The massive pilastered chimney in the center also is typical of the period. The pictured design is a faithful adaptation of a house built by Jonathan Corwin of Salem, Massachusetts in 1675.

than wealth. A civil war in England in the mid-17th Century brought even more settlers from places like Norfolk, Suffolk, Essex, Cambridge, Toppesfield, Canterbury and Wickford. These names are familiar today to New Englanders, whose forefathers often renamed their new communities after their old.

The 17th-Century villages these settlers left behind were still entirely Medieval in architecture. Houses were predominantly timber-framed, with stone used sparingly on only the most expensive buildings. Brick was reserved for wealthy manors and churches in places like Kent, Suffolk and Essex. This is the Medieval world these English immigrants attempted to recreate and build upon in their new world.

Architects today still disagree on labels for design styles. Our illustrations, however, depict historic homes in renditions from the nation's most popular creator of home designs. These illustrations capture the flavor of New England. Blueprints are available for each design at a modest cost.

3. Typical Georgian Townhouse with Tudor Chimneys *Design Y2688 p. 271*

This design is based on Williamsburg's historic Red Lion House (1730). Its clipped gables and pyramidal chimneys are reminiscent of Tudor dwellings of the late 1600s. The symmetrical windows, bracketed cornices and classic porch are nonetheless 18th-Century Georgian. Planters in 18th-Century Virginia built grand brick townhouses in Williamsburg, Virginia. Early planters would leave their plantations to reside and conduct business in these substantial houses. Virginia was the wealthiest of the colonies in the 18th Century, and Williamsburg served as its capital from 1699 to 1799, a period when Georgian-style architecture flourished. Examples of this period architecture are still evident in modern Williamsburg and Yorktown.

Design Y2654 p. 92

4. Transitional Saltbox

The long, low, rear roofline that is characteristic of Saltbox houses resulted from the addition of a lean-to in the rear of an otherwise simple two-room or four-room Medieval house. This change created more room—one reason this age-old design remains popular today. The rear wing of Colonial Saltbox homes often enclosed a kitchen flanked by a bedroom and a pantry. Design Y2654 at left illustrates a transition from a simple, functional Saltbox to Georgian symmetry and refinement.

Design Y2320 p. 127

5. Typical Connecticut River Valley Gambrel Design

This rendition of typical early Connecticut design illustrates gambrel roofs in the colonies. The charming facade of our adaptation exhibits balance between narrow clapboard siding and a shingled roof punctuated by triple dormer windows.

Design Y2556 p. 181

6. New Hampshire Gambrel

Design Y2556 illustrates the adaptation by New England colonists of Georgian styling when it made its way north. This faithful interpretation of the historic John Paul Jones home in Portsmouth, New Hampshire features symmetrical windows capped by angular pediments, a classical doorway with segmental pediment and a two-light tran-som—all capped by a gambrel roof. This historic boarding house, built in 1730, housed the legendary Revolutionary War captain. Note the dual corbelled chimneys, typical of much Georgian architecture, and the dormers, typical of Late Georgian or Federal styling.

7. Southern Colonial Gable

This design is a good example of Southern Colonial architecture. The elegant pillared house with gable roof is typical of estates in the Deep South between 1820 and 1860. This antebellum manor includes the Greek temple-look that swept much of the old South during the Greek Revival in Early America. A portico with columns suggested that the owners were cultured and civilized by classical standards. In those days, the Greek temple became the highest architectural ideal for a generation of Americans.

Gambrel Roofs

The gambrel roof became popular soon after introduction in the colonies in the middle of the 17th Century. In fact, it soon became a prominent feature of New England homes. The roof is believed to be French in origin. The term "gambrel" likely comes from the early French term "gamberel" for crooked sticks used by butchers. The gambrel roof has double slopes on either side of the house. It has a sharp, upper slope of low pitch and a long, lower slope of steep pitch.

Soon Colonial homes sported gambrel roofs on cottages, stately houses and farms. They were fairly common on houses of Williamsburg, Virginia.

The gambrel roof enabled almost a full second story of floor space. The style was an improvement over space allowed by designs of 1½ stories.

A substyle of the Early American gambrel roof design is the Dutch Colonial, which came later in history. It probably wasn't truly Dutch in origin, and was more bell-shaped.

Gabled Houses

Gables, the triangular wall parts formed by the intersection of two roof surfaces, appear in many different forms in accordance with various styles of architecture. Overhanging gables are typical of 17th-Century England.

Tudors frequently feature at least one front-facing cross gable, and many have two or three. The gables are generally decorated with half-timbers and stucco. Victorian designers decorated gables even more elaborately, using spindle-work, patterned shingles, half-timbers, sculpted masonry and finials at the peak.

Design Y2668 p. 244

Cape Cod Cottages

The ever-popular Cape Cod Cottage finds its roots in Medieval England. American colonists adapted the hearty structure to New England where harsh winds swept over the low profile of these clapboard structures with little resistance. Their steeply pitched gable roofs also provided space for a children's garret under the ridge.

Original Colonial cottages from Sandwich to Provincetown were tiny with small rooms clustered around a chimney stack. They were cozy, warm and practical dwellings. Their charm persists today, particularly in New England.

The compactness of Cape Cod cottages maximized living space by minimizing hallways. Their rectangular shape was easily fabricated. The typical Cape Cod was a "half house," characterized by a simple central doorway with the basic Medieval English hall. That great hall could be a single large room, borning room and buttery. Stairs led up to a sleeping attic.

Variations of this basic half house were generally simple expansions of the design. The three-quarter Cape Cod added one room opposite the parlor and one extra front window. This was generally a downstairs bedroom that could be entered from the front vestibule or keeping room. Its fireplace was located off the central chimney, like others in the house.

The full Cape Cod house doubled the half house. It resembles the popular Cape Cod cottage that survives today. While 17th-Century Cape Cods had gabled roofs with central chimneys, some later variations included bowed roofs and two corner fireplaces off one chimney, like Design Y2644, opposite.

Design Y2682 p. 30

8. The Half House
A simple Cape Cod cottage.

9. Three-Quarter House
One extra room and window added.

Design Y2661 p. 24

10. Bowed Full-Size Cape
Double the size of the simple half house.

Design Y2644 p. 52

Dutch Heritage

The Dutch settled the Hudson River Valley, west end of Long Island and Northern New Jersey, and controlled it until 1664 as New Netherlands.

The early Dutch were traders. Dutch architecture in Early America shows craftsmanship and pride in tradition. The Dutch built occasionally with stone, but preferably with brick, which they prized.

The Dutch never built exterior chimneys, but employed stacks within walls—often double stacks. When Dutch masons and craftsmen entered the Georgian period, their ideas melded with prevalent English styling.

11. Double Dutch Chimneys

Design Y1858 p. 228

Double Georgian chimney stacks put heat in all four corners of this Georgian rendition for a fireplace in virtually every room.

Design Y2633 p. 124

12. A German Farmhouse

This is a Georgian with a German accent from Pennsylvania Dutch country. The comfortable Georgian farms arrived with English settlers. This illustration recalls the 1805 home of Johannes and Anne Hersche of Lancaster County. Hersche built this large house with a front porch using bricks

made from the area's rich clay soil. The home was considered extravagant by his Mennonite Church, whose members almost expelled him. Elsewhere in Lancaster County, the Dutch country displays many roofs steeply pitched in the German Medieval style.

13. Northeast Country Vernacular

This design, patterned after the Bedford, New York homestead of former Secretary of Foreign Affairs John Jay, typifies the farmhouse styling of much American Traditional architecture. Notice the use of slender columns, typical of Pennsylvania farm country, as well. The columns and railing form a comfortable farmhouse porch. John Jay was born in 1745 and inherited the site for his home from his father, a wealthy New York merchant of French Huguenot descent. The modest yet comfortable two-story house features shutters. An orderly symmetry of design has been maintained.

American Traditional

The traditional style most often identified as truly American in origin is the farmhouse. Traditional farmhouses are simple, livable designs, built of wood, with fireplaces, country kitchens and covered front porches. The typical two-story design provides a combination of rustic charm and family livability.

The German Legacy

German craftsmanship is evident in much Early American architecture, although German workmanship and exquisite detailing was meshed in the Georgian period into more prevalent English styles of design.

German and Dutch Mennonites arrived in Pennsylvania in 1683, and by the 18th Century, Pennsylvania had the largest population of German descent of any state. German styling in many Pennsylvania religious communities remains an architectural statement today.

Many of the Germans who emigrated to America were Quakers, Amish and Mennonites who kept old-world customs. This is apparent in many buildings in settlements throughout Pennsylvania. The German immigrants often built in stone and generally repeated the patterns of architecture most familiar to them back in the old country.

One of their settlements was the Quaker Germantown near Philadelphia (part of present Philadelphia). What perhaps moved German settlers outward was the climate in outlying Lancaster, Berks, York, Dauphin, Bucks and Lehigh Valley. The soil and dense forest may have reminded them of the old country. Back home, land had been scarce, and German farmers there lived in close-knit communities. They emigrated to America because of scarce land, harsh taxes and religious oppression. Here in America they found plenty of land and freedom, but the once-necessary concept of close communities remained.

German preservation of old world traditions in Pennsylvania included German Medieval architecture. This is true of many German houses in Maryland, Wisconsin, North Carolina and Texas, as well. Much of present Pennsylvania reflects this Medieval German architecture with steeply-pitched roofs blended with more elegant classical forms.

Readily available English materials, such as windows, were incorporated into German houses. The German builders made good use of the rich, red clay soil in Pennsylvania for brickmaking.

Design Y2694 p. 120

Design Y2680 p. 132

The Dutch Colonial Farmhouse

When most Americans today think of Dutch architecture, they really are thinking Flemish. What sticks in their minds is the charming Dutch Colonial farmhouse with its bell-shaped gambrel roof and flaring eaves. Typically, this house was made of clapboard, shingle or stone. People commonly believe that Dutch colonists brought this delightful swept design with them to the new world.

It's likely, most scholars feel, that the farmhouse design is not Dutch and not even Colonial in its present 20th-Century form. Gambrel roofs were rare in Holland.

The design evolved to its present form as a graceful, simple cottage only a hundred years ago. That's long after the Dutch colony here disbanded and New Netherlands became New York. Possibly, therefore, the Dutch Colonial farmhouse is a truly American innovation.

Scholars believe the basic design with flaring eaves is Flemish or even French in origin. In maritime Flanders, an area that's now southern Holland, western Belgium and northern France, similar farmhouses were constructed with low walls built of clay mixed with lime and straw. To protect the clay walls from weather, flared eaves called "flying gutters" were added to project out two feet or longer.

Many native Flemings fled to Holland during Spanish occupation in the early 17th Century. Dutch farm land was scarce, however, so many Flemish farmers emigrated to New Netherlands in America.

The early Dutch in New Netherlands were traders or clustered in Dutch communities, but the Flemish were peasant farmers. The Flemish remain hard to trace in the United States, but some

scholars estimate two-thirds of certain counties in New Netherlands were Flemish, particularly in northern New Jersey. Elsewhere in southern New Netherlands the Flemish mixed with Dutch, Walloons and French in "Dutch" communities. The Flemish projecting curved eaves appeared on Long Island homes as early as the mid-17th Century. The Dutch Colonial farmhouse remains popular in rural Long Island and New Jersey.

Besides flaring eaves, these Flemish farmhouses were marked by a graceful version of the gambrel roof. However, this was not used until the 18th Century. The graceful curve of the roofline and its overhang provided a shelter. In the late 18th Century, posts were added under the projection to create a full-width porch. The overhang of the original Flemish farmhouse was designed to shield fragile walls of clay, lime and straw—a curious regional mixture. It's possible, therefore, to compare the American Dutch Colonial's stone and wood components as abundant substitutes for the building materials of Flanders. The American stone houses often were plastered and whitewashed. Certainly that visual impact reminds one of Flemish homes.

Another clue lies in the mortar between the stones. Curiously, the American version used a mortar mixture of clay, lime and straw. That mixture is identical to the wall material of Flemish houses. Most American mortar is harder.

Whether an American invention or a faithful import, the Dutch Colonial or Flemish farmhouse has not remained untouched as a pure art form in this country. The flaring Flemish eave can be seen in Bergen County, New Jersey, on

14. Dutch Colonial Farmhouse

The popular, cozy Dutch Colonial farmhouse may have been Flemish or French in origin and evolved in recent centuries here in America. Its bell-shaped low gambrel roof, flying eaves and posted porch make it a favorite—particularly in the Dutch counties of New England.

French Huguenot houses.

The added porch may reflect French Colonial influence, or it may have come from the West Indies where the Dutch traded in the late 19th Century. Regional examples abound in French Louisiana, Missouri and the Carolinas.

With all these changes and more than a century of local popularity, perhaps the so-called Dutch Colonial farmhouse should be considered an American creation, after all.

Design Y2650, p. 128

15. French Farmhouse

French immigrants built elegant raised cottages with broad porches the French called galleries. They evolved from simple dwellings from the Carolinas to Maryland. This design recalls a Chesapeake Bay home built around 1650. Characteristic of Tidewater design, it includes five dormers.

The French Connection

French immigrants, mostly Huguenots facing religious persecution, began settling in southern colonies in the 17th Century. For the most part, they built simple homes to mirror peasant cottages in the old world.

The pattern for these homes is rooted in the early Mediterranean. The originals were distinguished by a steep gabled roof that broke near the peak and sloped easily over the front and rear "galleries" or porches. The roofline broke farther down at the facade. The French farmhouse in America became a sort of cozy cottage and soon graced colonies all the way from the Carolinas to Maryland.

In Louisiana, the first French houses were one-story homes surrounded by a gallery or porch and hip roof. The framing was curious. Walls were made of posts sunk into the ground and positioned together, similar to log cabins, except that logs were laid vertically in the French homes. This sort of framing was called "poteau-en-terre," or posts in earth, by the French. Unfortunately, the posts rotted in the ground, so houses thereafter employed stone foundations. Builders raised these houses even higher above ground with piers in regions prone to floods. This, then, became the Louisiana plantation style. Such raised cottages became a popular French style in the South, regardless of flood conditions. Such raised cottages appeared in New Orleans in the early 18th Century. Framing of the revised French cottages resembled English style, rather than earlier French posts-in-ground fashion.

Design Y2660 p. 261

16. The Charleston "Single House"

Elegant Charleston Single Houses evolved from earlier French plantation houses with central block and attached porches. They were called Single Houses because originally they were a single room deep. These tall, slender townhouses became popular in Charleston, South Carolina, in the 18th and 19th Centuries. They can be seen in profusion in Charleston to this day. The facade of these stately Southern homes did not face the street. Rather, the narrow end of the townhouse was accessible to the street from stairs and double-tiered, collated porches which the French first had called "galleries" and then called "piazzas." The upper piazza typically overlooked a splendid front courtyard or garden. The French country farmhouse had been transformed from a cozy, raised cottage to an elegant townhouse with stately columns and even a pedimented gable in some cases. On hot summer days and muggy long nights, gentle sea breezes would blow across the piazza porches of these Southern homes.

17. Louisiana Plantation House

French raised cottages popular in the early South included French "galleries" or porches to catch summer breezes on hot, sultry days. The purpose of the raised elevation was originally to protect against floods. The elevated cottage features six Doric columns in this typical design, as well as four single-windowed dormers. Often, the house had paneled double French doors and tall chimneys. The classic French design remains functional and stately.

Design Y2686 p. 269

The Georgian Period

The Georgian Period of architecture in Colonial America was a time of formal style and elegance from approximately 1700 until 1780 when Georgian melted with subtle changes into Late Georgian or Federal. Pretentious Georgian mansions were marked by exquisite detailing, regular geometric shapes, ornament, formal symmetry and often size. Regional variations created a wide variety of Georgian architecture. Basically, Georgian in the South included brick and occasionally stone construction, while New England Georgian occurred slightly later with mainly wood construction.

Georgian was the dominant style in its time for the landed gentry who could afford its grandeur. Roots of Colonial Georgian are traced all the way to the Italian Renaissance and its emphasis on classical detailing. That early style resurfaced in England in the mid-17th Century where it dominated the architectural scene from approximately 1650 to 1750 under such masters as Christopher Wren. It reached the shores of Colonial America approximately 1700, at a time of new prosperity. New American commerce was thriving with plantations in the South and seaports in the North, and the prosperous welcomed the pretentious Georgian design as a statement of their wealth and elegant lifestyle. Many early Georgian homes were built from patterns

and carpentry books shipped from Europe.

While the basic Georgian house was a simple two-story or one-story box with symmetrical windows and doors and two rooms deep, many sub-types existed. These include Georgians with side-gabled roofs in the North, gambrel roofs mainly in the North, and hipped roofs in the South. Another sub-style was the Georgian with centered gable in which a triangular gable pediment was centered on the front facade. The Georgian townhouse was another sub-style. This is an urban house with narrow facade.

The front door was a major feature in Georgian architecture. Often the door was flanked with plain or fluted pilasters

of full height or raised on pedestals. Later versions involved columns with pediments or cornices above the door. Ornaments over the door included curved moulding topped by a row of small dentil blocks and moulded cornice. A simple triangular pediment over the door was most common.

Georgian style is the serene architecture of a confident people. Georgian architecture was the predominant style for homes of the wealthy from the Carolinas to Maine by the middle of the 18th Century, with regional variations. Common Georgian features include a symmetrical facade, a massive chimney, dentils, pedimented dormers and an elaborate doorway.

18. Georgian with Pediment Gable

This dignified Georgian design echoes Woodlawn, the gracious abode that George Washington built near Mount Vernon for his niece, as well as Tulip Hill, a stately manor in Ann Arundel County, Maryland. Its Georgian facade features a slender-column portico and round window that adorns the pediment.

Design Y2683 p. 214

Georgian Period in New England

Design Y2522 p. 189

19. New England Georgian

This stately design is based on the Lady Pepperrell House built approximately 1760 on a hill overlooking Portsmouth Harbor in Kittery Point, Maine. It is typical of New England Georgian design.

The house captures the simple elegance of the period. It employs the frame construction characteristic of New England Georgian homes, rather than the brick construction used predominantly in the South. Exquisite detailing indoors and outdoors recreates the simple grace of the period. A set of short steps leads to a projected pavilion that is distinguished from the clapboard walls by its smooth boards that simulate masonry. A grand entrance is framed by applied Ionic pilasters that are elevated on pedestals. Denticulated mouldings and paneled wainscotting decorate the spacious interior.

The evolution of Georgian styling progressed slowly from 16th-Century Renaissance Italy to 18th-Century England. There it took the name of three of England's ruling kings, all named King George.

When transported to the American colonies, Georgian architecture's classical elegance suited the taste of a new emerging elite class.

20. Cape Cod Georgian

This design recalls the Julia Wood House built approximately 1790 in Falmouth, Massachusetts, and is typical of many Georgian two-story homes built in Cape Cod. Earlier two-story houses on the Cape employed a central chimney, tiny entry porch and gabled roof. With Georgian and Federal style influences, later Cape Cod clapboard houses featured chimneys set either between front and rear rooms or at end elevations of the house. A hipped roof replaced the gable roof to relieve the boxlike proportions of the house. A center hall with elegant stairs replaced the cramped entry porch. Such homes generally had a balustraded roof deck where wives of captains looked to sea for signs of returning ships. Often they searched in vain, so the deck became known as a widow's walk.

Design Y2690 p. 191

Late Georgian Transition Into Federal Styling

The simple two-story symmetrical box that was early Georgian architecture went through a Late Georgian period of transition from approximately 1760 to 1780 into the Federal Period. Late-Georgian architecture made heavy use of classical details—notably doorways surrounded by pilasters or columns, surmounted by cornice or pediment, and semi-circular fanlight over doors. Use of columns and pilasters became more lavish, and so did the use of classical detailing in the cornice. More elaborate houses would feature a projected entrance pavilion with a pedimented gable on top. After the Revolutionary War, many designers would reject a lot of the classical decoration of Late Georgian, but retain its basic Greco-Roman symmetry.

Design Y2283 p. 256

21. Late Georgian Styling

This illustration recalls the transition from Georgian architecture into the Late Georgian Period with greater emphasis on brick permanence and crisp lines to replace the florid carvings and sweeping curves of Early-Georgian detailing. A hallmark of the new styles was the two-story projecting portico. The emerging style continued the Georgian use of classical symmetry.

Design Y2667 p. 221

22. 18th-Century Tidewater Virginia

This design, patterned after the historic Semple House in Williamsburg, Virginia, is reminiscent of 18th-Century Tidewater Virginia homes. Classic renaissance innovations were added to Georgian styling. The configuration featured a pedimented center section flanked by lower wings, typical in much Palladian design transported from Europe to the colonies. This classical form was derived from the classical architecture of ancient Rome, as interpreted by 16th-Century Italian Renaissance architect Andrea Palladio. His styling was revived in England in the Early 18th Century. The imposing gable of the design dramatized the entire structure and gave the center section the jutting prominence of an ancient temple. Cornice treatments of the gable reappear at rooflines on all elevations and the porch.

Design Y2639 p. 190

23. Massachusetts Palladian Manor

This elegant Massachusetts manor recalls the late 18th-Century Alexander Field House in Longmeadow. It demonstrates early New England regard for simple order and symmetry with classical implementation of Palladian detailing. An elevated doorway is defined by pilasters and pediment, topped by a second-story Palladian window. The window is capped by a pediment that projects from the hipped roof. Clapboard covered most New England homes of the Late Georgian period.

The Federal Period

Many people today still confuse Georgian and Federal styles of architecture. It's basically correct to say that Federal style emerged from the Georgian Period as a sedate Late-Georgian style more concerned with classical correctness and understatement than Georgian concern for classical form and overstatement.

It is also generally correct to associate Federal styling with the Northern colonies, although it appears in brick Late-Georgian homes of the South. It is also correct to associate it with Palladian style, which introduced a stripped-down classical look to Georgian after Christopher Wren architected a rebuilding of London after the Great Fire. At any rate, the Federal Style dominated Colonial architecture from approximately 1780 to 1830. The Federal Period also is sometimes referred to as the Adams Period, after transitional designer Robert Adams.

Particularly in the North, post-Revolutionary designers and builders rejected much of the classical decoration of Georgian architecture, particularly its heavy ornamentation in the later years of Greek and Roman influence. The new Federal look, however, kept the basic Roman symmetry found in Georgian design. Doorways kept their pilasters and columns, and were often topped with flat entablature. Elliptical fanlights above doorways also were popular. Corners were unmarked by quoins or ornamental pilasters. Hipped roofs became more common, and were occasionally rimmed by a balustrade. Flat boarding was sometimes used on the exterior for a more classical effect.

By the time Georgian architecture caught on in the seaports of the North, Georgian ornate grandeur had pretty well played itself out. That was fine, perhaps, for the God-fearing, practical New Englanders, who appreciated classical symmetry and grand homes, but not particularly pretentious splendor. Their resulting compromise of styles may be described as New England eclectic.

A desire for classical quality and correctness continued. White smoothness of flush-boarded walls or painted brick or stucco demonstrate this understatement, as does the bare simplicity of painted plaster walls.

The Federal house often featured a giant portico and almost always employed a doorway of narrow flanking side lights and embracing elliptical fanlight. This is the so-called Federal doorway. The Federal house also typically featured a curved or polygon-shaped bay on an exterior wall and balustrade or parapet over eaves (rather than high on the roof). Often such homes included fragile carved wood or moulded plaster ornaments, inspired by Robert Adams, a devotee of the decorated walls of Pompeii.

The box shape of Georgian homes was expanded in the Federal period in many instances to include wings from temple-form house shape.

While hipped-roof houses were frequent in New England, there were many side-gabled houses and center-gabled houses with triangular pediments centered on the front facade. Many Federal townhouses became so-called row houses in urban areas.

The Greek Revival Period

Colonial interest in classical Greek and Roman arts as well as English design trends led to a Greek Revival Period in American architecture. Focus on the Golden Age was prompted initially by archeological discoveries in the late 18th Century. It started with excavation of two lost Roman cities buried by the eruption of Vesuvius in AD 79. Herculaneum was discovered in 1719, followed by Pompeii in 1748. Around the world, people heard new stories about how people of these once glorious Roman cities had lived. Books on Greek classicism followed. Detailed documentation of the 5th Century BC structures of the Acropolis in Athens soon was incorporated into builders' handbooks and the textbooks of influential architects. Knowledge of classical architecture was also spread by new museums and the advent of photography. The Greek temple became the highest architectural ideal for Americans from 1820 to approximately 1860.

In truth, much of the American so-called Greek Revival in architecture employs Roman styling, particularly the heavy unfluted Roman columns. While the era might well be defined as a Greco-Roman revival, the concept was classical idealism best exemplified by Greek thinking. In America, what's meant to be elegant often becomes a bit pompous. It's best to remember that early Americans were enterprising imitators with a brash mind of their own. Greek Revival archi-

tects pretty much decided for themselves which classic order in both Greek and Roman design they chose to follow, often mixing and matching.

The typical Early American house of the Greek Revival period was a two-story or three-story symmetrical building that was essentially a copy of a Greek temple with columns, architraves, friezes and cornices. Windows were small and hidden, since they were not truly a part of Greek temple architecture. Of course, the style has continued in modern America in the design of public buildings.

Exterior walls of Greek Revival Period structures were clapboard, flush-board, stucco, stone, or even brick—but they were invariably white. Interior walls were smooth plaster. Trim was rich yet refined, with mouldings adapted from classical orders. Ceiling trim often enhanced the elegance. The general tone of such period architecture was that of tranquility and order.

Southern Colonial architecture of the period absorbed the Greek Revival and adapted it to post-Georgian styling. Often the Doric or Ionic pillars were abbreviated to form entry porches or full-width porches supported by square or round columns only half the height of a two-story house.

Rooflines could be gabled or hipped with a low pitch. A cornice line on the main roof and porch roof often was accentuated with a wide band of trim to

represent classic entablature.

Columns can be distinguished by their capitals on top and their bases. Doric columns employ plain capitals, while Ionic columns employ capitals with scrolled spirals. Less frequent Corinthian capitals are shaped somewhat like inverted bells with leaves.

The Greek Revival style employed round columns, never square. The thick Greek Doric fluted column with no base is most prominent, although thinner fluted Roman Dorics with base and unfluted Roman Tuscans with base also are found in Early American houses.

24. The Greek Temple House

The Greek temple was the highest architectural ideal for many wealthy Americans from 1820 until the Civil War. Variations include everything from modest farmhouses in Maine to luxurious plantations in Mississippi. The hallmark of the dignified style is the classic white portico. The illustration below shows a symmetrical entry facade with a projecting center pavilion. A giant portico with fluted columns rises two stories to support a pedimented gable. Flat pilasters are used on external corners in the same composite classical order as the portico columns. Entry facade details are repeated in the rear.

Design Y2184 p. 258

Design Y2974 p. 301

25. Queen Anne Cottage

Victorian houses are well known for their orientation on narrow building sites. Even when this occurs, none of the captivating exterior styling is lost. This house is but 38 feet wide. The ubiquitous porch/veranda with delicate spindlework contributes mightily to style as well as livability.

The Victorian Period

After the formality and symmetry of the Greek Revival period, some people began to react against classicism by experimenting and incorporating curved lines and exotic details in public and private buildings. So arose the Victorian style, characterized by freedom of expression, liveliness, whimsy and optimism. Named after Queen Victoria, who reigned from 1837 to 1901, the Victorian Period spanned seven decades from 1840 to 1910.

Several factors brought about the change in architecture. Industrial and technological advances created a new, wealthy middle class and provided new carving tools. The expansion of railroads in America made building supplies readily available. New building techniques allowed houses to be built faster and with more wings and appendages.

Gothic Revival (1840 to 1880) and Italianate style (1840 to 1885) marked the beginning of the Victorian Period. A steeply pitched roof with cross gables with decorative trim pieces called vergeboards exemplified Gothic Revival. Italianate style emphasized Italian villa-style architecture with low-pitched roofs, a central tower, wide overhangs and tall, narrow windows, often covered with hooded crowns.

The Middle Victorian Period brought the Second Empire and Stick styles. Second Empire, or Mansardic, homes offered the dual-pitched, hipped mansard roof named after 17th-Century French architect Francois Mansart. Wood replaced masonry in the building of Stick houses. Walls were decorated with patterns of horizontal, vertical or diagonal boards raised from the wall surface.

The High Victorian Period provided Queen Anne Style, typified by elaborate detailing including patterned shingles, carved fretwork, finials, and spindlework. Many Queen Anne Victorians are found in the San Francisco area.

Glossary of Architectural Terms

Arcade A row of arches supported by columns.

Arch Curving structure comprised of wedge-shaped blocks, supported at the sides. Examples of types of arches include: semicircular, elliptical, trefoil, and four-centered Tudor.

Baluster A small column or pillar which supports a rail.

Balustrade A series of balusters joined by a rail used for porches and balconies.

Bay Window A projecting window of various shapes, though usually at least three sided.

Beam Ceiling A ceiling that has exposed beams, either real or ornamental.

Belt Course Horizontal band on the outside walls of a building which usually defines interior floor levels.

Casement Window Popular window type with sashes that swing out from the structure.

Clerestory Windows Upper story, usually multi-paned windows.

Cornice A moulded projection that topsoff the part to which it is attached.

Cupola A small domed roof or turret usually built upon the main roof.

Dentil A series of rectangular blocks arranged in a row like a set of teeth.

Dormer A projecting window set in the sloping plane of a roof.

Double Hung Window A window having two sashes which may be opened from the top, the bottom, or both.

Double Portico A two-story porch usually with columns and a pediment.

Dutch Door A door that has two halves — upper and lower — that swing independently of one another.

Eaves The lower edge of the part of the roof which overhangs a wall.

Facade The face of a building.

Fanlight A semicircular window usually found above a door or large set of multi-paned windows.

Fenestration The way in which windows are arranged in a wall.

Finial An ornament fixed to the top of a spire, gable, pediment, roof, or other structure.

French Doors Doors that have large areas of glass, usually multi-paned.

Gable The triangle-shaped part at the edge of a ridged roof.

Gable Roof A roof that slopes on only two sides.

Gambrel A ridged roof having two slopes on each side with the lower slope having the steeper pitch.

Georgian A style that borrows from houses typically found during the reigns of the four King Georges of England.

Glass Sliding Doors Doors with one stationary and one moving panel, both of glass.

Half House Small Cape Cod-style house, characterized by two windows to one side of the front door.

Half-Timbering Ornamentation on walls in which spaces between timber framing have been filled with masonry or other material.

Hearth The floor directly in front of a fireplace and the floor of a fireplace where the fire is built.

Hipped Roof A roof that has four sides, each uniformly pitched.

Lintel The horizontal piece spanning the top of an opening such as a door or window.

Mansard Roof A roof which has two slopes on all four sides.

Masonry Material for building consisting of stone, brick, tile, adobe, or concrete.

Mouldings Bands used as ornamentation for a wall or other surface.

Norman Architecture which derives its style from houses of Eleventh and Twelfth Century England.

Palladian Window Window with a large arched center and rectangular flanking pieces.

Pediment A triangular gable piece which finishes the ends of a sloping roof.

Pent Roof A small roof ledge located between the first and second floors of a house.

Pilaster A rectangular column that projects outward from a wall.

Quoin Decorative pieces of stone or brick at the corners of buildings.

Saltbox Style of house which has a gabled roof with the rear slope much longer than the front.

Three-Quarter House A Cape Cod-style house with two windows on one side of the door and one window on the other.

Transom A small window over a door.

Turret A small round or polygonal tower.

Veranda An open porch with a roof.

Wainscot Paneling in general, or more specifically, paneling which reaches only part way up a wall.

CAPE COD HOUSES

The charm of Cape Cod houses is delightfully captured on the following pages. This selection of designs ranges in size from 1,428 to 4,222 square feet. There are houses for narrow urban building sites and restricted building budgets, as well as for large rural sites and luxury budgets. Family living patterns are well-planned whether the interior be compact or spacious. Compare the fine livability offered by such contrasting designs as Y2661 and Y2921 on the following pages. Don't miss the two expandable house features represented by designs Y2682 and Y2983 on pages 30/31 and 34/35 respectively. Observe the country kitchens, the formal and informal dining areas, the fine bath facilities, the excellent traffic patterns and the pleasing indoor/outdoor living relationships.

Compact Three-Quarter Cape

Design Y2661
First Floor: 1,020 square feet
Second Floor: 777 square feet
Total: 1,797 square feet

L **D**

● Here is the embodiment of the three-quarter Cape. The front entrance detailing consists of pilasters, a paneled door and a glass transom. Twin carriage lamps, muntined double-hung windows and louvered shutters add to the exterior appeal. The massive chimney serves two fireplaces. The rear of the house has a long dormer to provide an abundance of space to the second floor. Note the projecting boxed bay window.

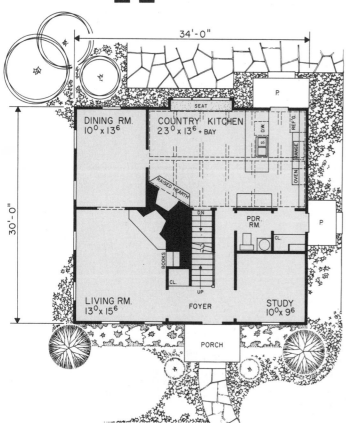

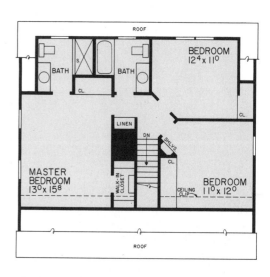

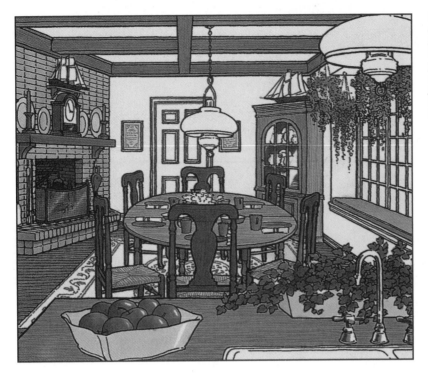

Viewed from the work center, the open planning of the country kitchen is a delight to behold. The bay window, with its seat, provides plenty of natural light. The family will enjoy informal dining and games near the raised-hearth corner fireplace in what is sure to be the family's social center.

CUSTOMIZABLE

Custom Alterations? See page 381 for customizing this plan to your specifications.

● The center entrance and foyer lead to outstanding traffic circulation. To the left are the formal living room with fireplace and the dining room. To the right are the study and powder room, as well as a handy side service entrance. The spacious country kitchen, with its beamed ceiling and efficient work center, is straight ahead. The kitchen has a commanding view of the family's favorite gathering spot and is handy to the rear outdoor living areas. Off the country kitchen are the stairs to the basement—a bonus area for the development of laundry space and further livability. Up the stairs from the foyer is the three-bedroom second floor, including two full baths highlighted by a stall shower in the master bedroom. This home serves admirably as a starter house or as a home for a retired couple.

A Cape Cod Rambler

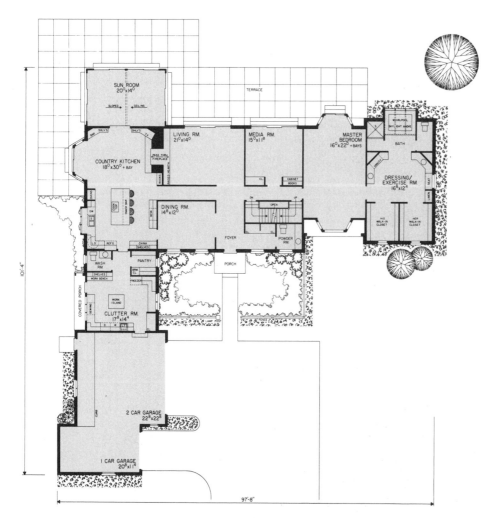

Design Y2921

First Floor: 3,215 square feet
Sun Room: 296 square feet
Second Floor: 711 square feet
Total: 4,222 square feet

L **D**

● Here is a floor plan that offers all the amenities. It is designed to cater to the living patterns of either a maturing, active family, or those of a couple whose children have left home but return for holiday visits.

● The ambience of Cape Cod is pleasingly captured by this rambling 1½-story home. Like many of its forebears, it has varying roof planes that seem to emphasize the addition of a variety of areas. The L-shaped configuration results in an impressive front drive court. Inside the white picket fence, the flower court leads to the center entrance. Unlike most houses of this style, this one has an exterior of brick veneer painted white, while black shutters and roof shingles, or cedar shakes, contrast effectively. The transom-capped paneled front door, the muntined double-hung windows, the wide cornices, the cupola and the massive chimney with its black Tory top set the exterior character. Properly oriented for solar exposure, the bay windows and projecting sun room garner an abundance of natural light. The interior is wonderfully zoned. The informal family area centers around the spacious country kitchen. Space abounds for a dining/games table near the bay window and a conversational furniture placement in front of the dramatic through-fireplace. The work center, with plenty of counter and cupboard space, is outstanding. The clutter room is directly accessible from the garage and features the laundry equipment, a serving area, work bench, work island, freezer and a nearby walk-in pantry and washroom. The sun room, with its sloped ceiling, functions through sliding glass doors with an outdoor terrace. The media room may serve alternatively as a quiet study or library. The master suite could hardly be more appealing. The large master bedroom has twin bays and fine blank wall space for furniture placement. The personal care area is highlighted by twin lavatories, His and Hers walk-in closets, a stall shower, whirlpool, linen storage and space for exercise equipment. Upstairs, two bedrooms and a bath cater to the older children.

A raised-hearth fireplace warms the living room. The country kitchen shares the glow of this through-fireplace. The masonry wall may be of brick or fieldstone. Observe the raised mouldings of the adjacent wall. You may opt for wallpaper.

Cape Cod Houses   27

Budget-Minding Cape Cod

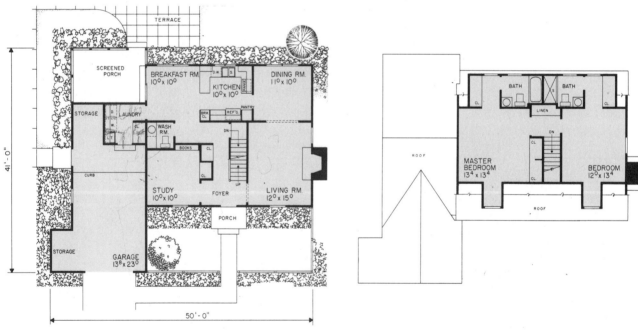

Design Y2655 First Floor: 893 square feet; Second Floor: 652 square feet; Total: 1,545 square feet

L

● Although 17th-Century Cape Cod houses were known for their steep gabled roofs, houses with gambrel roofs were not uncommon. Such a roof configuration afforded additional second floor headroom. This charming cottage has an abundance of well-lit upstairs bedroom space as a result of projecting twin dormers on the front and a long dormer on the rear. Two nice-sized bedrooms and two full baths along with good wardrobe and linen storage facilities serve the small family. Within only 1,545 square feet there is plenty of livability for the construction dollar. The clapboard exterior and the door and window treatment set the character. The projecting garage and the picket fence help form an inviting flower court on the way to the centered entrance and foyer. A quiet study to the left of the foyer includes a closet for games or storage and built-in bookshelves. Space for recreation or hobbies can be developed in the basement. The garage provides bonus space for storage of garden paraphernalia.

To the right of the formal foyer, with its open staircase and handy coat closet, is the living room. The centered fireplace sets the stage for a pleasant family conversation spot. Paneled walls with raised mouldings offer a possible decorating theme. The dining room is adjacent.

● Traffic flows to the rear of the plan where the U-shaped kitchen is flanked by the formal dining room and the informal breakfast room. A handy wash room is nearby and the first-floor laundry is around the corner on the way to the garage. Outdoor dining and relaxing can be enjoyed in the screened porch conveniently accessed through sliding glass doors from the breakfast room.

Expanding the Half-House

Design Y2682

First Floor (Basic Plan): 976 square feet
First Floor (Expanded Plan): 1,230 square feet
Second Floor (Both Plans): 744 square feet
Total (Basic Plan): 1,720; Total (Expanded Plan): 1,974 square feet

L D

CUSTOMIZABLE

Custom Alterations? See page 381 for customizing this plan to your specifications.

● Here is an expandable Colonial with a full measure of Cape Cod Charm. For those who wish to build the basic house, there is an abundance of low-budget livability. Twin fireplaces serve the formal living room and the informal country kitchen. Note the spaciousness of both areas. A dining room and powder room are also on the first floor of this basic plan. Upstairs three bedrooms and two full baths.

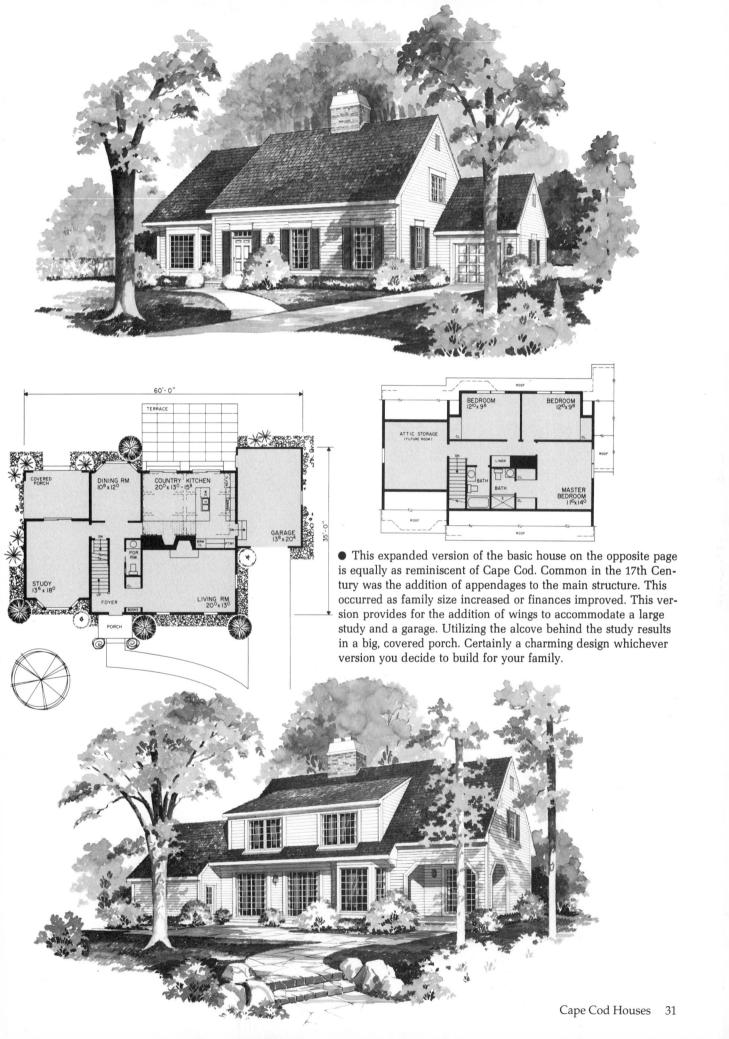

60'-0"

TERRACE

COVERED PORCH

DINING RM.
10⁸ x 12⁰

COUNTRY KITCHEN
20⁰ x 13⁰ - 15⁸

GARAGE
13⁸ x 20⁴

35'-0"

STUDY
13⁶ x 18⁰

PDR. RM.

FOYER

BOOKS

LIVING RM.
20⁰ x 13⁰

PORCH

ATTIC STORAGE
(FUTURE ROOM)

BEDROOM
12¹⁰ x 9⁸

BEDROOM
12¹⁰ x 9⁸

ROOF

LINEN

BATH

BATH

MASTER BEDROOM
11¹⁰ x 14⁰

ROOF

ROOF

ROOF

● This expanded version of the basic house on the opposite page is equally as reminiscent of Cape Cod. Common in the 17th Century was the addition of appendages to the main structure. This occurred as family size increased or finances improved. This version provides for the addition of wings to accommodate a large study and a garage. Utilizing the alcove behind the study results in a big, covered porch. Certainly a charming design whichever version you decide to build for your family.

Design Y2657 First Floor: 1,217 square feet; Second Floor: 868 square feet; Total: 2,085 square feet

L

● What could be more classic than this full Cape with its delightful symmetry. The white picket fence and resulting entrance court complete a picture of charm. Of course, the projecting one-car (make it a two-car if you prefer) garage is a necessary 20th Century addition. The exterior has clapboard siding,

muntined double-hung windows and a transom-lit entrance flanked by shutters and carriage lamps. The massive chimney serves two fireplaces—one in the living room, the other in the country kitchen. Measuring slightly less than fifty feet across the front, this house will fit a modest-sized building site. It

has a basement, a rear covered porch and a laundry with adjacent wash room behind the garage. There are many highlights to the fine floor plan. Imagine a 23-foot living room with a bay window and access to a porch. A separate formal dining room has blank wall space for effective furniture placement.

Spacious Living Areas

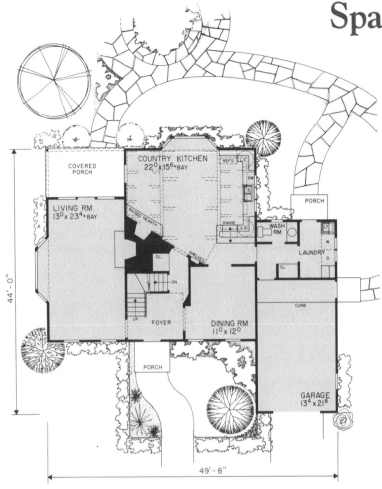

● Open-planned is the by-word for the spacious country kitchen. The U-shaped work center has good counter space, a couple of Lazy Susans and a pass-through to the snack bar. The open, angular staircase leads to the second floor with its three bedrooms and two full baths. Don't miss the seats in the dormer areas with storage below.

The focal point of the big country kitchen with its beamed ceiling is the raised-hearth masonry fireplace in an interior corner. This truly sets the ambience for cozy, family-oriented activities. Built-in shelves accommodate cookbooks or family souveiners.

Expandable Cape Ann Cottage

Design Y2983 First Floor (Basic Plan): 776 square feet
First Floor (Expanded Plan): 1,072 square feet
Second Floor (Both Plans): 652 square feet
Total (Basic Plan): 1,428; (Expanded Plan): 1,724 square feet

● This charming gambrel-roofed Colonial cottage is reminiscent of the simple houses built and occupied by seafarers on Cape Ann, Mass. in the 17th and 18th Centuries. However, this adaptation offers a new twist. It is designed to expand as your need and/or budget grows. Of course, building the expanded version first will deliver the bonus livability promised by the formal dining room and quiet study, plus the convenience of the attached garage.

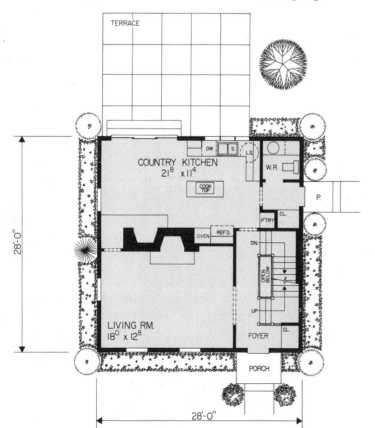

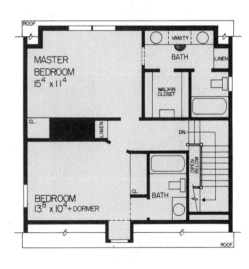

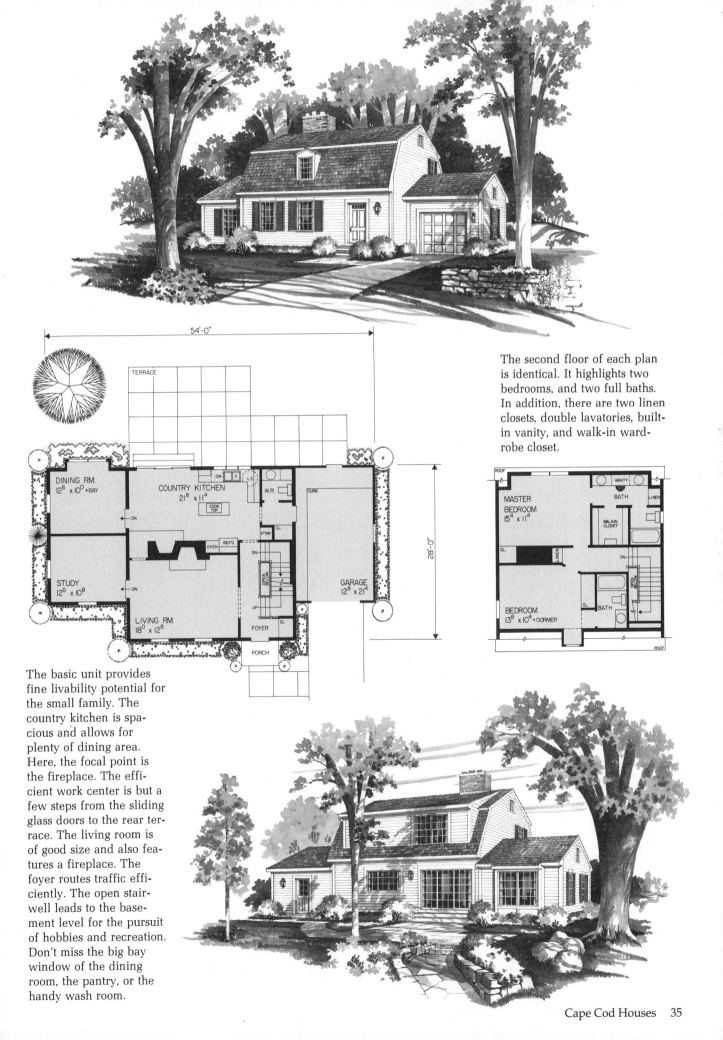

54'-0"

TERRACE

DINING RM.
12⁶ x 10⁰ +BAY

COUNTRY KITCHEN
21⁸ x 11⁴

DW

S

L.S.

W.R.

CURB

COOK
TOP

OVEN

REF'G

P'TRY

CL.

DN.

DN.

STUDY
12⁶ x 10⁸

DN.

OPEN
BELOW

UP

GARAGE
12⁸ x 21⁴

LIVING RM.
18⁰ x 12⁸

FOYER

CL.

PORCH

28'-0"

The second floor of each plan
is identical. It highlights two
bedrooms, and two full baths.
In addition, there are two linen
closets, double lavatories, built-
in vanity, and walk-in wardrobe closet.

ROOF

VANITY

MASTER
BEDROOM
15⁴ x 11⁴

BATH

LINEN

WALK-IN
CLOSET

CL.

LINEN

DN.

BEDROOM
13⁸ x 10⁴ +DORMER

CL.

BATH

OPEN
BELOW

ROOF

The basic unit provides
fine livability potential for
the small family. The
country kitchen is spa-
cious and allows for
plenty of dining area.
Here, the focal point is
the fireplace. The effi-
cient work center is but a
few steps from the sliding
glass doors to the rear terrace. The living room is
of good size and also features a fireplace. The
foyer routes traffic efficiently. The open stair-
well leads to the base-
ment level for the pursuit
of hobbies and recreation.
Don't miss the big bay
window of the dining
room, the pantry, or the
handy wash room.

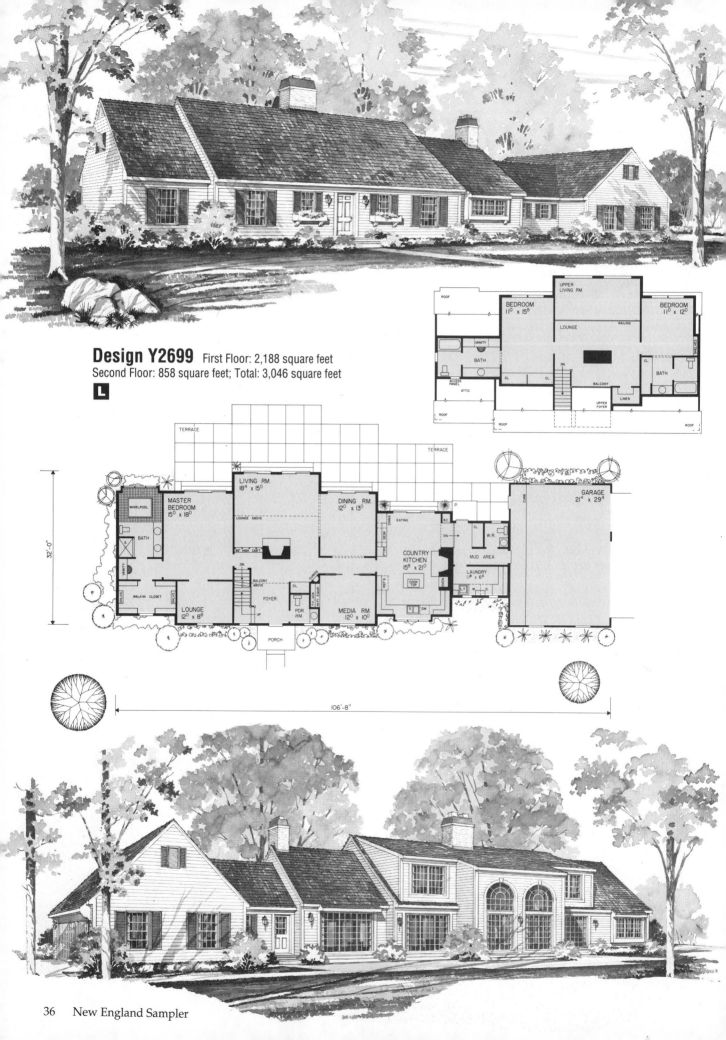

Design Y2699 First Floor: 2,188 square feet
Second Floor: 858 square feet; Total: 3,046 square feet

L

Here are two more examples of the rambling Cape Cod house that illustrate just how delightful the appearance of those added dependents can be. The appealing result is houses with varying roof planes, projecting and recessed exterior walls and interesting, irregular configurations. In addition to charm, these two houses deliver exceptional country-estate livability for the growing, active family. Each one has a central entrance leading to a foyer, but from there the many features are distinct.

Design Y2615
First Floor: 2,563 square feet
Second Floor: 552 square feet
Total: 3,115 square feet

L **D**

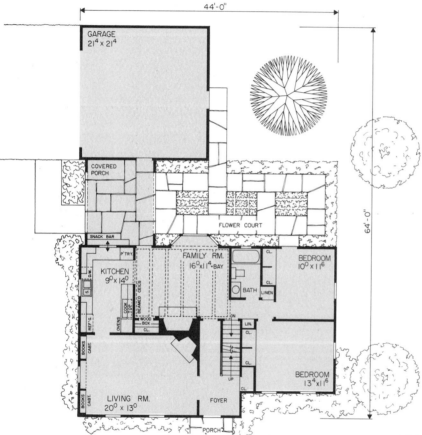

GARAGE
21⁴ x 21⁴

COVERED PORCH

FLOWER COURT

SNACK BAR

KITCHEN
9⁰ x 14⁰

FAMILY RM.
16⁰ x 11⁴·BAY

BEDROOM
10⁰ x 11⁶

BATH

LINEN

LIVING RM.
20⁰ x 13⁰

FOYER

BEDROOM
13⁴ x 11⁶

PORCH

44'-0"

64'-0"

Design Y2145

First Floor: 1,182 square feet
Second Floor: 708 square feet
Total: 1,890 square feet

L

● Historically referred to as a "half house", this authentic adaptation has its roots in the heritage of New England. With the completion of the second floor, the growing family doubles its sleeping capacity. Notice that the overall width of the house is only 44 feet. It will adapt well to a narrow or a corner building site.

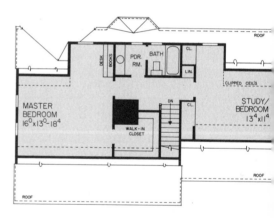

MASTER BEDROOM
16⁰ x 13⁰·18⁴

WALK-IN CLOSET

STUDY/BEDROOM
13⁴ x 11⁴

PDR. RM.

BATH

ROOF

CLIPPED CEIL'G.

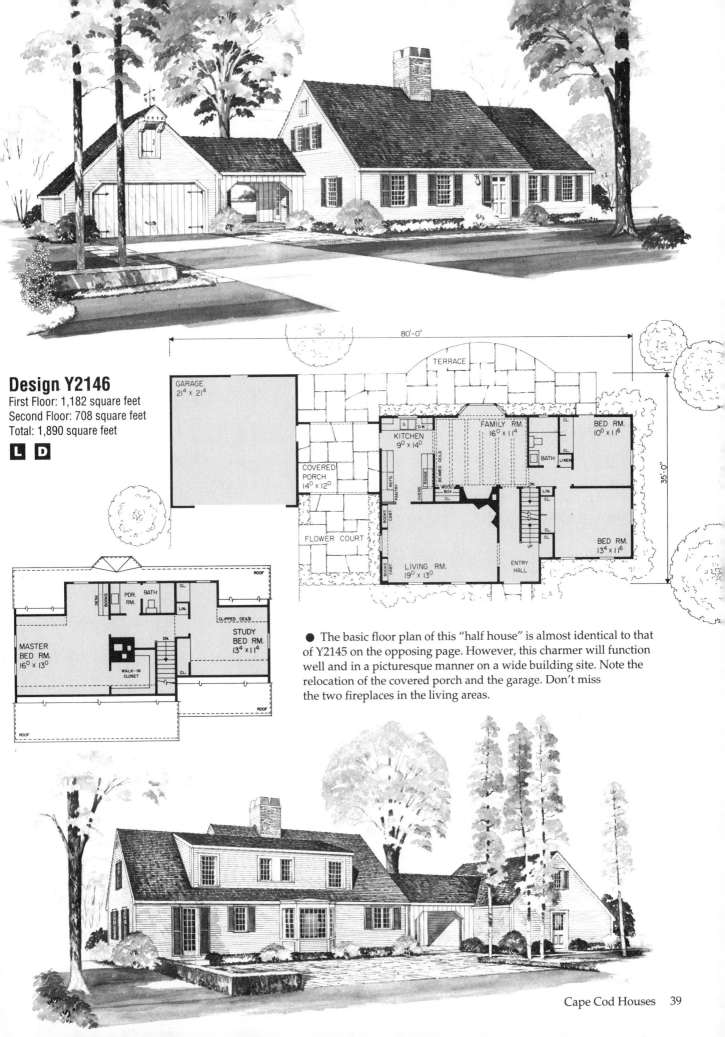

Design Y2146

First Floor: 1,182 square feet
Second Floor: 708 square feet
Total: 1,890 square feet

L **D**

GARAGE
21⁴ x 21⁴

COVERED
PORCH
14⁰ x 12⁰

FLOWER COURT

80'-0"

TERRACE

KITCHEN
9⁰ x 14⁰

FAMILY RM.
16⁰ x 11⁴

BED RM.
10⁰ x 11⁶

BATH

LINEN

S.

D.W.

REF'G

PANTRY

OVENS

RANGE

WOOD
BOX

CL.

BOOKS

CABT.

DN.

LIN.

CL.

CL.

UP

35'-0"

LIVING RM.
19⁰ x 13⁰

ENTRY
HALL

BED RM.
13⁴ x 11⁶

BOOKS

CABT.

DESK

BOOKS

PDR.
RM.

BATH

CL.

LIN.

CLIPPED CEIL'G

ROOF

MASTER
BED RM.
16⁰ x 13⁰

DN.

STUDY
BED RM.
13⁴ x 11⁴

WALK-IN
CLOSET

CL.

ROOF

ROOF

● The basic floor plan of this "half house" is almost identical to that of Y2145 on the opposing page. However, this charmer will function well and in a picturesque manner on a wide building site. Note the relocation of the covered porch and the garage. Don't miss the two fireplaces in the living areas.

Design Y2888
Square Footage: 3,018

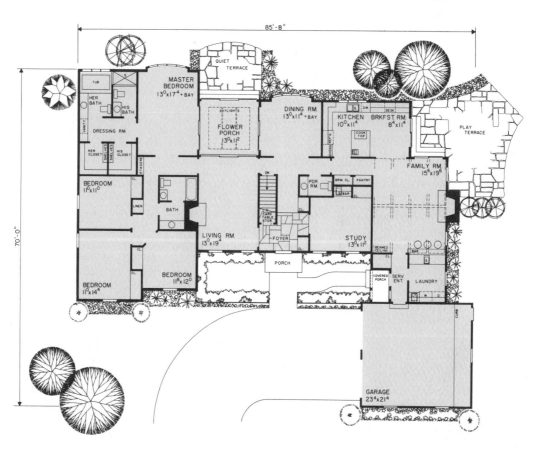

● This is an outstanding Early American design for the 20th-Century. The exterior detailing with narrow clap boards, multi-paned windows and cupola are the features of yesteryear. Interior planning, though, is for today's active family. Formal living room, in-

formal family room plus a study are present. Every activity will have its place in this home. Picture yourself working in the kitchen. There's enough counter space for two or three helpers. Four bedrooms are in the private area. Stop and imagine your daily routine if

you occupied the master bedroom. Both you and your spouse would have plenty of space and privacy. The flower porch, accessible from the master bedroom, living and dining rooms, is a very delightful "plus" feature. Study this design's every detail.

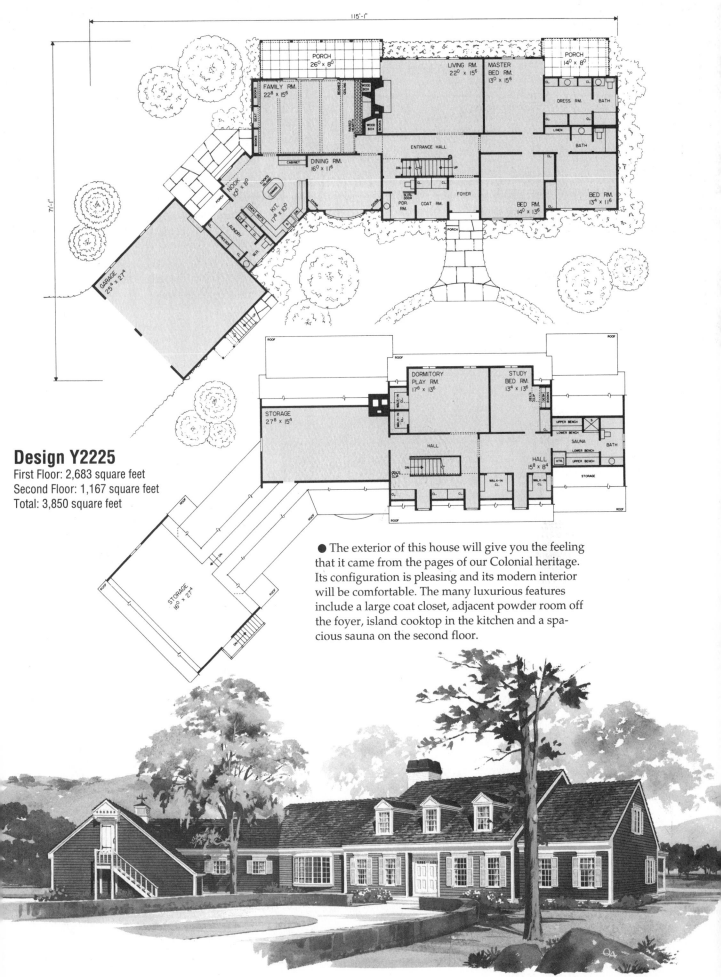

Design Y2225

First Floor: 2,683 square feet
Second Floor: 1,167 square feet
Total: 3,850 square feet

● The exterior of this house will give you the feeling that it came from the pages of our Colonial heritage. Its configuration is pleasing and its modern interior will be comfortable. The many luxurious features include a large coat closet, adjacent powder room off the foyer, island cooktop in the kitchen and a spacious sauna on the second floor.

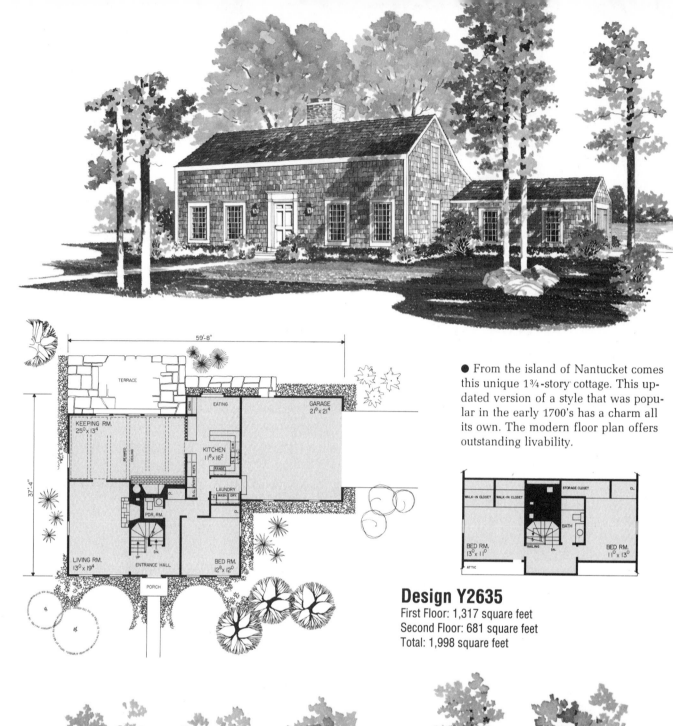

● From the island of Nantucket comes this unique 1¾-story cottage. This updated version of a style that was popular in the early 1700's has a charm all its own. The modern floor plan offers outstanding livability.

Design Y2635

First Floor: 1,317 square feet
Second Floor: 681 square feet
Total: 1,998 square feet

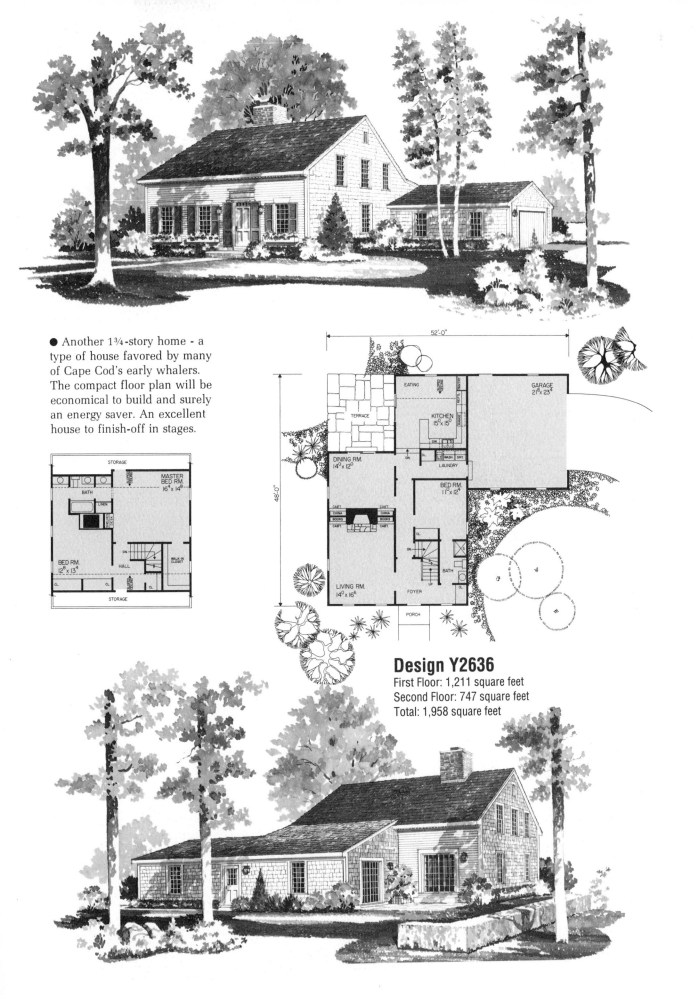

● Another 1¾-story home - a type of house favored by many of Cape Cod's early whalers. The compact floor plan will be economical to build and surely an energy saver. An excellent house to finish-off in stages.

Second Floor Plan:

STORAGE

MASTER BED RM.
16⁴ x 14⁸

BATH

LINEN

BED RM.
12⁸ x 13⁴

DN

HALL

WALK-IN CLOSET

CL

CL

CL

STORAGE

First Floor Plan:

52'-0"

48'-0"

TERRACE

EATING

REF'S. PANTRY

GARAGE
21⁸ x 23⁴

KITCHEN
15⁰ x 15⁰

RANGE

DK.

CL

DN.

WASH. DRY.

DINING RM.
14⁰ x 12⁰

LAUNDRY

BED RM.
11⁴ x 12⁴

CAB'T. CAB'T.
CHINA CHINA
BOOKS BOOKS
CAB'T. CAB'T.

CL

BATH

LIVING RM.
14⁰ x 16⁶

DN.

UP

FOYER

PORCH

Design Y2636

First Floor: 1,211 square feet
Second Floor: 747 square feet
Total: 1,958 square feet

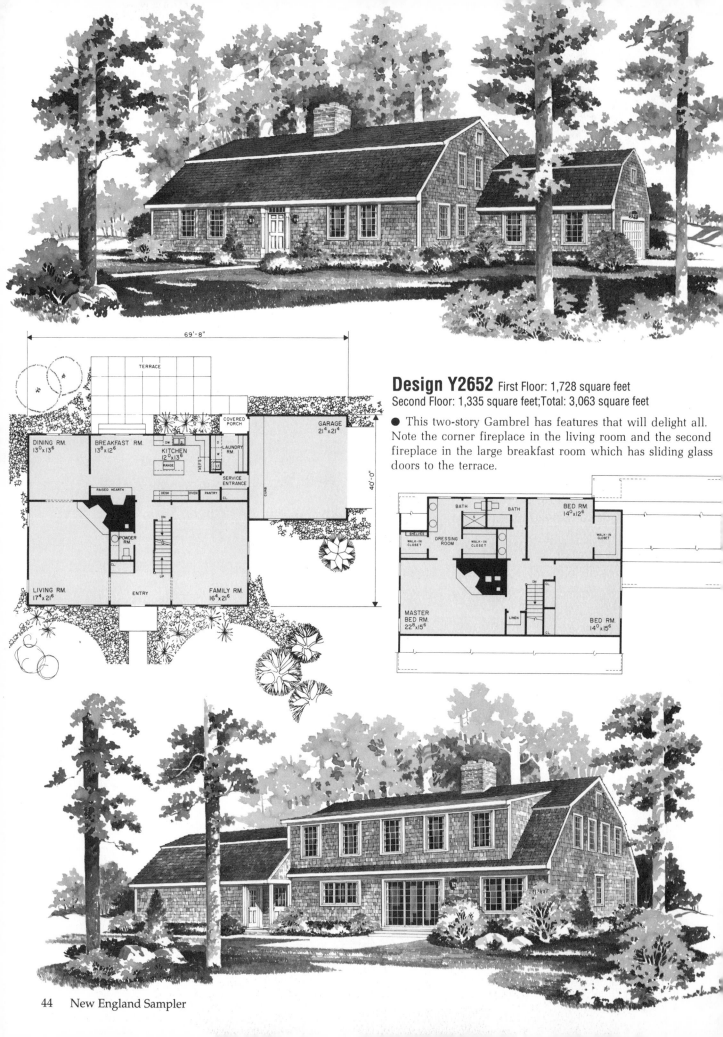

Design Y2652 First Floor: 1,728 square feet
Second Floor: 1,335 square feet;Total: 3,063 square feet

● This two-story Gambrel has features that will delight all.
Note the corner fireplace in the living room and the second
fireplace in the large breakfast room which has sliding glass
doors to the terrace.

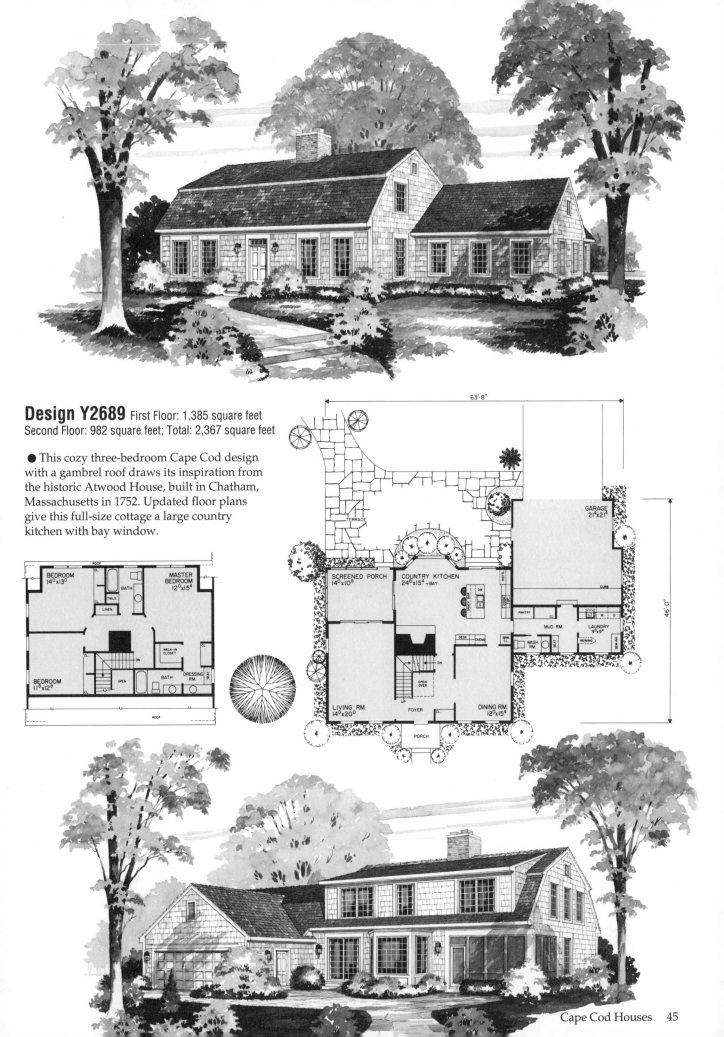

Design Y2689 First Floor: 1,385 square feet
Second Floor: 982 square feet; Total: 2,367 square feet

● This cozy three-bedroom Cape Cod design with a gambrel roof draws its inspiration from the historic Atwood House, built in Chatham, Massachusetts in 1752. Updated floor plans give this full-size cottage a large country kitchen with bay window.

● This Colonial has all the exterior charm of its Early American ancestry, yet its modern interior plan belies its roots. To the immediate left of the entry is a living room with music alcove and fireplace; to the right a formal dining room. In its own wing, a few steps down from the living room, is a cheery sun room. The country kitchen with island range, built-in china cabinet, and a fireplace offers plenty of space for informal eating and overlooks the rear terrace. A laundry, washroom, and garage are also found on this floor. Three bedrooms and two baths on the second floor include the master suite with whirlpool bath.

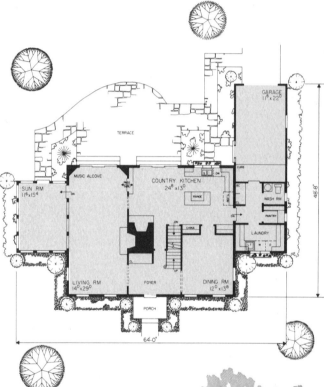

Design Y2986
First Floor: 1,592 square feet
Second Floor: 1,054 square feet
Total: 2,646 square feet

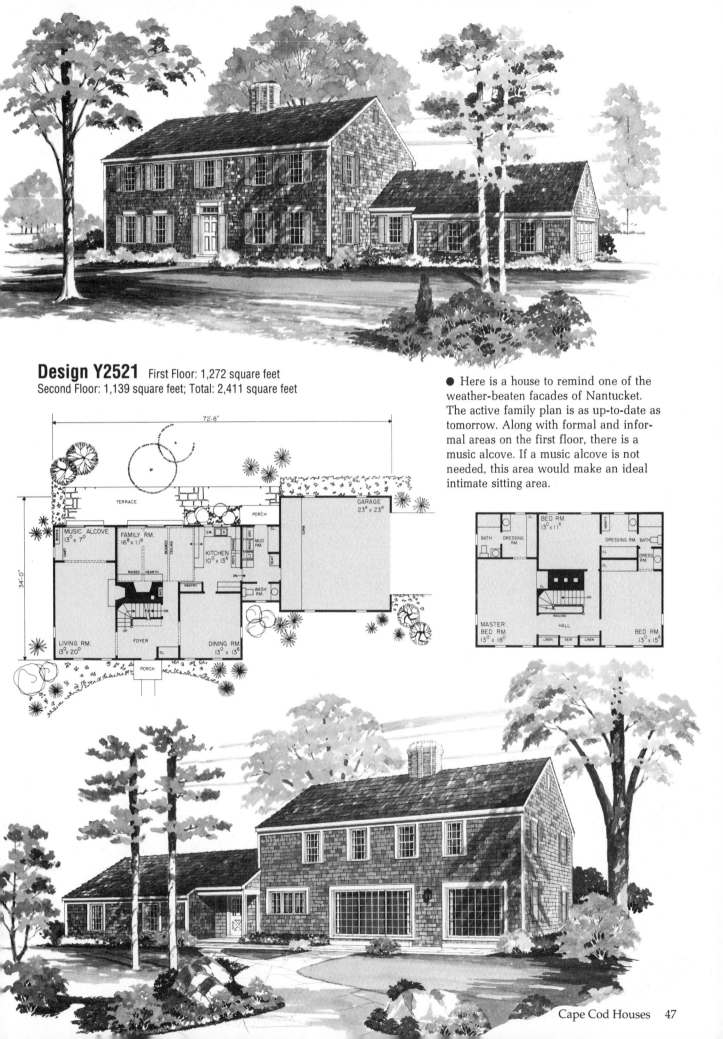

Design Y2521 First Floor: 1,272 square feet
Second Floor: 1,139 square feet; Total: 2,411 square feet

● Here is a house to remind one of the weather-beaten facades of Nantucket. The active family plan is as up-to-date as tomorrow. Along with formal and informal areas on the first floor, there is a music alcove. If a music alcove is not needed, this area would make an ideal intimate sitting area.

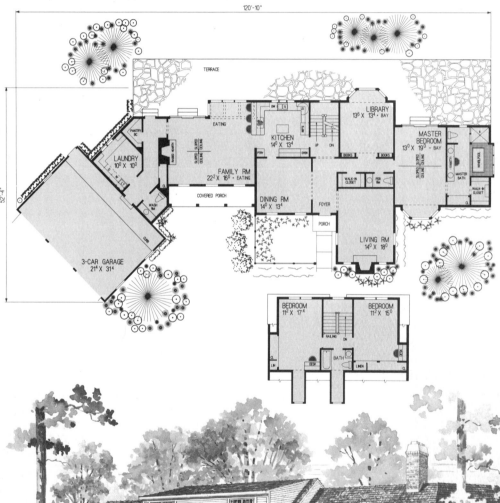

Design Y2995

First Floor: 2,465 square feet
Second Floor: 617 square feet
Total: 3,082 square feet

L **D**

● The New England charm of this 1½-story house is created by varying roof planes and detailing in the facades. The central foyer is flanked by the formal dining and living rooms. The living room is free from cross-room traffic and has its focal point at the end fireplace. Behind the living room is the library with twin bookcases and a projecting bay window. The well-equipped U-shaped kitchen functions well with the snack bar, family room and dining room. A pampering bath adjoins the master suite.

Design Y1787

First Floor: 2,656 square feet
Second Floor: 744 square feet
Total: 3,400 square feet

D

● Can't you picture this dramatic home sitting on your property? The curving front drive is impressive as it passes the walks to the front door and the service entrance. The roof masses, the centered masonry chimney, the window symmetry and the 108 foot expanse across the front are among the features that make this a distinctive home. Of interest are the living and family rooms — both similar in size and each having its own fireplace.

STUDY - LOUNGE
16⁴ x 12⁴
BOOKS
DN.
STORAGE
LIN.
MASTER BED RM.
15⁰ x 21⁶
DRESSING RM.
BATH
CL.
CL.

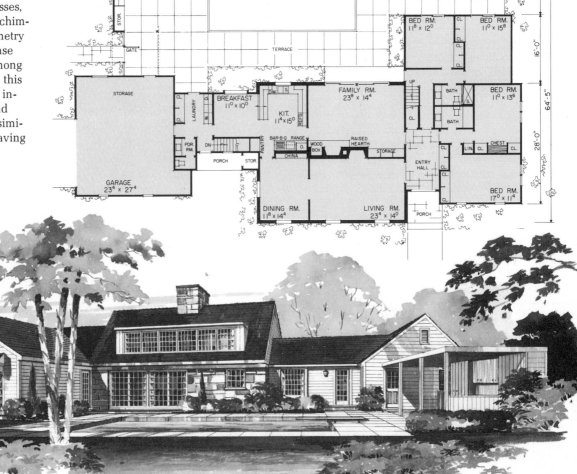

108'-0"

24'-0" 20'-0" 36'-0" 28'-0"

STOR.
COOKING
POOL HOUSE
STOR.
GATE

POOL
36⁰ x 20⁰

TERRACE

16'-0"

BED RM.
11⁸ x 12⁰
BED RM.
11⁰ x 15⁸

16'-0"

STORAGE

LAUNDRY
CL.
BREAKFAST
11⁰ x 10⁰
DW S
KIT.
11⁴ x 15⁰
REFG.

FAMILY RM.
23⁸ x 14⁴

UP

BATH
BED RM.
11⁰ x 13⁶

64'-5"

BATH

PDR. RM.
DN
PANTRY
BAR-B-Q RANGE O.
CHINA
WOOD BOX
RAISED HEARTH
STORAGE
CL. LIN. CHEST CL.

PORCH
STOR.

ENTRY HALL
CL.
CL.

28'-0"

GARAGE
23⁴ x 27⁴

DINING RM.
11⁸ x 14⁴

LIVING RM.
23⁴ x 14⁰

PORCH

BED RM.
17⁰ x 11⁴

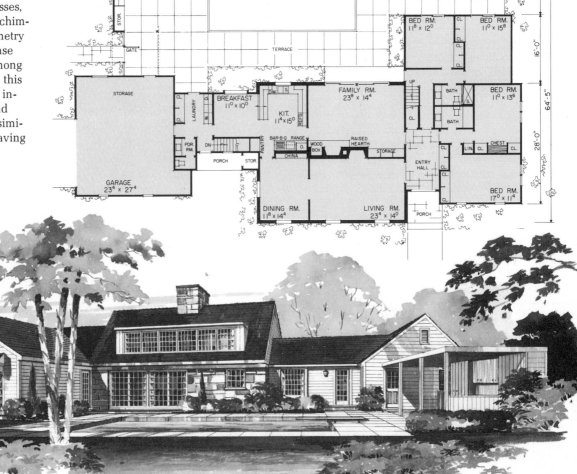

Design Y2658 First Floor: 1,218 square feet
Second Floor: 764 square feet; Total: 1,982 square feet

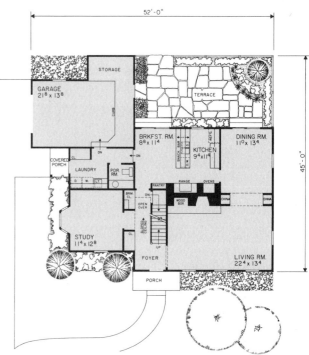

● Traditional charm of yesteryear is exemplified delightfully in this one-and-a-half story home. The garage has been conveniently tucked away in the rear of the house which makes this design ideal for a corner lot. Interior livability has been planned for efficient living. The front living room is large and features a fireplace with wood box. The laundry area is accessible by way of both the garage and a side covered porch. Enter the rear terrace from both eating areas, the formal dining room and the informal breakfast room.

Design Y1970

First Floor: 1,664 square feet
Second Floor: 1,116 square feet
Total: 2,780 square feet

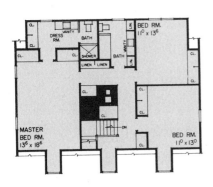

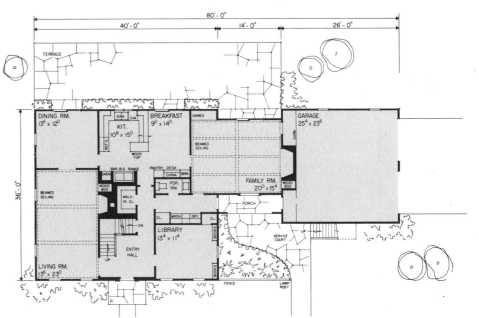

● The prototype of this Colonial house was an integral part of the 18th-Century New England landscape; the updated version is a welcome addition to any suburban scene. The main entry wing, patterned after a classic Cape Cod cottage design, is two stories high but has a pleasing groundhugging look. The steeply pitched roof, triple dormers, and a massive central chimney anchor the house firmly to its site. Entry elevation is symmetrically balanced; doorway, middle dormer, and chimney are in perfect alignment. The one story wing between the main house and the garage is a spacious, beam-ceilinged family room with splay-walled entry porch at the front elevation and sliding glass windows at the rear opening to terrace, which is the full length of the house.

Design Y2644

First Floor: 1,349 square feet
Second Floor: 836 square feet
Total: 2,185 square feet

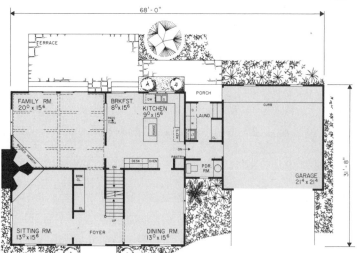

● A bowed-roof Cape cottage. This unusual roof structure survives from the 17th Century and was also known as a ship's bottom or rainbow roof. Inside is an outstanding plan with loads of livability. One raised-hearth fireplace warms the family room while a second fireplace serves the sitting room. The kitchen area features open planning.

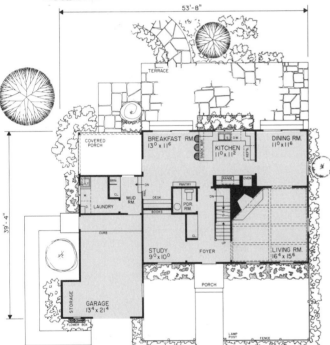

Design Y2656 First Floor: 1,122 square feet
Second Floor: 884 square feet; Total: 2,006 square feet

L **D**

● This charming Cape cottage possesses a great sense of shelter through its gambrel roof. Dormers at front and rear pierce the gambrel roof to provide generous, well-lit living space on the second floor which houses three bedrooms. This design's first floor layout is not far different from that of the Cape cottages of the 18th century. The large kitchen and adjoining dining room recall cottage keeping rooms both in function and in location at the rear of the house.

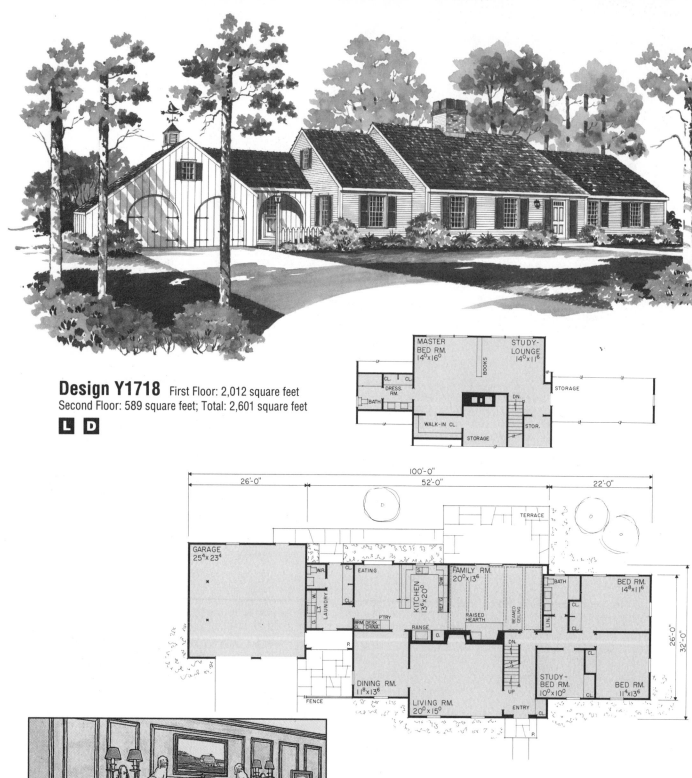

Design Y1718 First Floor: 2,012 square feet
Second Floor: 589 square feet; Total: 2,601 square feet

L D

MASTER BED RM. 14⁰x16⁰

STUDY-LOUNGE 14⁰x11⁶

BOOKS

STORAGE

CL. CL.

DRESS. RM.

BATH

DN.

WALK-IN CL.

STOR.

STORAGE

100'-0"
26'-0" 52'-0" 22'-0"

TERRACE

GARAGE 25⁴x23⁴

W.R.

CL.

EATING

S.

FAMILY RM. 20⁰x13⁶

BATH

BED RM. 14⁸x11⁶

CL.

W.

D.

LAUNDRY

CL.

KITCHEN 13⁶x20⁰

REF'G

DW.

RAISED HEARTH

BEAMED CEILING

LIN.

CL.

26'-0" 32'-0"

BRM CL.

DESK CHINA

P'TRY

RANGE

O.

DN.

STUDY-BED RM. 10⁰x10⁰

CL.

BED RM. 11⁴x13⁶

DINING RM. 11⁸x13⁶

LIVING RM. 20⁰x15⁰

UP

FENCE

ENTRY

CL.

P.

● Here is a good example of how the historic half-house may have grown as its various appendages were attached. The result is a well-proportioned, interesting and practical facade. This 20th Century version can be built all at one time. There is also the option of leaving the second floor unfinished for completion at a later date when family requirements change or finances improve. In this plan the two most frequently used rooms are located to the rear of the house and function with the rear yard. The living room, shown at left, provides a formal conversation spot before the fireplace.

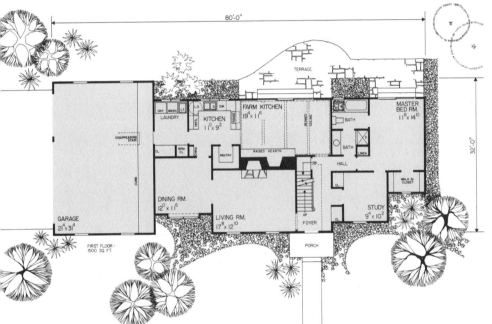

Design Y2563

First Floor: 1,500 square feet
Second Floor: 690 square feet
Total: 2,190 square feet

L **D**

CUSTOMIZABLE

Custom Alterations? See page 381
for customizing this plan to your
specifications.

● This Cape Cod Home combines a favorite
exterior style with a popular floor plan to
provide an outstanding investment with
fine family livability. Appealing window
and door treatment, interesting roof lines
and an irregular configuration catch the eye.
This plan locates formal living areas to the
front and informal to the rear. As viewed at
the right, the raised-hearth fireplace will be
enjoyed from both the family room and
kitchen. Notice that the two sleeping areas
function with their own study and sitting
room. Observe the separate laundry and the
three-car garage.

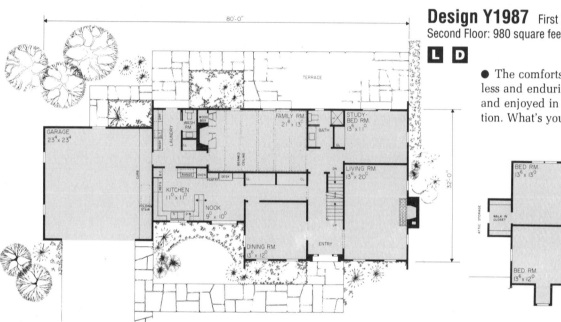

Design Y1987
First Floor: 1,632 square feet
Second Floor: 980 square feet; Total: 2,612 square feet

L D

● The comforts of home will be end-less and enduring when experienced and enjoyed in this Colonial adaptation. What's your favorite feature?

Design Y1791 First Floor: 1,157 square feet
Second Floor: 875 square feet; Total: 2,032 square feet

L **D**

● Wherever you build this moderately sized house an aura of Cape Cod is sure to unfold. The symmetry is pleasing, indeed. The authentic center entrance seems to project a beckoning call.

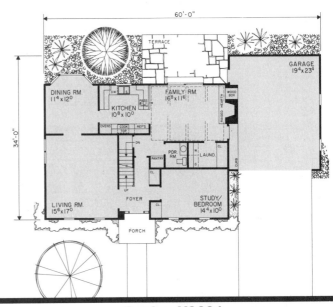

Design Y2631

First Floor: 1,634 square feet
Second Floor: 1,011 square feet
Total: 2,645 square feet

L **D**

● Here is a modified version of Design Y1987 above left. It is offered in reverse with the garage opening on the right.

Design Y2131

First Floor: 1,214 square feet
Second Floor: 1,097 square feet
Total: 2,311 square feet

L **D**

● A Gambrel roof design from our Colonial past. The growing family will have plenty of space in this modest house.

Design Y1701
First Floor: 1,344 square feet
Second Floor: 948 square feet; Total: 2,292 square feet

D

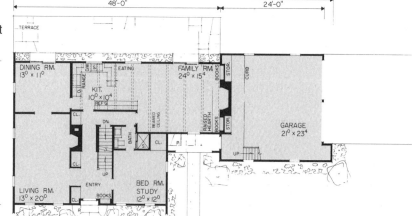

Design Y2396 First Floor: 1,616 square feet
Second Floor: 993 square feet; Total: 2,609 square feet

D

● Another picturesque facade right from the pages of our Colonial heritage. There are many authentic features. Stairs lead to a studio over the garage.

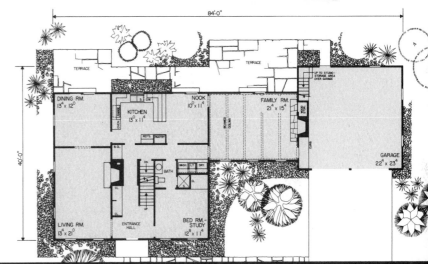

Design Y1870

First Floor: 1,136 square feet
Second Floor: 936 square feet
Total: 2,072 square feet

● Besides an enchanting exterior, this home has formal dining and living rooms, plus informal family and breakfast rooms. Note 2½ baths.

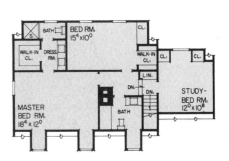

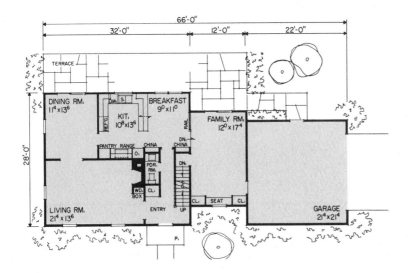

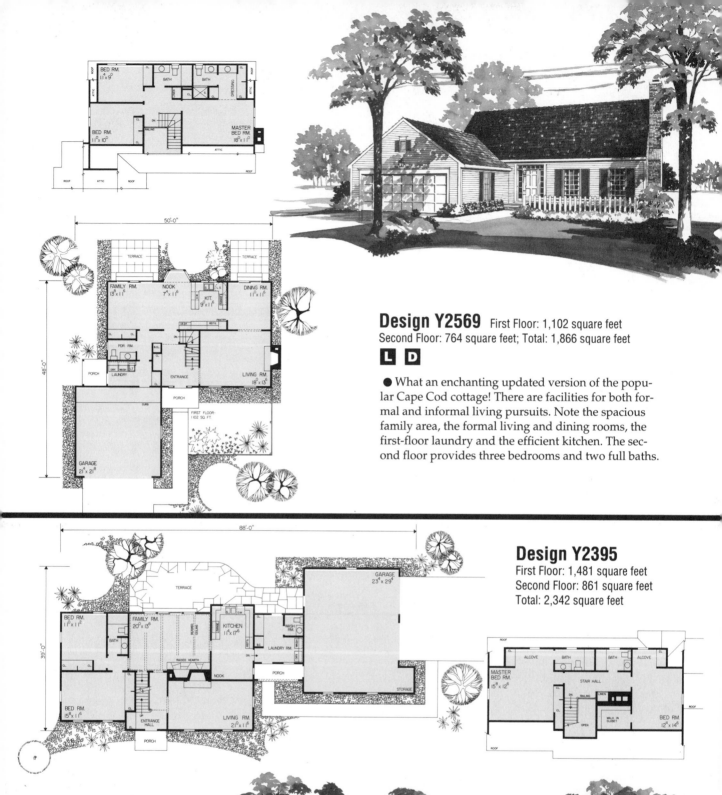

Design Y2569
First Floor: 1,102 square feet
Second Floor: 764 square feet; Total: 1,866 square feet

L D

● What an enchanting updated version of the popular Cape Cod cottage! There are facilities for both formal and informal living pursuits. Note the spacious family area, the formal living and dining rooms, the first-floor laundry and the efficient kitchen. The second floor provides three bedrooms and two full baths.

Design Y2395
First Floor: 1,481 square feet
Second Floor: 861 square feet
Total: 2,342 square feet

● This is New England revisited, with an appeal that is ageless. With two bedrooms downstairs, you may want to finish the second floor at a later date. Alternatively, one first-floor bedroom may serve as a guest suite while the other provides space for an office.

● Captivating as a New England village! From the weather vane atop the garage to the roofed side entry and paned windows, this home is perfectly detailed. Inside, there is a lot of living space. An exceptionally large family room which is more than 29' by 13' including a dining area. The adjoining kitchen has a laundry just steps away. Two formal rooms are in the front.

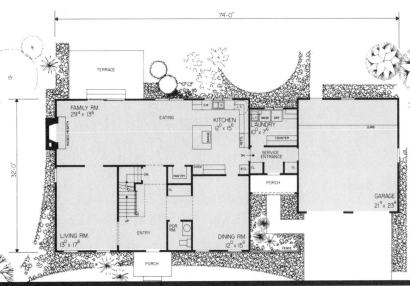

Design Y2596

First Floor: 1,489 square feet
Second Floor: 982 square feet
Total: 2,471 square feet

L **D**

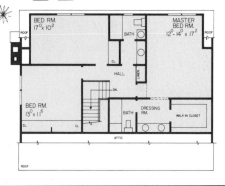

Design Y2559

First Floor: 1,388 square feet
Second Floor: 809 square feet
Total: 2,197 square feet

D

● Offering great livability including a 26-foot living room with fireplace, a quiet study with built-in bookshelves, and excellent dining facilities, this home also has an appealing exterior. There are three bedrooms on the second floor — one a master suite with private bath.

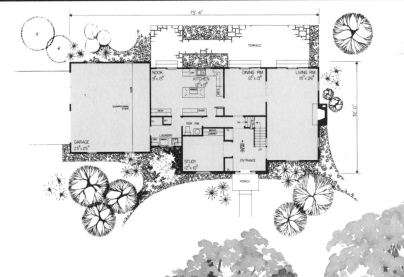

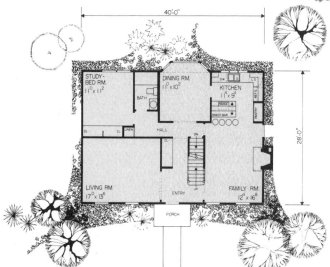

Design Y2571 First Floor: 1,137 square feet
Second Floor: 795 square feet; Total: 1,932 square feet

L **D**

● Cost-efficient space! That's the bonus with this attractive Cape Cod. An efficient kitchen with a pass-through to the family room and a large storage pantry. Three bedrooms are located on the second floor.

Design Y2852
First Floor: 919 square feet
Second Floor: 535 square feet; Total: 1,454 square feet

L D

● Compact enough for even the smallest lot, this cozy design provides comfortable living space for a small family. At the heart of the plan is a spacious country kitchen. It features a cooking island - snack bar and a dining area that opens to a house-wide rear terrace. The nearby dining room also opens to the terrace. At the front of the plan is the living room, warmed by a fireplace. Across the centered foyer is a cozy study. Two second floor bedrooms are serviced by two baths. Note the first floor powder room and storage closet located next to the side entrance. This home will be a delight.

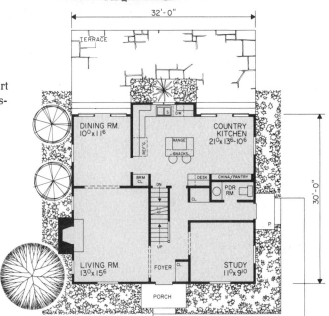

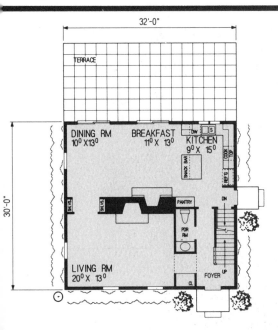

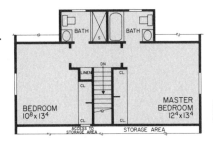

Design Y3501
First Floor: 960 square feet
Second Floor: 733 square feet
Total: 1,693 square feet

● This Cape Cod half-house may look like half a house, but it includes three bedrooms and two full baths plus a handy powder room on the first floor. A large living room in the front of the home features a fireplace. The rear of the home is left open, with room for a kitchen with snack bar, breakfast area with fireplace and dining room with outdoor access. If you wish, use the breakfast area as an all-purpose dining room and turn the dining area into a library or sitting room.

Informal Family Living Areas

The main room of early Colonial houses was known as the hall or keeping room. It functioned as the living room, dining room, kitchen and workroom. As houses grew in size, the kitchen and work activities such as sewing, candle-making and weaving occupied a room of their own. Further expansion led to the incorporation of the parlor into Colonial plans. As the only source of heat, the fireplace became a dominant feature of these rooms.

Design Y2157, page 137.
(Right) Informal living area with beamed ceiling, a step down from the kitchen.

Around the corner from the work center.

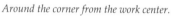

A spacious conversation area.

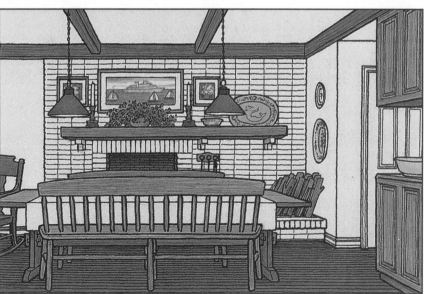

Design Y2563, page 55.
Country kitchen with snack bar.

A functional room for music by firelight.

By the end of the 19th Century even houses of modest size included, in addition to the kitchen, a parlor and what had become known as the living room. The parlor was a seldom-used formal room reserved for use during weddings, funerals and visits from the minister. The living room was the informal living area. Since World War II changes in terminology have taken place. The parlor has become the living room; the living room has become the family room.

On the following pages is a collection of artist's sketches depicting informal family living areas. Of interest, and of help to the home planner, are views which include: fireplaces, beamed ceilings, decorating ideas, furniture and its groupings, and overall ambience. Many of the sketches are from home designs featured in the book.

Design Y2635, page 42.
The fireplace and mantel form a commanding presence.

The Family/Gathering Room

Fireplaces have many faces. Some are made of brick, others of stone. Patterns and textures of the masonry vary: Some fireplaces have mantels that reflect a variety of sizes and styles; others forego the mantel altogether Fireplaces can be the focal point of an impressive masonry wall, or they can be one of a number of features on a wall with bookshelves, a wood bin, pictures and windows. They may be located so they can be enjoyed from a couple of rooms simultaneously. Fireplaces may have raised hearths that project into the rooms, adding an extra measure of appeal and providing a spot for the placement of firewood, fireplace tools and a variety of decorations.

Design Y2223, page 151.
A cozy corner for conversation.

Design Y2540, page 105.
An eye-catching corner.

Sloped ceiling and flanking windows.

Design Y2774, page 147.
Textured wall and a practical hearth.

Design Y2542, page 140.
Books, firewood and a warm glo[w]

Open-ended enjoyment.

The Family/Gathering Room

Large picture windows create a bright and cheerful atmosphere and provide the opportunity to view and enjoy the surrounding landscape. Such large glass areas are effectively utilized in projecting bays, adjacent to massive masonry walls, and to break up long wall expanses. Multi-lite windows with their muntins become a highly decorative factor in traditionally styled homes. These large glass areas may be fixed, immovable windows, or in the form of sliding glass doors that permit access to outdoor living areas. Of interest in these illustrations are the placements of the room furniture in relation to the glass areas. Some furniture is pleasingly arranged in front of windows; others, beside. Whatever the furniture placement, windows serve the primary function of providing a full measure of natural light to the interior.

Design Y2500, page 152.
Window bay provides group seating.

Flanking the stone fireplace.

Assuring a bright, cheerful interior.

Enjoying the outdoor panorama.

Sliding doors flanked by fixed panels.

A cozy gathering spot.

The Family Room

Family rooms are areas that cater to the informal living patterns of the active family. As these interior views show, the style, type and placement of furniture, as well as the presence of accessories, mementos, and knick-knacks all contribute to an ambience conducive to pleasurable living. Conversational corners, eating areas, games tables, music spaces and lounging facilities go together to foster wholesome family livability.

Design Y1701, page 58.
Backdrop for multi-purpose activity.

Design Y2644, page 52.
A cheerful multi-purpose room.

Masonry wall for cooking and fireplace.

Design Y2681, page 145.
A through-fireplace provides double enjoyment.

Design Y2614, page 152.
Enjoy game-time or tea-time by the fire.

The Gathering Room

Gathering rooms can have a formal look, too, with a pleasant and interesting atmosphere. Arched openings, mouldings, mantels, coffered ceilings and radial head windows are among the architectural elements that contribute to this formal ambience. The formality is further enhanced by the drapery, wall and floor covering, accessories and, of course, furniture. These views exemplify the elegance of formality around the fireplace. As seen on prior pages, large glass areas make a wonderfully important contribution to livability.

Design Y2977, page 251.
Inviting the outdoors in.

Design Y2230, page 246.
An arched opening creates a welcoming portal.

Accessories enhance a room.

Design Y2897, page 95.
(Below, left) Radial head windows make a
statement.

Design Y2283, page 256.
(Below) Coffered ceiling and paneled walls.

Informal Family Living Areas   73

Family Living

Family activities often include such convivial pursuits as playing games. Who cannot remember from their childhood the games of checkers, dominoes or backgammon? The gathering or family room is just the place to make a provision for these family endeavors. As a dual-use area, such a room with a games table caters to informal dining, hobbies, homework and organizing. It is in this room that the family's library may be conveniently located. The younger generation may congregate here near the TV and entertainment equipment.

The games table awaits action.

A home library or study area.

A convenient spot for a hand of bridge.

Design Y2174, page 153.
A game of backgammon in progress.

The sloped, beamed ceiling creates space.

A warming influence for family activity.

EARLY
NEW ENGLAND
HOUSES

arly New England Houses of the 17th Century were Medieval in character. They were almost exclusively of frame construction and were devoid of much elaboration or adornment. Many reflected their earlier Gothic and Tudor origins. The following houses capture much of this ambience. Such designs as Y2101, Y2642 and Y2978 are quite authentic exterior interpretations of their forebears—the Parson Capen, the Paul Revere and the Nathaniel Hawthorne houses. Of course, their floor plans in no way resemble those of the original structures. Most of the designs in this section are of modest size, ranging from 1,248 to 3,465 square feet. Centered entry halls, formal living and dining rooms, family rooms and country kitchens, functional kitchens, first-floor laundries, master bedrooms and baths are all among the 20th-Century highlights of these 17th- and early 18th-Century facade adaptations.

Four-Bedroom Colonial Saltbox

● The history of the Colonial Saltbox goes back some 200 years. This adaptation of the historic Thomas Bannister House in Podunk, Massachusetts captures all the warmth and charm of the early days both inside and out. To reflect today's living patterns, an up-dating of the floor plan was inevitable. The result is a room arrangement which will serve the active family wonderfully. Formal living and dining take place at one end of the house, free from cross-room traffic. Informal living activities will center around the family room and expand through sliding glass doors to the terrace. The mud room area is strategically located and includes the laundry and a full bath. An extra study/bedroom supplements four bedrooms upstairs. Closets and other storage areas are abundant.

Design Y1900
First Floor: 1,672 square feet
Second Floor: 1,287 square feet
Total: 2,959 square feet

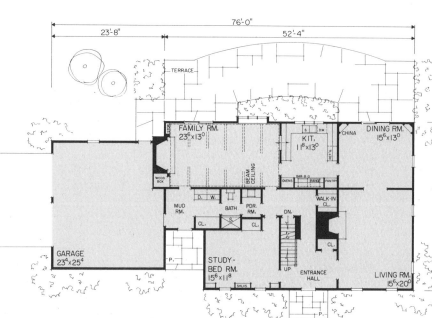

The study, with its built-in bookshelves, can also be called upon to function as a guest or family bedroom. Shown here with a functional bedroom, the room could instead be furnished with a sofa bed to serve the purposes of both. Full bath facilities are just around the corner.

Activities in the formal living room center around the paneled fireplace wall. The mouldings and the mantel strike a pleasing decorative note. Tea time will be an enjoyable time amidst these surroundings. This large room with its blank wall space lends itself to a variety of room arrangements.

Early New England Houses   79

A Garrison House from Yesteryear

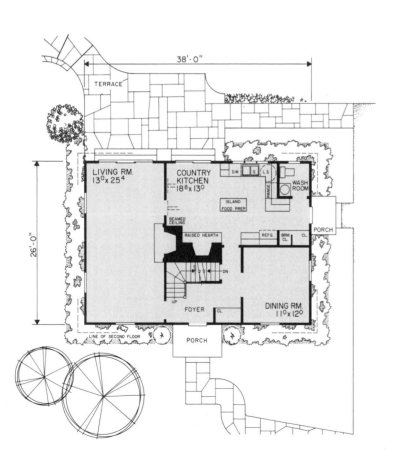

38'-0"

TERRACE

26'-0"

LIVING RM.
13⁰ x 25⁴

COUNTRY KITCHEN
18⁸ x 13⁰

D.W. S. L.S.

WASH ROOM

RANGE

ISLAND FOOD PREP.

BEAMED CEILING

RAISED HEARTH

REFG.

BRM CL.

CL.

PORCH

DN

UP

FOYER

CL.

DINING RM.
11⁰ x 12⁰

LINE OF SECOND FLOOR

PORCH

Design Y2666
First Floor: 988 square feet
Second Floor: 1,147 square feet
Total: 2,135 square feet

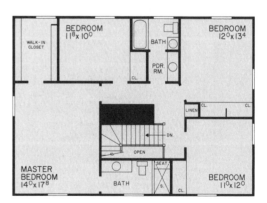

BEDROOM
11⁸ x 10⁰

WALK-IN CLOSET

BATH

PDR. RM.

BEDROOM
12⁰ x 13⁴

CL.

LINEN

CL.

CL.

DN.

OPEN

MASTER BEDROOM
14⁰ x 17⁸

SEAT

S

BATH

CL.

BEDROOM
11⁰ x 12⁰

● Garrison houses have their roots farther back than 17th-Century New England. The prominent second-floor overhang was a popular feature of English houses between the 11th and 16th Centuries. There is little agreement among historians concerning the function of the overhang. Popular folklore tells of it serving as a haven from which to drop boiling water on attacking Indians. Some maintain it protected lower-floor timbers and wattling from rain. Others say it provided shelter for patrons of first-floor shops in cities. However, it is possible that its purpose was more decorative than practical. Even today, it serves the utilitarian purpose of providing the second floor with more square footage than the first floor. Observe the bracketed gables, the wooden pendant drops under the overhang and the carriage lamps flanking the paneled door. The central foyer assures efficient and flexible traffic patterns. The entire left side of the interior is devoted to the 25-foot living room with its centered fireplace. To the right of the foyer is the formal dining room. Four bedrooms and two baths are found upstairs.

Straight ahead from the foyer is the open-planned country kitchen. As viewed from near the refrigerator, this area, with its beamed ceiling and muntined windows, has plenty of character. Imagine all that cupboard and counter space. There is plenty of room for a big dining table near the raised-hearth fireplace.

Historic Yankee Homestead

Design Y2978

First Floor: 1,451 square feet
Second Floor: 1,268 square feet
Third Floor: 746 square feet
Total: 3,465 square feet

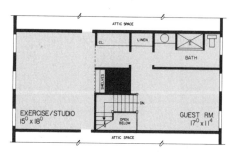

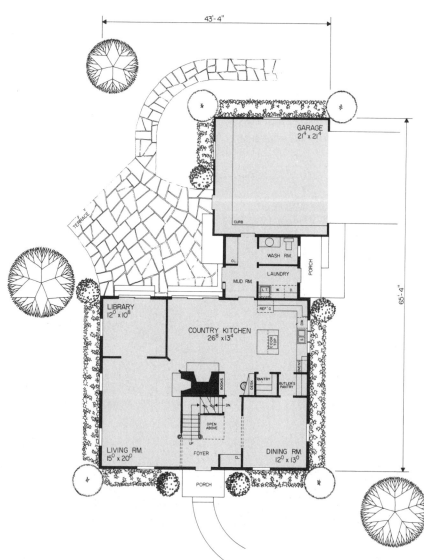

Looking over the island cooktop and counter with its ample storage capacity below, there is much on which to focus attention. To the left of the view is a partial look at the built-in shelving unit. Utilize this for books or, as shown, pottery. Don't miss the richly detailed fireplace with its charming mantel. To the right of the paneled door to the living room, a long wall offers great potential for furniture placement.

● The Nathaniel Hawthorne house in Salem, Massachusetts was the inspiration for this New England gambrel-roofed design. It was originally constructed around 1730. This 20th-Century version offers a heap of living potential. The family's favorite spot will be in front of the fireplace in the spacious country kitchen. However, there are other places to retire to, such as the formal living room with a second fireplace, the adjacent library with terrace access and the dining room. Three bedrooms on the second floor include a master suite with a dressing room that offers His and Hers walk-in closets. The third floor accommodates a guest bedroom and a large exercise room or studio. Additional recreational space can be developed in the basement. Don't overlook the mud room strategically located with access from the garage and both yards. With the garage projecting to the rear (ideal for a corner lot), a sheltered terrace forms.

Design Y2101

First Floor: 1,338 square feet
Second Floor: 1,114 square feet
Total: 2,452 square feet

● This is a modified version of one of America's most famous Colonial dwellings, the Parson Capen of Topsfield, Mass. Dating back to the 17th-Century, the English colonists built this medieval adaptation reproducing its bracketed second floor overhang, pendant drops at the corners, massive pilastered chimney and narrow clapboards. The floor plan, of course, has been updated to cater to today's living requirements.

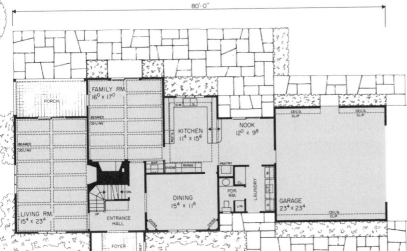

80'-0"

38'-0"

PORCH

FAMILY RM.
16⁰ x 17⁰

BEAMED CEILING

BEAMED CEILING

LIVING RM.
15⁴ x 23⁴

ENTRANCE HALL

FOYER

KITCHEN
11⁴ x 15⁶

BAR

OVENS

RANGE

PANTRY

PDR. RM.

CL.

LIN

DINING
15⁴ x 11⁶

NOOK
12⁰ x 9⁸

CEIL'G CLIP

CEIL'G CLIP

LAUNDRY

GARAGE
23⁴ x 23⁴

CEIL'G CLIP

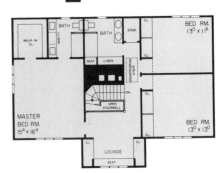

WALK-IN CL.

BATH

VANITY

BATH

STOR.

SEAT

LINEN

DN

OPEN STAIRWELL

BED RM.
13⁰ x 11⁶

MASTER BED RM.
15⁴ x 16⁴

CL.

BED RM.
13⁰ x 13⁰

LOUNGE

SEAT

Design Y2191
First Floor: 1,553 square feet
Second Floor: 1,197 square feet
Total: 2,750 square feet

L

● This exquisite house reproduces the architectural details from 17th-Century Medieval and Tudor influences. It is reminiscent of the so-called Witch's House in Salem, Massachusetts. The floor plan delivers wonderful livability. Don't miss the lounge and covered porch.

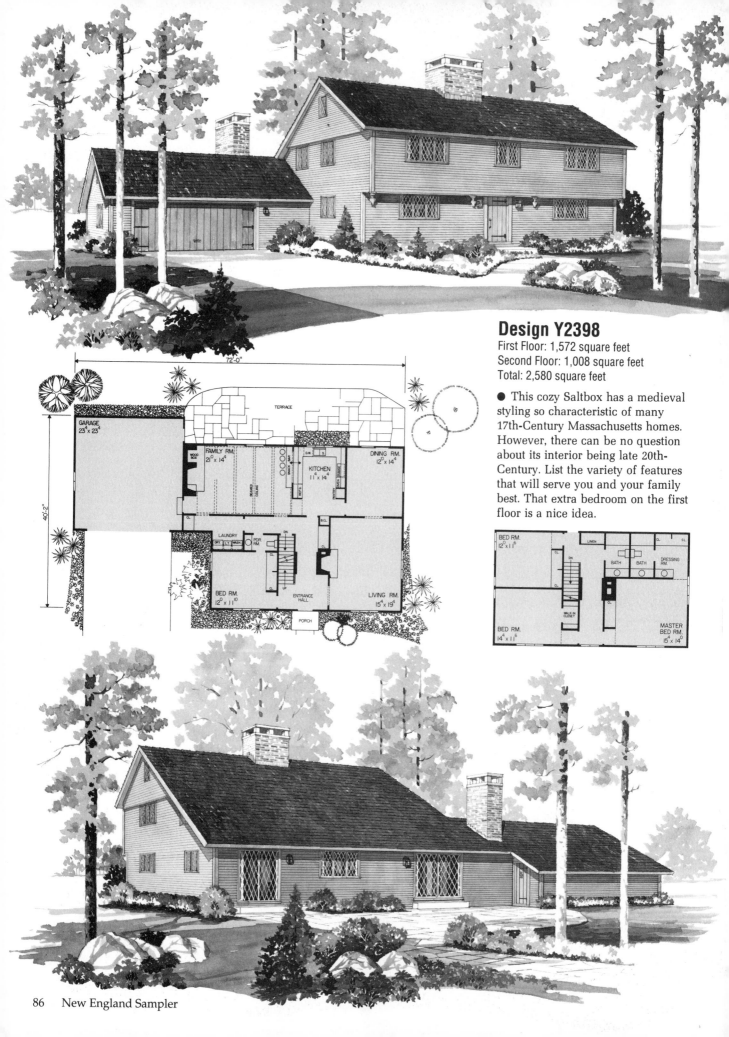

Design Y2398

First Floor: 1,572 square feet
Second Floor: 1,008 square feet
Total: 2,580 square feet

● This cozy Saltbox has a medieval styling so characteristic of many 17th-Century Massachusetts homes. However, there can be no question about its interior being late 20th-Century. List the variety of features that will serve you and your family best. That extra bedroom on the first floor is a nice idea.

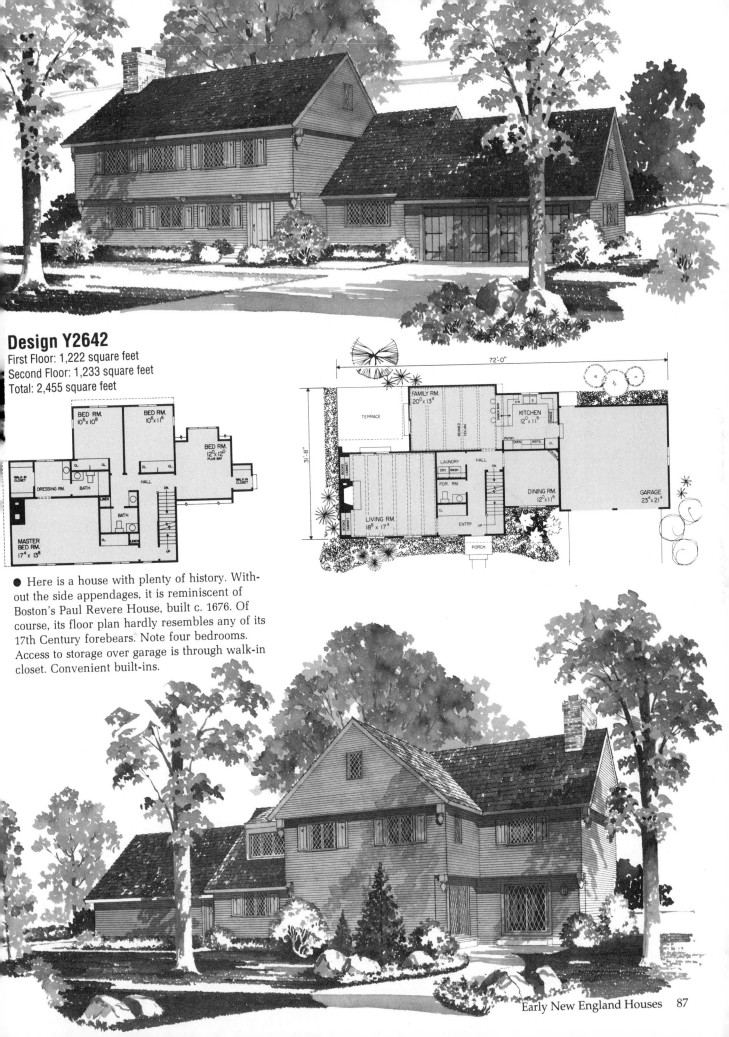

Design Y2642

First Floor: 1,222 square feet
Second Floor: 1,233 square feet
Total: 2,455 square feet

● Here is a house with plenty of history. Without the side appendages, it is reminiscent of Boston's Paul Revere House, built c. 1676. Of course, its floor plan hardly resembles any of its 17th Century forebears. Note four bedrooms. Access to storage over garage is through walk-in closet. Convenient built-ins.

Design Y2651

First Floor: 1,404 square feet
Second Floor: 1,323 square feet
Total: 2,727 square feet

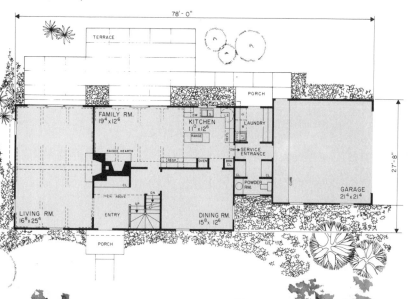

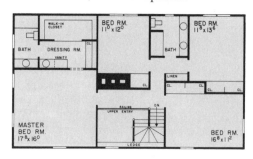

● This Garrison house recalls that of Micum McIntyre built in Scotland, Maine, reputedly between 1640 and 1645. The central entry hall is open to the second floor and has a curving open staircase. The end living room has a beamed ceiling as in the family room. Both rooms are spacious and have a fireplace. Note the service area leading from the garage and the four-bedroom, two-bath upstairs.

Design Y2692

First Floor: 1,818 square feet
Second Floor: 1,395 square feet
Total: 3,213 square feet

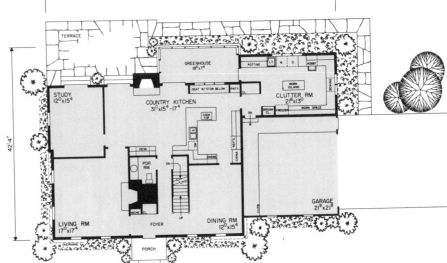

● This feature-filled Colonial saltbox adaptation is just as delightful inside as on the outside! Highlights include a large country kitchen, practical clutter room in the rear, spectacular rear greenhouse, and four bedrooms isolated for peace and quiet upstairs. The greenhouse adds 147 square feet not included in the totals above and is certain to be a focal point in this very comfortable home. An adjacent large clutter room with work island provides plenty of useful space for hobbies, sewing, freezer, storage, and greenhouse potting area. The large country kitchen incorporates a cozy family fire-place and efficient U-shaped kitchen with built-ins. The first floor also includes a front dining room, large front living room with fireplace, powder room, and rear study. A large master bedroom with separate bath is located upstairs along with three other bedrooms and a second bath.

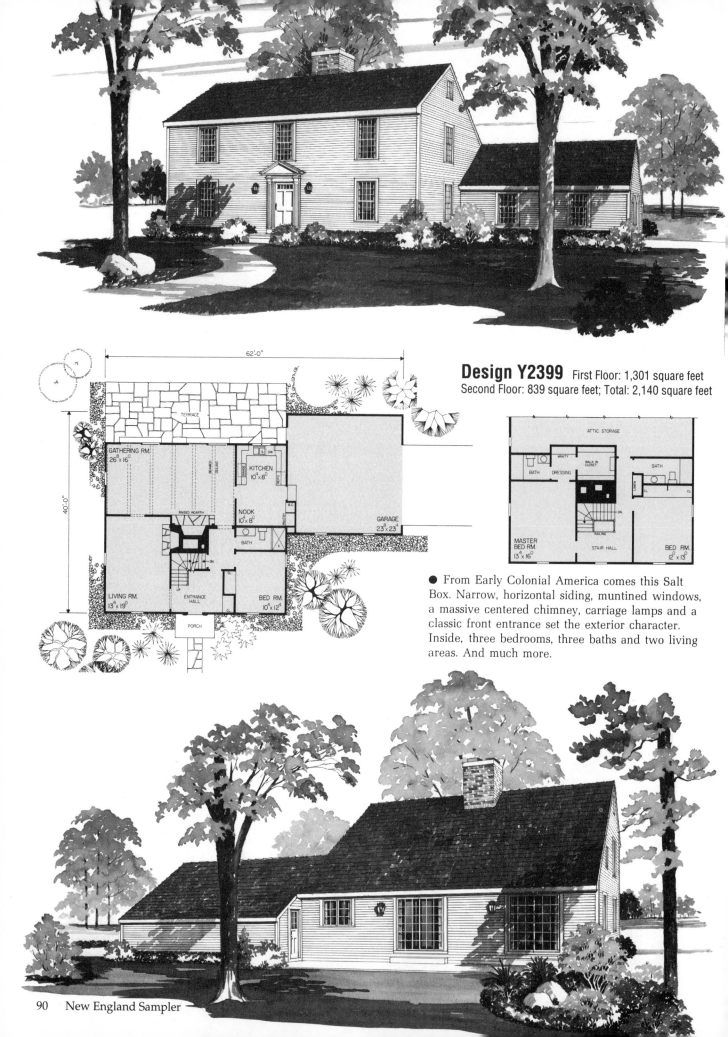

Design Y2399 First Floor: 1,301 square feet
Second Floor: 839 square feet; Total: 2,140 square feet

● From Early Colonial America comes this Salt
Box. Narrow, horizontal siding, muntined windows,
a massive centered chimney, carriage lamps and a
classic front entrance set the exterior character.
Inside, three bedrooms, three baths and two living
areas. And much more.

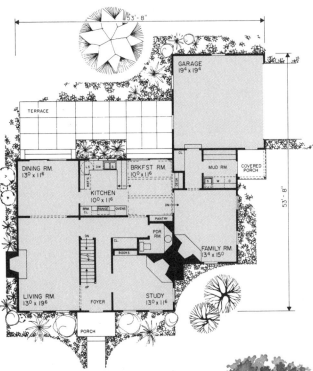

Design Y2616 First Floor: 1,415 square feet
Second Floor: 1,106 square feet; Total: 2,521 square feet

● Unlike the majority of the Salt Boxes of Colonial New England, this design has a distinguishing feature: a saw-tooth-shaped side wing that shares the same rear roofline as the house to which it was appended. History is exquisitely detailed in this exterior yet its floor plan has been planned to serve today's family conveniently.

Design Y2654

First Floor: 1,152 square feet
Second Floor: 844 square feet
Total: 1,996 square feet

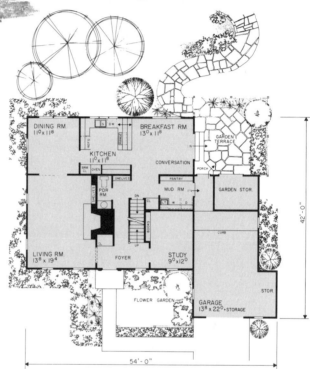

● This is certainly an authentic traditional salt-box. It features a symmetrical design with a center fireplace, a wide, paneled doorway and multi-paned, double-hung windows. Tucked behind the one-car garage is a garden shed which provides work and storage space. The breakfast room features French doors which open onto a flagstone terrace. The U-shaped kitchen has built-in counters which make efficient use of space. The upstairs plan houses three bedrooms.

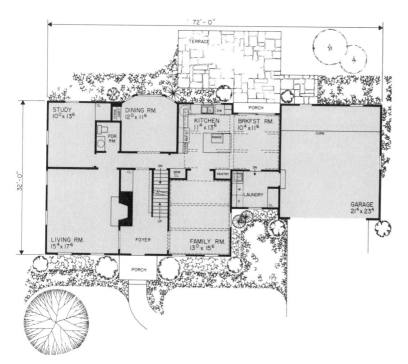

Design Y2649

First Floor: 1,501 square feet
Second Floor: 1,280 square feet
Total: 2,781 square feet

● This design's front exterior is highlighted by four pedimented nine-over-nine windows, five second-story eyebrow windows and a massive central chimney. Note the spacious kitchen of the interior. It is large in size and features an island range, pantry and broom closets, breakfast room with sliding glass doors to the rear porch and an adjacent laundry room which has access to the garage.

Design Y1887

First Floor: 1,518 square feet
Second Floor: 1,144 square feet
Total: 2,662 square feet

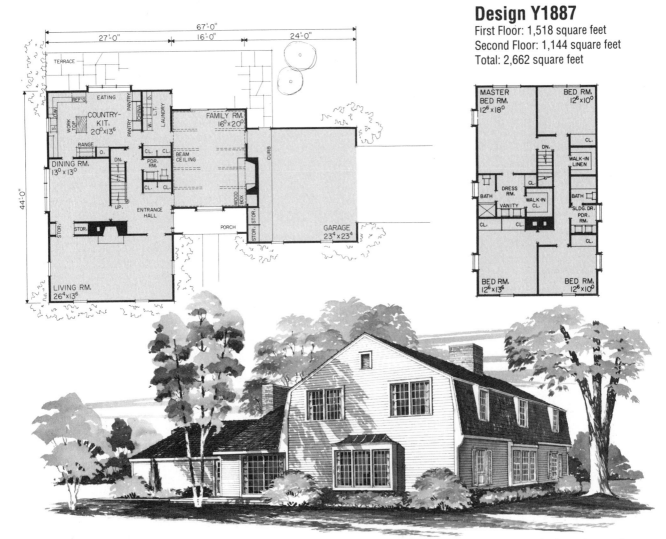

● This Gambrel roof Colonial is steeped in history. And well it should be, for its pleasing proportions are a delight to the eye. The various roof planes, the window treatment, and the rambling nature of the entire house revive a picture of rural New England. The covered porch protects the front door which opens into a spacious entrance hall. Traffic then flows in an orderly fashion to the end living room, the separate dining room, the cozy family room, and to the spacious country-kitchen. There is a first floor laundry, plenty of coat closets, and a handy powder room. Two fireplaces enliven the decor of the living areas. Upstairs there is an exceptional master bedroom layout, and abundant storage. Note the walk-in closets.

Design Y2897

First Floor: 1,648 square feet
Second Floor: 1,140 square feet
Total: 2,788 square feet

● A covered service entrance and attached two-car garage enhance the appeal of this gambrel roof design. A wing projecting to the rear greatly increases livability by providing a big family room with a sloped ceiling and a raised-hearth fireplace. The outstanding master bedroom and first-floor study provide views into this sunken room. Flanking the central foyer are the formal living and dining rooms. Note the efficient kitchen, breakfast room, powder room and laundry.

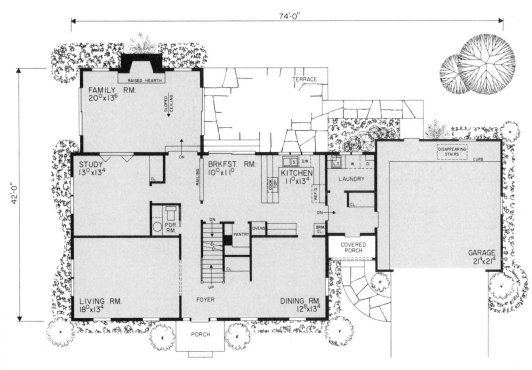

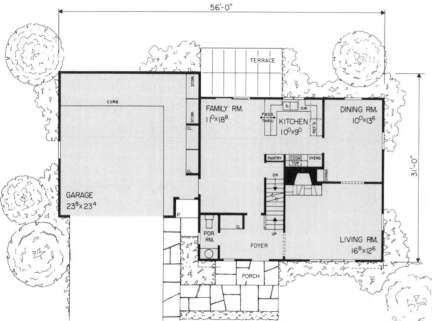

56'-0"

TERRACE

STOR.

STOR.

CURB

FAMILY RM.
11⁰x18⁸

PASS
THRU

KITCHEN
10⁰x9⁰

S.

D.W.

REF'G.

DINING RM.
10⁰x13⁶

CL.

CL.

PANTRY

COOK
TOP

OVENS

CHINA

DN

31'-0"

GARAGE
23⁸x23⁴

P

PDR.
RM.

CL.

UP

FOYER

LIVING RM.
16⁸x12⁶

PORCH

Design Y1719 First Floor: 864 square feet
Second Floor: 896 square feet; Total: 1,760 square feet

L **D**

BEDROOM
11⁰x10⁰

CL.

BATH

VANITY

BEDROOM
10⁰x11⁴

CL.

LINEN

WALK-IN
CLOSET

LINEN

DN

CL.

CL.

CL.

WALK-IN
CLOSET

BEDROOM
11⁰x13⁸

S.

BATH

MASTER
BEDROOM
13⁴x13⁴

● What an appealing low-cost Colonial
adaptation. Most of the livability features
generally found in the largest of homes
are present to cater to family needs.

Design Y2799 First Floor: 1,196 square feet
Second Floor: 780 square feet; Total: 1,976 square feet

● This two-story traditional design's facade
with its narrow clapboards, punctuated by
tall multi-paned windows, appears decep-
tively expansive. Yet the entire length of
the house, including the garage, is 66 feet.

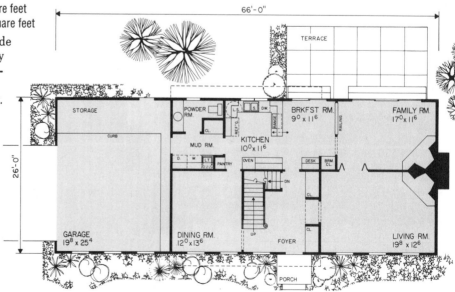

66'-0"

TERRACE

STORAGE

CURB

POWDER
RM.

CL.

MUD RM.

REF'G.

S.

D.W.

BRKFST RM.
9⁰x11⁶

RANGE

RAILING

FAMILY RM.
17⁰x11⁶

KITCHEN
10⁰x11⁶

26'-0"

D

W

LT

PANTRY

OVEN

DN

DESK

BRM
CL.

GARAGE
19⁸x25⁴

DINING RM.
12⁰x13⁶

UP

FOYER

CL.

LIVING RM.
19⁸x12⁶

PORCH

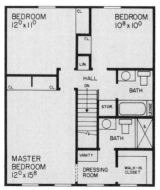

BEDROOM
12⁰x11⁰

CL.

BEDROOM
10⁸x10⁰

CL.

LIN.

CL.

CL.

HALL

DN

CL.

BATH

STOR.

LEDGE

BATH

S.

MASTER
BEDROOM
12⁰x15⁸

VANITY

DRESSING
ROOM

WALK-IN
CLOSET

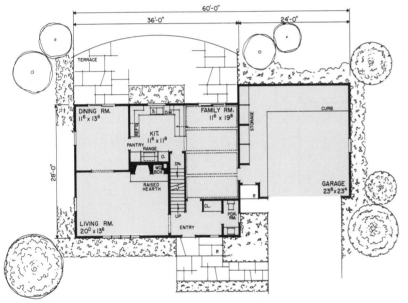

A Garrison type adaptation that projects all the romance of yesteryear. The narrow horizontal siding, the wide corner boards, the window detailing, the overhanging second floor and the massive, centered chimney help set this home apart.

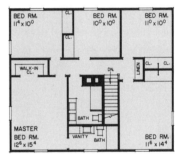

Design Y1849 First Floor: 1,008 square feet
Second Floor: 1,080 square feet; Total: 2,088 square feet

Design Y2539

First Floor: 1,450 square feet
Second Floor: 1,167 square feet
Total: 2,617 square feet

● This appealingly proportioned gambrel exudes an aura of coziness. The beauty of the main part of the house is delightfully symmetrical and is enhanced by the attached garage and laundry room. The center entrance routes traffic directly to all major zones of the house.

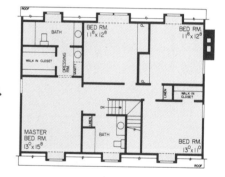

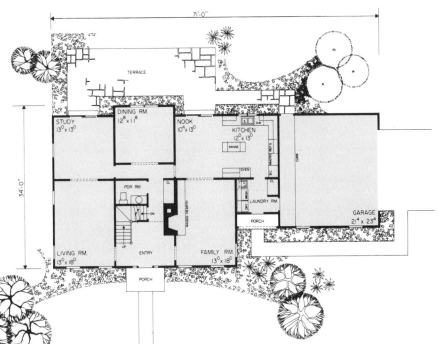

Design Y2538

First Floor: 1,503 square feet
Second Floor: 1,095 square feet
Total: 2,598 square feet

L **D**

● This Salt Box is charming, indeed. The livability it has to offer to the large and growing family is great. The entry is spacious and is open to the second floor balcony. For living areas, there is the study in addition to the living and family rooms.

Design Y2731   First Floor: 1,039 square feet

Second Floor: 973 square feet; Total: 2,012 square feet

L **D**

● The multi-paned windows with shutters of this two-story highlight the exterior delightfully. Inside the livability is ideal. Formal and informal areas are sure to serve your family with ease. Note efficient U-shaped kitchen with handy first-floor laundry. Sleeping facilities on second floor.

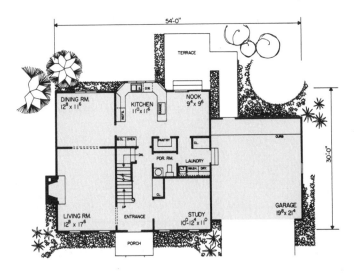

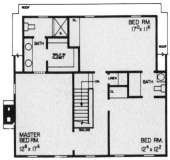

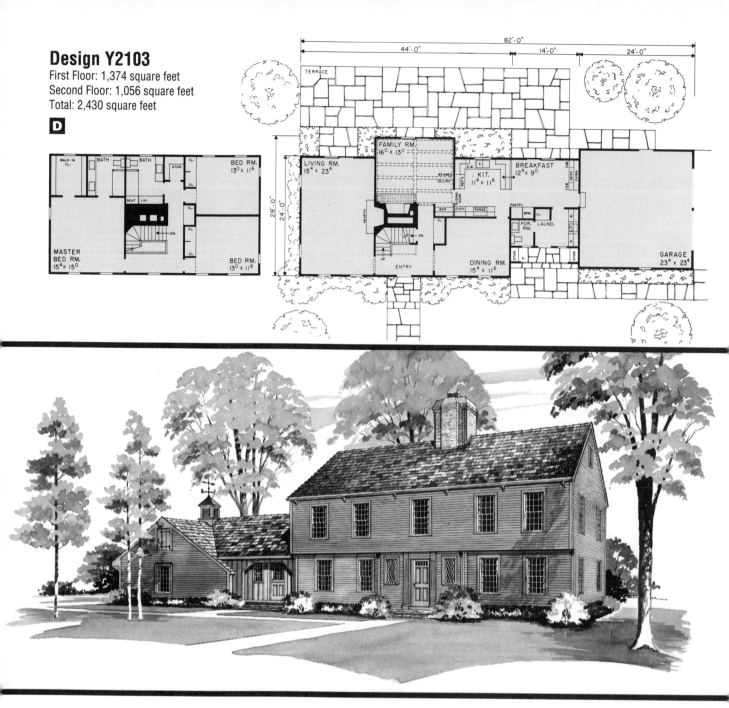

Design Y2103

First Floor: 1,374 square feet
Second Floor: 1,056 square feet
Total: 2,430 square feet

D

First floor plan labels: 82'-0", 44'-0", 14'-0", 24'-0", TERRACE, FAMILY RM. 16⁰ x 13⁰, LIVING RM. 15⁴ x 23⁴, BEAMED CEILING, BREAKFAST 12⁴ x 9⁰, KIT. 11⁴ x 11⁶, DW, S, REF'G, CAB, DESK, CHINA, 28'-0", 24'-0", HEARTH, BAR, OVEN, RANGE, CL, PANTRY, BRM, CL, PDR. RM, LAUND, STOR, D, ENTRY, UP, DN, DINING RM. 15⁴ x 11⁶, GARAGE 23⁴ x 23⁴

Second floor plan labels: WALK-IN CL., BATH, BATH, STOR, BED RM. 13⁰ x 11⁶, CL, SEAT, LIN, DN, CL, CL, CL, MASTER BED RM. 15⁴ x 15⁰, BED RM. 13⁰ x 11⁶

Design Y1700
First Floor: 1,836 square feet; Second Floor: 1,232 square feet; Total: 3,068 square feet

● Good zoning, fine traffic circulation, efficient work center, first floor laundry are among convenient living features.

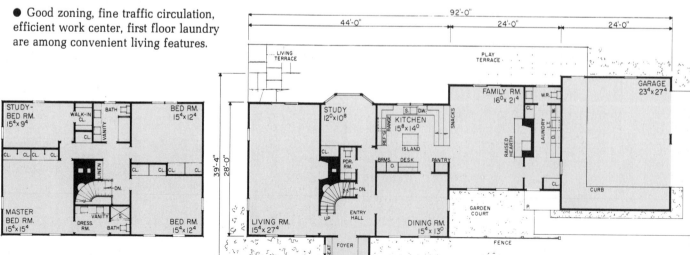

First floor plan labels: 92'-0", 44'-0", 24'-0", 24'-0", LIVING TERRACE, PLAY TERRACE, STUDY 12⁰ x 10⁸, FAMILY RM. 16⁰ x 21⁴, GARAGE 23⁴ x 27⁴, W.R., S, DW, KITCHEN 15⁸ x 14⁰, SNACKS, RANGE, REF'G, ISLAND, RAISED HEARTH, LAUNDRY, W, D, CL, PDR. RM, BRMS, DESK, O, PANTRY, 39'-4", 28'-0", DN, UP, SEAT, FOYER, LIVING RM. 15⁴ x 27⁴, ENTRY HALL, DINING RM. 15⁴ x 13⁰, GARDEN COURT, FENCE, P, CURB

Second floor plan labels: STUDY-BED RM. 15⁴ x 9⁴, WALK-IN CL., BATH, VANITY, BED RM. 15⁴ x 12⁴, CL, CL, CL, CL, LINEN, CL, CL, CL, DN, MASTER BED RM. 15⁴ x 15⁴, DRESS. RM, VANITY, S, BATH, BED RM. 15⁴ x 12⁴

Design Y2253 First Floor: 1,503 square feet; Second Floor: 1,291 square feet; Total: 2,794 square feet

● The overhanging second floor sets the character of this Early American design. Study the features, both inside and out.

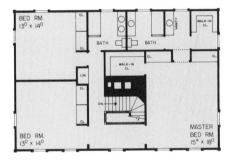

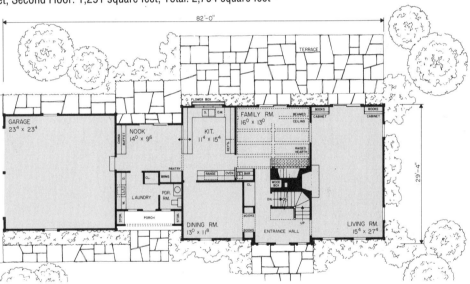

Design Y2610
First Floor: 1,505 square feet
Second Floor: 1,344 square feet; Total: 2,849 square feet

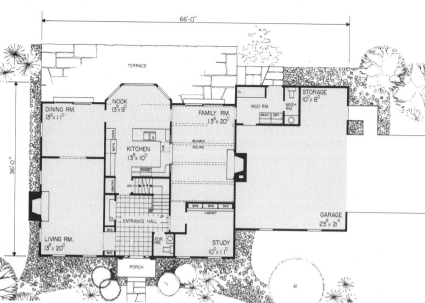

CUSTOMIZABLE
Custom Alterations? See page 381
for customizing this plan to your
specifications.

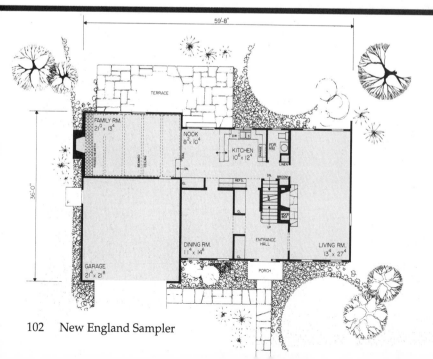

Design Y2623
First Floor: 1,368 square feet
Second Floor: 1,046 square feet;
Total: 2,414 square feet

● A four-bedroom Saltbox with a
beamed ceiling in the family room and
a 27 foot living room; plus formal and
informal dining areas— just right for
the large family.

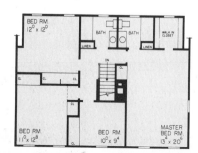

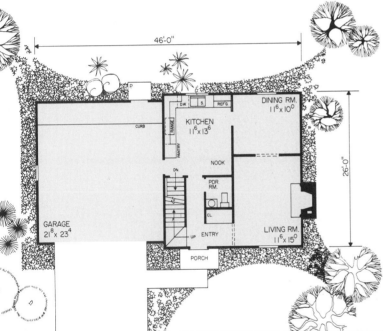

DINING RM.
$11^6 \times 10^0$

KITCHEN
$11^6 \times 13^6$

NOOK

GARAGE
$21^8 \times 23^4$

PDR. RM.

ENTRY

LIVING RM.
$11^6 \times 15^0$

PORCH

46'-0"

26'-0"

Design Y2622 First Floor: 624 square feet
Second Floor: 624 square feet; Total: 1,248 square feet

L **D**

● Appealing design can envelope little packages, too. Here is a charming, Early Colonial adaptation with an attached two-car garage to serve the young family with a modest building budget.

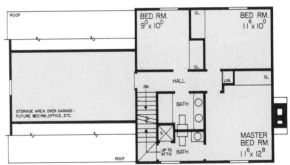

ROOF

BED RM.
$9^0 \times 10^0$

BED RM.
$11^6 \times 10^0$

HALL

STORAGE AREA OVER GARAGE – FUTURE BED RM, OFFICE, ETC.

BATH

LIN.

MASTER BED RM.
$11^6 \times 12^8$

UP TO ATTIC

BATH

ROOF

Design Y1856

First Floor: 1,023 square feet
Second Floor: 784 square feet
Total: 1,807 square feet

D

● This small house includes big house features and livability. On the first floor are a washroom, laundry and two fireplaces, each with a wood box. Two sets of sliding glass doors lead to the rear terrace. Upstairs are two full baths and extra storage.

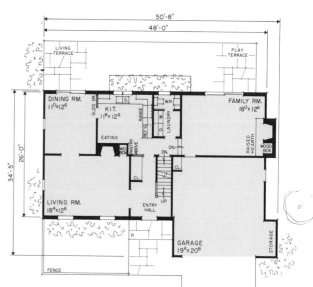

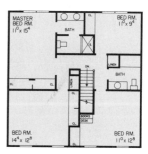

Design Y2733 First Floor: 1,177 square feet
Second Floor: 1,003 square feet; Total: 2,180 square feet

L **D**

● This is definitely a four-bedroom Colonial with charm galore. The kitchen features an island range and other built-ins. All will enjoy the sunken family room with fireplace and sliding glass doors leading to the terrace. A basement provides room for recreational activities while the laundry remains on the first floor for extra convenience.

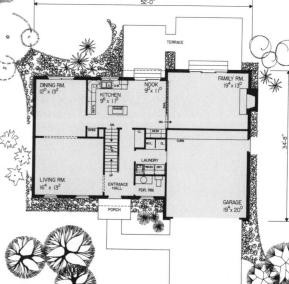

Design Y2211

First Floor: 1,214 square feet
Second Floor: 1,146 square feet
Total: 2,360 square feet

L **D**

● The appeal of this Colonial home will be virtually everlasting. It will improve with age and service the growing family well. The architectural detailing is exquisite, indeed. The window treatment, the narrow siding, the masive chimneys, the service porch and the garage are attractive features.

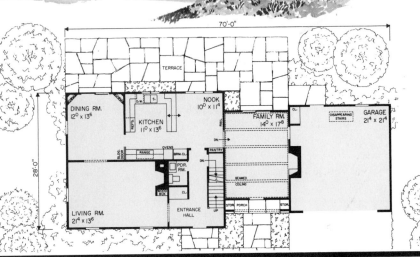

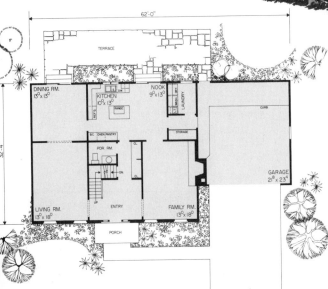

Design Y2540

First Floor: 1,300 square feet
Second Floor: 1,360 square feet; Total: 2,660 square feet

L **D**

● This efficient Colonial abounds in features. A spacious entry is flanked by living areas, one with a fireplace. The island kitchen features an adjacent breakfast nook and nearby dining room. Upstairs are four bedrooms, including a master suite with a sitting room and walk-in closet.

Informal Dining Areas

Early Colonial houses had their dining areas integrated with the hall or keeping room. Since so many functions were performed here, eating was perfunctorily executed in cramped multi-use spaces before the fireplace. As we know, fireplaces in early houses were the sole providers of heat and served as cooking centers. As houses got larger, the space allotted to dining grew. Even with the introduction of the separate dining room, houses still maintained informal dining areas. Sometimes these were part of the floor areas of country kitchens. During the 19th and 20th Centuries they became highly identifiable areas known as nooks, breakfast rooms and morning rooms. Whatever the location or configuration, informal dining has kept its proximity to the fireplace. As these illustrations show, the fireplace provides a warm, homey quality to the family environment around the dining table. Informal eating is also wonderfully serviced by the snack bar, often found as an appendage to one of the kitchen counters. Meals in the nook, breakfast, morning or family rooms can be served handily and quickly.

Design Y2684, page 235.
Country kitchen ambience.

Design Y2682, page 30.
Eating in front of the fireplace.

Design Y2975, page 226.
Informal dining with the kitchen nearby.

A setting for preparation and consumption.

Waiting for meal-time.

Design Y2692, page 89.
Soup's on!

Informal Dining Areas

Informal dining areas may open directly to the kitchen or they may be separated from the kitchen by a counter or cabinets with a pass-through. Whatever may be the case, the kitchen and its activities and aromas are ever present. The interaction of these two areas is practical and efficient. While the cook may, on occasion, prefer a measure of solitude, the kitchen table traditionally is the family hang-out. Even if the neighborhood coffee klatch does not regularly descend on one's house, the kitchen table is useful for a myriad of sit-down pursuits. Here are a number of cozy settings which promise a reenactment of enjoyable family experiences.

Design Y2559, page 61.
(Right) Open planning creates space.

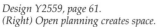

(Left) Just a couple of steps from the oven to the table.

Design Y2658, page 50.
A pass-through facilitates serving.

Design Y1791, page 57.
The fireplace wall is an appealing backdrop.

Design Y2707, page 332.
(Above) Informal and formal dining—side by side.

Providing spaciousness with dining.

Informal Dining Areas

Dining areas will acquire an extra measure of enjoyment when there is a large glass area nearby offering a view of the outdoors. Here there are a number of settings that present an inviting picture of the appeal created by planning the informal dining area near windows. What could be a more pleasing backdrop than having a panoramic view of the surrounding countryside at breakfast? Of course, such broad expanses of glass also provide an abundance of natural light not only to the informal eating center but to all adjacent areas. Making open planning the goal can result in a kitchen that

Design Y2695, page 230.
A pleasant breakfast setting.

Design Y2610, page 102.
A bay window dining area.

is the beneficiary of an abundance of natural light. Bay windows and other strategically located glass areas can surely make a beautiful contribution to informal family dining.

Design Y2641, page 186.
The scene from the kitchen.

Design Y2539, page 98.
(Above, left) Enjoy the greenery inside
and out.

Design Y2635, page 42.
(Above) Informal dining niche with
utility.

Design Y1887, page 94.
Let the snacking begin!

Design Y2596, page 61.
A cheerfully convenient eating spot.

Informal Dining Areas

Dining areas can be as distinctive as your floor planning, decorating and furnishing ideas permit. As we have seen, the informal eating area can be at a bay window. It can also be near a sliding glass door to an outdoor porch, or it can be situated between a kitchen and a family room. Then again, it can be comprised of just a couple of chairs and a small table adjacent to a built-in snack bar. Whatever its size and configuration, the informal dining area must be located near the kitchen. As shown in the pictures and floor plans in this book, informal dining areas can be right in the kitchen itself.

(Right) Two handy snack facilities.

Dining informally in the kitchen.

Outdoor environment indoors.

Dining amidst open planning.

Informal dining near a porch.

Dining with the deck a step away.

Kitchen Work Centers

K itchen work centers have come a long way since they occupied a portion of the 17th-Century hall or keeping room. As houses got larger, kitchens developed into central rooms. In the warmer climates of the South, kitchens actually became out-buildings. Today's kitchens have become highly sophisticated work centers. They have many configurations and offer a variety of cupboard and work-surface layouts. L-shaped counters save many steps. The short leg of a long counter can be just the spot for the cooktop. Bonus counter space can create a

Design Y2654, page 92.
A pass-through to the breakfast room.

Placing the china cupboard nearby.

Design Y2688, page 271.
Island cooking surface with hood.

handy pass-through to an eating area. Island work surfaces are step-savers and provide extra base cabinet storage space. This may be the location of the cooktop with a ventilating fan and hood above, or it may function as a generous food-preparation surface.

Design Y2731, page 99.
U-shaped kitchen bay.

Design Y2666, page 80.
Open planning makes a difference.

The Kitchen

Let the areas flow together.

Design Y1970, page 51.
A recessed cooking niche.

The kitchen offers a great opportunity to define the character and ambience in a house. As the settings on these pages illustrate, the kitchen can establish individuality. In addition to the many configurations of cabinets, cupboards and counters or the locations of windows, there is the matter of decoration that offers the opportunity to achieve a mark of distinction. Wall and floor coverings, ceiling treatment, lighting fixtures, cabinet surfaces and styling, window treatments and the selection of furniture and appliances all provide the elements to coordinate a pleasing family environment. Favorite colors brighten the scene and complement the decorating scheme.

A handy planning desk.

A place for food preparation.

FARMHOUSES
OF THE
NORTHEAST

The 17th- and 18th-Century farmhouses of the Northeast were a varied lot. They had exteriors of wood, stone and brick. Some had gabled roofs; others had gambrel roofs. Houses of this period and region were primarily 1½ or two stories. While the main portion of the house was generally rectangular in shape, the overall structure frequently had an irregular configuration. This was the result of the addition of various dependencies. In addition to the country kitchen and prominent chimney, a popular characteristic of the farmhouse was the covered porch. Of course, all farmhouses did not have front porches. Those that did, however, followed no stringent rules concerning their size, style or location. Some were large, others small. Some had pillars and railings and wrapped around a side of the house. Others were barely large enough to accommodate more than a couple of rocking chairs. Study and contrast the variety of family-oriented lifestyles offered by the plans in this section. Designs Y2542 on page 140 and Y3307 on page 155 provide an interesting contrast.

Design Y2694
First Floor: 2,026 square feet
Second Floor: 1,386 square feet; Total: 3,412 square feet

L

● Here is a rambling two-story house that recalls the farmhouses occupied by prosperous families in upstate New York in the 18th Century. John Jay, the first chief of justice of the United States, built such a house around 1800 in Katonah, New York. The highly identifiable raised porches of the front and rear of this design were common in New York's Hudson River Valley. The various appendages add to both the appeal and the livability of this impressive house.

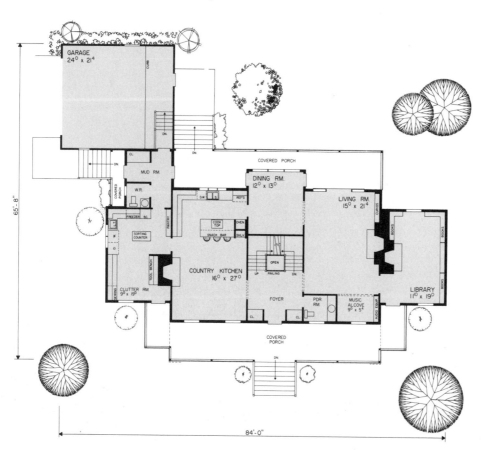

The separate dining room is strategically located between the kitchen and living room. A window wall looks out over the rear porch into the yard. Two doors provide access to the porch.

A Rambling Upstate Farmhouse

● A sweeping covered front porch provides sheltered passage to the centered foyer of this farmhouse. Of particular interest are the two secondary entrances from this porch. Stepping into the spacious foyer, even the most casual visitor cannot help but be impressed by the open staircases. Two large living areas flank the foyer. To the right is the

formal living room with its music alcove and adjacent library with lots of bookshelves. Note the three fireplaces. Convenient to the country kitchen with snack bar is the 19-foot clutter room. It serves as an excellent multi-purpose area with laundry equipment, freezer, pantry, tool bench, sewing area, broom closet and island sorting counter. Don't

miss either the wash room or the powder room. Upstairs there are two big children's bedrooms plus the master bedroom with an outstanding bath; Noteworthy are the whirlpool, stall shower, twin lavatories, built-in seats and walk-in closet. Space for recreational activities can be developed in the basement.

Columned Two-Story Balcony

● This two-story with impressive columns supporting the covered porch and balcony is reminiscent of Southern manors. However, rural areas of the Northeast produced a variety of houses of this type. Even today, a trip through New York or Pennsylvania provides a glimpse of such farmhouse adaptations. Much of its charm is to be found in the symmetry. The center entrance, the spacing of the windows and columns and the straightforward rectangular shape of the house help to create the appeal. The break in the projecting roof line adds extra interest. The floor plan is wonderfully zoned for the active family. Formal and informal living rooms flank the central foyer. The big country kitchen has a commanding fireplace, an island cooktop and plenty of space for interesting furniture placement and informal dining. It is but a step from the separate dining room and functions well with the outdoor terrace. Don't miss the beamed ceilings, the bar, the laundry and the strategically-placed powder room. Upstairs there are three children's rooms and a full bath, plus a fine master bedroom suite.

Design Y2664
First Floor: 1,308 square feet
Second Floor: 1,262 square feet
Total: 2,570 square feet

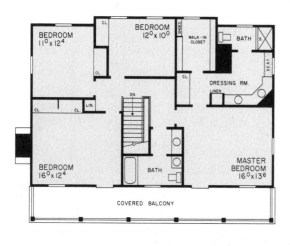

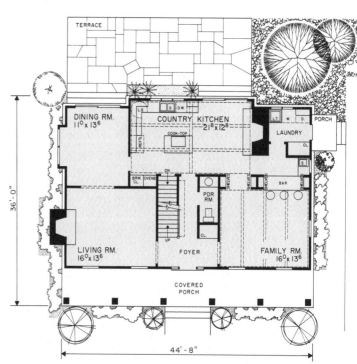

The formal living room provides an inviting spot for entertaining in front of the fireplace. Adjacent to this quiet haven is the formal dining room.

Pennsylvania Farmhouse with Georgian Roots

BEDROOM 9⁸ x 9⁰
BEDROOM 11⁰ x 12⁴
SEAT
WALK-IN CLOSET
WALK-IN CLOSET
BATH
CL
CL
DN
OPEN ABOVE
BATH
LINEN
UP
CL
MASTER BEDROOM 15⁰ x 18⁰
BEDROOM 12⁸ x 10⁸

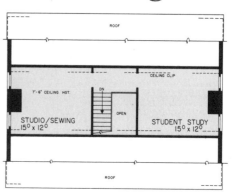

ROOF
CEILING CLIP
7'-6" CEILING HGT.
DN
OPEN
STUDIO/SEWING 15⁰ x 12⁰
STUDENT STUDY 15⁰ x 12⁰
ROOF

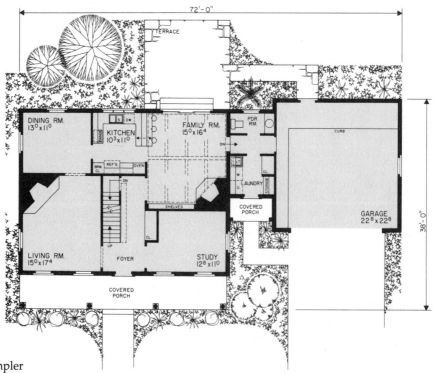

72'-0"
TERRACE
DINING RM. 13⁰ x 11⁰
KITCHEN 10³ x 11⁰
FAMILY RM. 15⁰ x 16⁴
PDR. RM.
S DW
CURB
BRM CL
REF'G
OVEN
DN
W
LAUNDRY
D
CL
STORAGE
COVERED PORCH
SHELVES
GARAGE 22⁸ x 22⁸
38'-0"
DN
LIVING RM. 15⁰ x 17⁴
UP
FOYER
CL
STUDY 12⁸ x 11⁰
COVERED PORCH

The corner fireplace of the family room can be enjoyed from the U-shaped kitchen. The pass-through to the snack bar enhances the feeling of spaciousness.

Design Y2633

First Floor: 1,338 square feet
Second Floor: 1,200 square feet
Third Floor: 506 square feet
Total: 3,044 square feet

● The Middle Colonies of the 18th Century produced many houses with early Georgian architecture. This variation with its brick exterior features a covered front porch across the entire main portion of the house. The center entrance, muntined double-hung windows with paneled shutters, stolidly proportioned columns and twin chimneys set the character. The two-car garage appended to the house by the one-story utility area completes the interesting facade. A second covered porch provides shelter for the convenient service entrance. The rear exterior is equally impressive with its interesting window treatment. Like so many houses with central foyers, this one has fine traffic circulation. The formal living and dining rooms are located to one side of the plan and function well together. The informal family room area is spacious. Two corner fireplaces are focal points of the two living areas. The U-shaped kitchen with snack bar is efficient and strategically located. In addition to the four-bedroom, two-bath second floor there is the bonus space of the third floor.

A Gambrel of the Connecticut River Valley

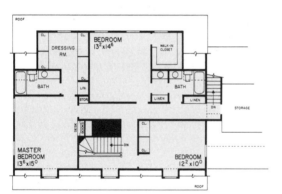

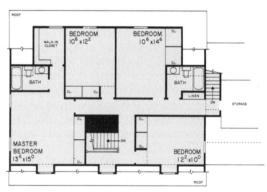

Alternate Floor Plan

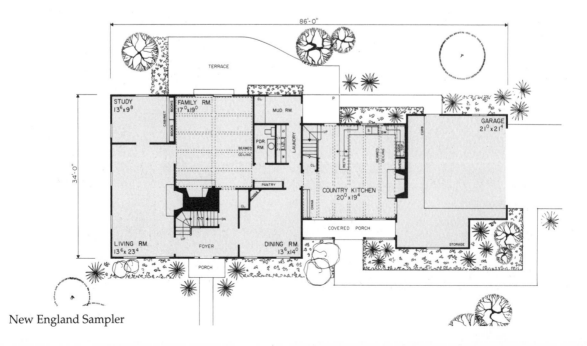

Design Y2320 First Floor: 1,856 square feet; Second Floor: 1,171 square feet; Total: 3,027 square feet

● Here is a distinctive Colonial adaptation with two interesting roof configurations that were popular with early settlers in the American colonies. The front exterior features a gambrel roof; the rear, a Saltbox roof. The attached dependencies, which were so common in early houses, add to the appeal of this house. As the demands of family living increased, so did the houses. The main portion of the house provides the formal facilities: 23-foot living room, beamed-ceiling family room and quiet study. The formal dining room, shown below, can provide the perfect setting for convivial, yet formal, dining. The horizontal wainscoting and diagonal china closet with paneled doors are typical features of early American homes. This home features two fireplaces. There is also a strategically-placed powder room, a laundry and a mud room. Connecting this main portion of the house to the garage is the huge family kitchen. This will function as a real gathering room and cater to a multitude of functions. Its open planning, with the fireplace as the focal point, creates a delightful atmosphere for food preparation or mealtime. In addition to the staircase in the foyer, there is a second flight of stairs in the kitchen. The blueprints for this family-oriented floor plan offer details for either a three- or four-bedroom second floor.

Dormers and Porch Create Appeal

Design Y2650

First Floor: 1,451 square feet
Second Floor: 1,091 square feet
Total: 2,542 square feet

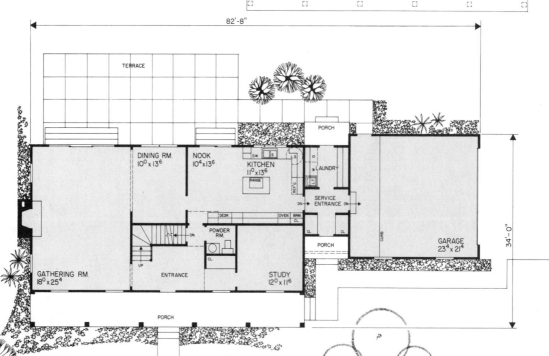

● Early farmhouses had a simple appeal that is still popular today. Dormers, shuttered windows, paneled doors, well-spaced columns and massive chimneys, when put together in a perfectly proportioned manner, result in a charming facade. This rectangular plan attaches a recessed secondary service entrance and an end-opening two-car garage to produce an impressive, yet modest-sized, house. To the left of the formal entrance hall is the 25-foot gathering room. Its size allows for the creation of a number of functional family-oriented living areas with the fireplace providing a cheerful backdrop. Sliding glass doors provide access to the outdoor living facilities. Adding further to the spaciousness of this area is the open planning with the formal dining room. Space is also the byword for the kitchen/nook area. There is an abundance of counter and cupboard space, an island cooking range, a planning desk and a large area for a table and chairs. Here again, there is direct access to the outside through sliding glass doors. Completing the first-floor livability are the somewhat isolated study and convenient powder room. Upstairs there are two bedrooms and a shared bath for the children. The master bedroom is large and, as shown above, even features a cozy fireplace and a full bath with walk-in closet.

A Flemish Colonial Farmhouse

Design Y2697   First Floor: 1,764 square feet; Second Floor: 1,506 square feet; Total: 3,270 square feet

● A Flemish style of architecture became popular in New Jersey and in Long Island, New York after the American Revolution. It has since become known as "Dutch Colonial." This design recalls the Vreeland House built in 1818 near Englewood, New Jersey. Characteristic of this pleasing style are the gambrel roof lines with their impressive sweep, the clapboard siding, the stately verandas and the chimneys at each end. Though not Dutch, the elliptical fanlight and delicate classical enframement of the front doorway reflect the Federal period of the time. By today's standards the floor plan satisfies the requirements needed to deliver fine family livability. There are separate rooms for formal living and dining, each with a fireplace and no unnecessary cross-room traffic. For informal living there is the 27-foot family room with raised-hearth fireplace, desk, sliding glass doors, eating space and a snack bar. For food preparation the U-shaped kitchen with plenty of counter and cupboard space could hardly be better. The butler's pantry with wet bar is a great feature. On the way to the garage is the laundry room and the walk-in pantry. The second floor has three sizeable bedrooms and two full baths for the children. For the parents there is the 17 x 17 foot bedroom and its adjacent master bath with tub, stall shower and walk-in closet.

The largest of the children's rooms has its own private bath, a long wardrobe closet and an interesting recessed window seat. To add to its utility, the seat can be built to provide shoe or game storage below.

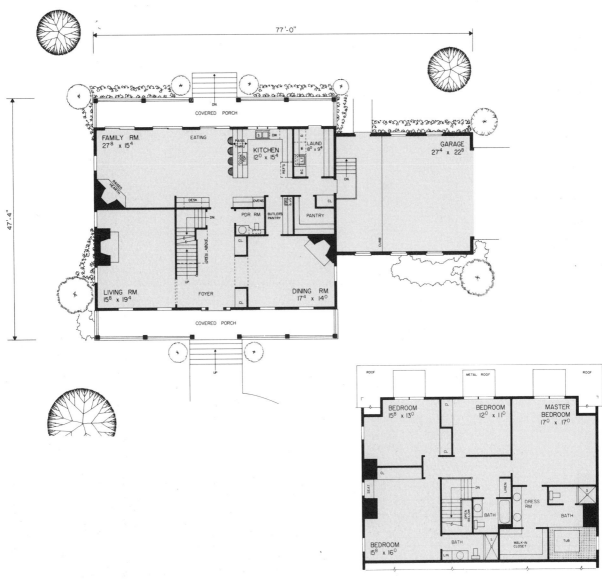

FAMILY RM.
27⁸ x 15⁴

EATING

KITCHEN
12⁰ x 15⁴

LAUND.
16⁰ x 9⁴

GARAGE
27⁴ x 22⁸

COVERED PORCH

DN

PASS THRU

RAISED HEARTH

DESK

OVENS

PDR. RM.

BUTLERS PANTRY

PANTRY

CL

OPEN ABOVE

UP

DN

LIVING RM.
15⁸ x 19⁴

FOYER

DINING RM.
17⁴ x 14⁰

CL

COVERED PORCH

UP

77'-0"

47'-4"

ROOF

METAL ROOF

ROOF

BEDROOM
15⁸ x 13⁰

BEDROOM
12⁰ x 11⁰

MASTER BEDROOM
17⁰ x 17⁰

CL

CL

SEAT

DN

OPEN BELOW

BATH

LINEN

DRESS RM

BATH

BEDROOM
15⁸ x 16⁰

BATH

WALK-IN CLOSET

TUB

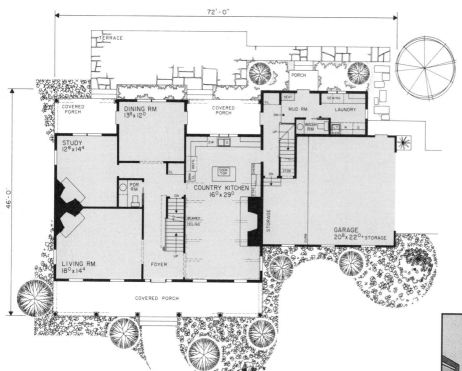

TERRACE

72'-0"

COVERED PORCH

PORCH

COVERED PORCH

DINING RM.
13⁸ x 12⁰

SEWING

MUD RM.

LAURNDRY

WASH RM.

STUDY
12⁸ x 14⁴

PDR. RM.

COUNTRY KITCHEN
16⁰ x 29⁰

COOK TOP

STORAGE

46'-0"

LIVING RM.
18⁰ x 14⁴

FOYER

BEAMED CEILING

GARAGE
20⁸ x 22⁰ + STORAGE

COVERED PORCH

Design Y2680

First Floor: 1,707 square feet
Second Floor: 1,439 square feet
Total: 3,146 square feet

D

ROOF

ROOF

BEDROOM
13⁰ x 12⁰

BATH

BATH

DRESS'G RM.

WALK-IN CLOSET

LINEN

OPEN

DESK

LINEN

RAIL

BEDROOM
16⁰ x 12⁰

BATH

DN

BEDROOM
16⁰ x 12⁰

RAIL

MASTER BEDROOM
16⁰ x 16⁰

ATTIC

ROOF

ATTIC ACCESS

ATTIC ACCESS

ATTIC ACCESS

ATTIC ACCESS

Dutch Colonial

● This Early American Dutch Colonial not only has charm, but offers many fine features. The foyer, below left, allows easy access to all rooms on the first and second floors for excellent livability. The large country kitchen, below, includes a beamed ceiling, fireplace and island cooktop. A large formal dining room and powder room are only a few steps away. Fireplaces can also be found in the study and living room. The service area, mud room, wash room and laundry are tucked away near the garage. Two large bedrooms, a full bath and master bedroom suite are found on the second floor. A fourth bedroom and bath are accessible through the master bedroom or via stairs from the service entrance.

Design Y2996 First Floor: 2,191 square feet

Second Floor: 1,928 square feet; Total: 4,119 square feet

L **D**

● This New York manor house reminds one of the Folger House built circa 1800 in Geneva, New York. Covered porches upstairs and down are charming additions to the well-appointed two-story. Four chimney stacks herald four hearths inside: living room, dining room, family room and study. The second floor holds four bedrooms including a master suite with its own fireplace and a huge walk-in closet.

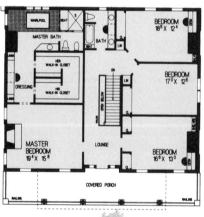

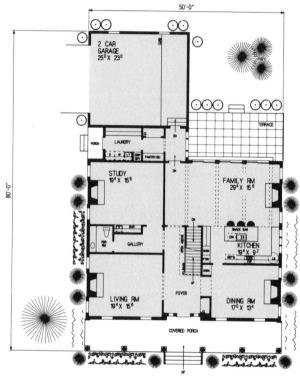

Design Y2981

First Floor: 2,104 square feet
Second Floor: 2,015 square feet
Total: 4,119 square feet

● Here is another version of what prosperous farmers in western New York might have built in the 1840s. Such dwellings often incorporated the Ionic columns and the pediment gable that echo the Greek Revival style. Highlighting the interior is the bright and cheerful spaciousness of the informal family room area. It features a wall of glass stretching to the second-story sloping ceiling. Enhancing the drama of this area is the adjacent glass area of the breakfast room. Note the His and Hers areas of the master bedroom.

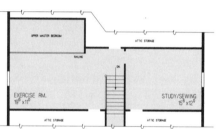

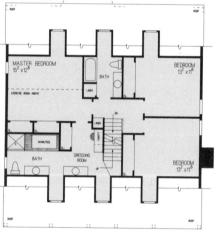

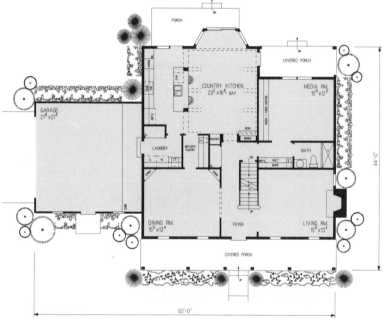

Design Y2988

First Floor: 1,458 square feet
Second Floor: 1,075 square feet
Third Floor: 462 square feet
Total: 2,995 square feet

L **D**

● A picturesque Dutch
Colonial with flared gambrel
roof lines and a covered front
porch. Particularly noteworthy are the country kitchen,
the media room, the first-
floor full bath and the
upstairs master suite. Don't
miss the rear covered porch.

● What a tremendous amount of livability this house has to offer. Of particular note is the spaciousness of the various rooms. Study the room sizes. The traffic circulation is outstanding. The center entrance hall directs the flow most conveniently. The living room and library, each with its own fireplace, will enjoy complete privacy.

Design Y2157

First Floor: 1,720 square feet
Second Floor: 1,205 square feet
Total: 2,925 square feet

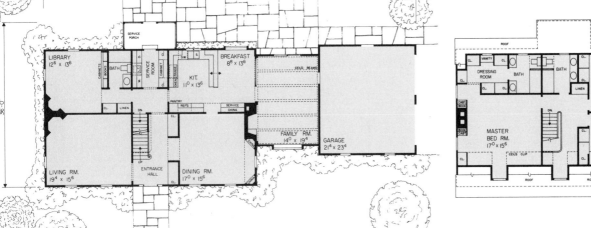

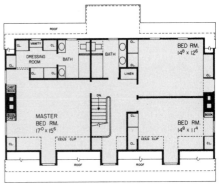

Design Y2776

First Floor: 1,134 square feet
Second Floor: 874 square feet
Total: 2,008 square feet

L **D**

● This board-and-batten farmhouse design has all of the country charm of New England. The front covered porch will be appreciated during the warm weather months. Immediately off the front entrance is the delightful corner living room. The dining room with bay window, shown below, will be easily served by the U-shaped kitchen. Informal family activities will take place in the family room with a raised-hearth fireplace and sliding glass doors to the rear terrace. The second floor houses all of the sleeping facilities. There is a master bedroom with a private bath and walk-in closet. Two other bedrooms share a bath.

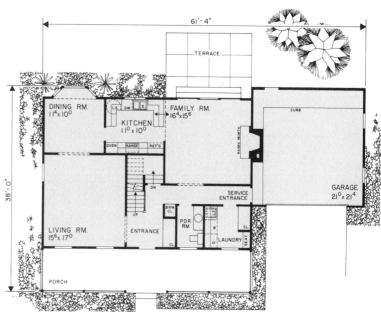

CUSTOMIZABLE

Custom Alterations? See page 381 for customizing this plan to your specifications.

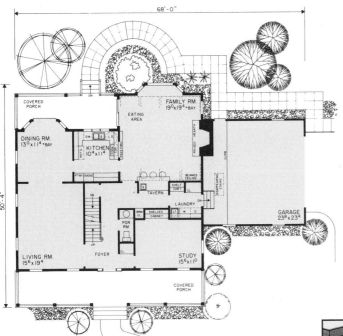

Design Y2890

First Floor: 1,612 square feet
Second Floor: 1,356 square feet
Total: 2,968 square feet

D

● An appealing Farmhouse complemented by an inviting front porch. Entering this house, you will notice a nice-sized study to your right and a spacious living room to the left. The adjacent dining room is enriched by an attractive bay window. Just a step away, an efficient kitchen will be found. Many family activities will be enjoyed in the large family room with fireplace, shown below. The tavern/snack bar will make entertaining guests a joy. A powder room and laundry are also on the first floor. Upstairs is a master bedroom suite featuring a bath with an oversized tub, a shower and a dressing room. Also on this floor: two bedrooms, a full bath and attic storage.

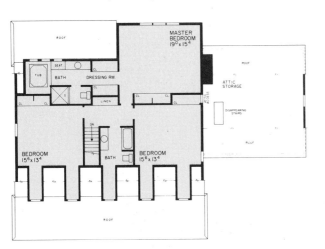

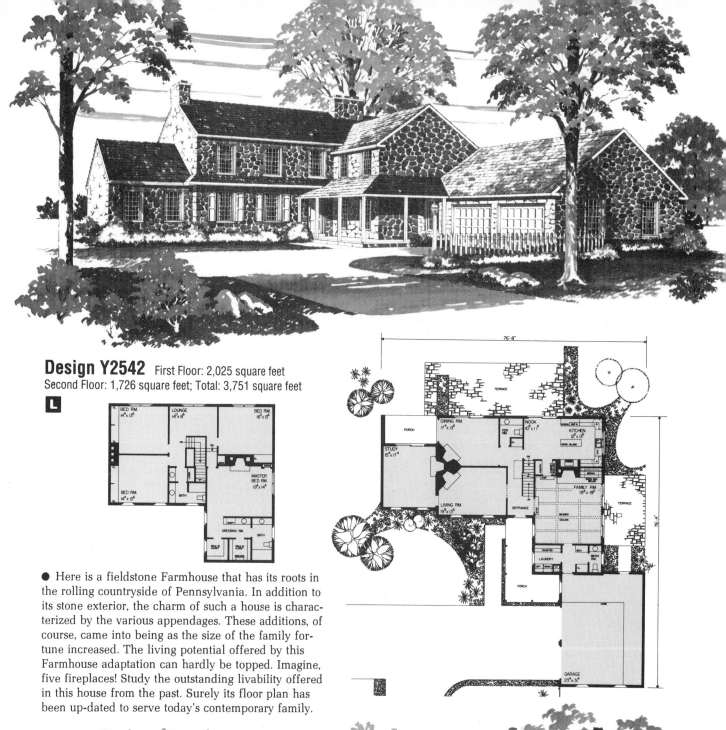

Design Y2542

First Floor: 2,025 square feet
Second Floor: 1,726 square feet; Total: 3,751 square feet

L

● Here is a fieldstone Farmhouse that has its roots in the rolling countryside of Pennsylvania. In addition to its stone exterior, the charm of such a house is characterized by the various appendages. These additions, of course, came into being as the size of the family fortune increased. The living potential offered by this Farmhouse adaptation can hardly be topped. Imagine, five fireplaces! Study the outstanding livability offered in this house from the past. Surely its floor plan has been up-dated to serve today's contemporary family.

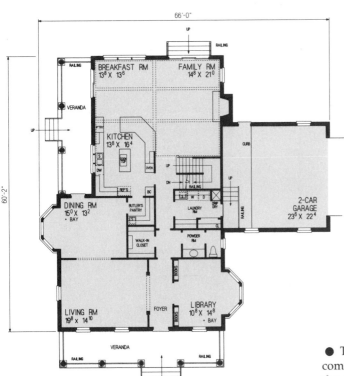

Design Y3502

First Floor: 2,114 square feet
Second Floor: 2,045 square feet
Total: 4,159 square feet

● This lovely stone farmhouse is reminiscent of the solid, comfortable homes once so prevalent on homesteads throughout America. The columned front porch leads to a formal foyer with living room on the left and library on the right. The formal dining room connects directly to the living room and indirectly to the island kitchen through a butler's pantry. The family room and breakfast room have beamed ceilings and are both open to the kitchen. A covered veranda is accessed from the breakfast room and leads to a side yard. On the second floor are three bedrooms and a guest room with private bath. The master bedroom has a fireplace and a fine bath with separate shower and whirlpool tub. Two walk-in closets grace the dressing area. The two secondary bedrooms share a full bath with double vanity.

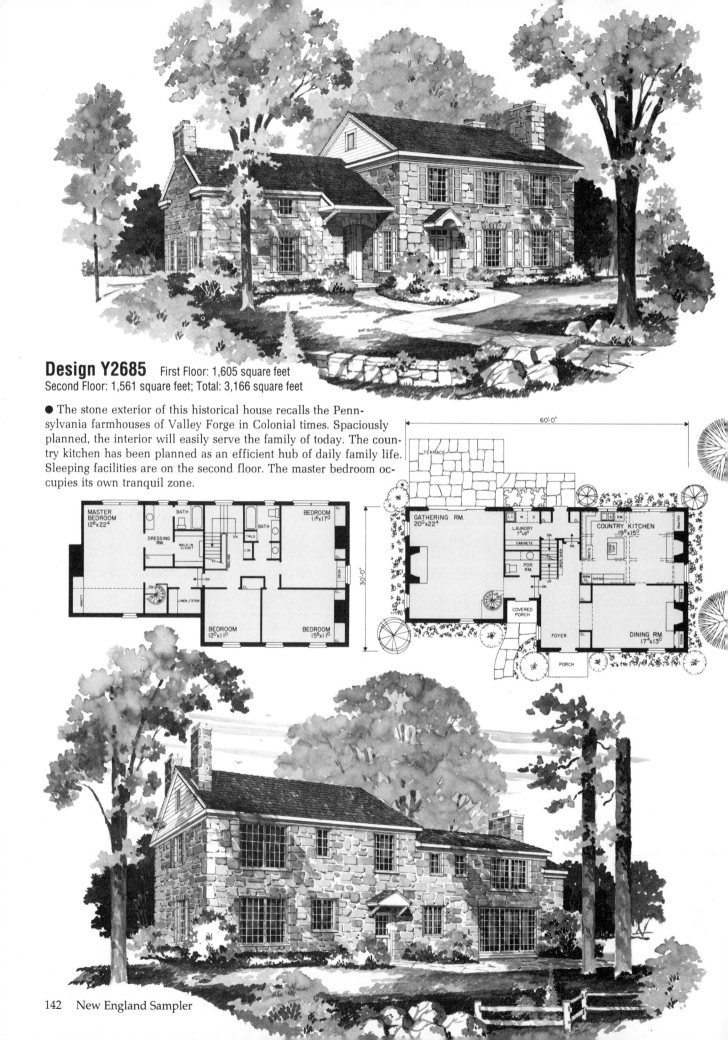

Design Y2685
First Floor: 1,605 square feet
Second Floor: 1,561 square feet; Total: 3,166 square feet

● The stone exterior of this historical house recalls the Pennsylvania farmhouses of Valley Forge in Colonial times. Spaciously planned, the interior will easily serve the family of today. The country kitchen has been planned as an efficient hub of daily family life. Sleeping facilities are on the second floor. The master bedroom occupies its own tranquil zone.

MASTER BEDROOM 12⁸×22⁴
BATH
DRESSING RM.
WALK-IN CLOSET
BEDROOM 11⁶×17⁰
BATH
TWLS
LIN
DESK
CL
DN
DN
VANITY
LINEN / STOR.
BEDROOM 12⁰×11⁰
BEDROOM 15⁸×11⁰

60'-0"
30'-0"

TERRACE
GATHERING RM. 20⁰×22⁴
LAUNDRY 7⁴×8⁰
CABINETS
PDR. RM.
COUNTRY KITCHEN 19⁸×15⁰
COOK TOP
OVENS
BRM. CL.
CHINA
PANTRY
COVERED PORCH
FOYER
PORCH
DINING RM. 17⁸×13⁰
CHINA

● This two-story farmhouse brings to mind the stone houses of Bucks County, Pa. The recessed center entrance opens to the foyer. To the left is the living room with its adjacent music alcove. The sunken study offers a guest retreat. The efficient, U-shaped kitchen functions

well with the large breakfast room and separate dining room with fireplace. The three bedroom upstairs features nice sized rooms and a fourth fireplace. Note the laundry.

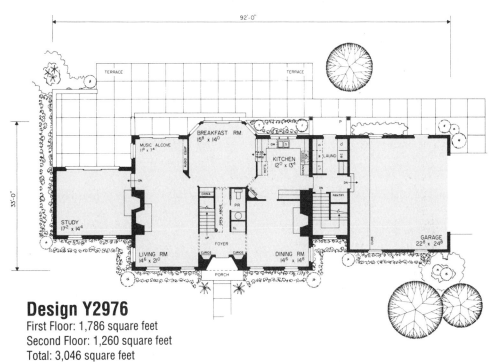

Design Y2976

First Floor: 1,786 square feet
Second Floor: 1,260 square feet
Total: 3,046 square feet

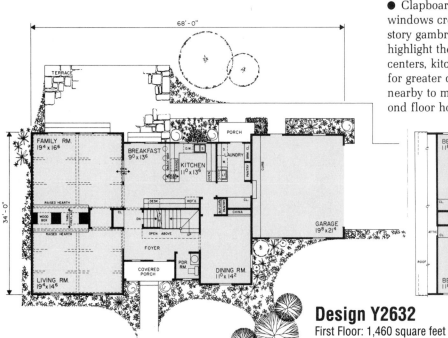

68'-0"

34'-0"

TERRACE

FAMILY RM.
19⁴ x 16⁶

PORCH

BREAKFAST
9⁰ x 13⁶

KITCHEN
11⁰ x 13⁶

LAUNDRY

PANTRY

RAISED HEARTH

WOOD BOX

DESK

REF'G

CL

BUTLER'S

CHINA

RAISED HEARTH

OPEN ABOVE

FOYER

DN

GARAGE
19⁸ x 21⁴

LIVING RM.
19⁴ x 14⁶

COVERED PORCH

PDR RM

DINING RM.
11⁰ x 14²

● Clapboard siding and shuttered, multi-paned windows create the delightful detailing of this two-story gambrel. Beamed ceilings and a thru-fireplace highlight the living and family rooms. The work centers, kitchen and laundry, are clustered together for greater convenience. The formal dining room is nearby to make the serving of meals easy. The second floor houses all of the sleeping facilities.

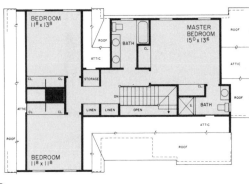

BEDROOM
11⁸ x 13⁸

ROOF

ATTIC

BATH

CL

MASTER BEDROOM
15⁰ x 13⁶

ROOF

ATTIC

ATTIC

STORAGE

CL

CL

CL

CL

ATTIC

DN

LINEN

LINEN

OPEN

CL

BATH

ROOF

BEDROOM
11⁸ x 11⁸

ROOF

Design Y2632

First Floor: 1,460 square feet
Second Floor: 912 square feet
Total: 2,372 square feet

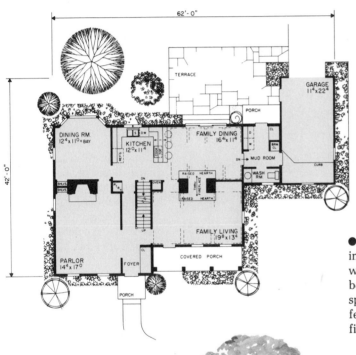

Design Y2681

First Floor: 1,350 square feet
Second Floor: 1,224 square feet
Total: 2,574 square feet

● The charm of Early America is exemplified in this delightful design. Note the three areas which are highlighted by a fireplace. The three-bedroom second floor is nicely planned. Make special note of the master bedroom's many fine features. Study the rest of this design's many fine qualities.

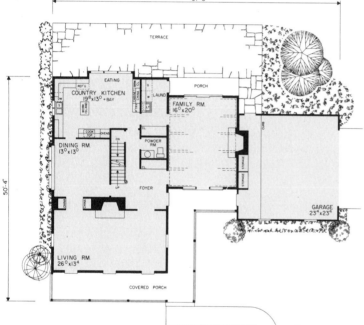

TERRACE

EATING

COUNTRY KITCHEN
19⁸x13⁰ +BAY

PORCH

LAUND.

FAMILY RM.
16⁰x20⁰

REF'G.

DINING RM.
13⁰x13⁰

POWDER RM.

FOYER

UP

67'-0"

50'-4"

STORAGE

GARAGE
23⁴x23⁴

LIVING RM.
26⁰x13⁴

COVERED PORCH

MASTER BEDROOM
12⁴x18⁰

BEDROOM
12⁴x10⁰

LINEN

BATH

DRESSING RM.

BATH

BEDROOM
12⁴x13⁴

BEDROOM
12⁴x10⁰

Design Y2907 — First Floor: 1,546 square feet
Second Floor: 1,144 square feet; Total: 2,690 square feet

● These three popular designs have many common features: wraparound porches, four bedrooms, 2½ baths, first-floor laundries, separate dining rooms, breakfast rooms or eat-in kitchens, family and living rooms, fireplaces, attached garages and basements. The floor plans for each offer a tremendous amount of living potential for the large family.

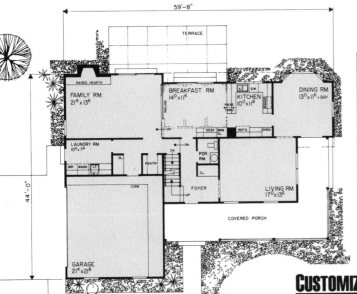

Design Y2774 First Floor: 1,370 square feet
Second Floor: 969 square feet; Total: 2,339 square feet

L D

TERRACE

FAMILY RM. 21⁴ x 13⁶

BREAKFAST RM. 14⁰ x 11⁶

KITCHEN 10⁰ x 11⁸

DINING RM. 13⁰ x 11⁶ + BAY

LAUNDRY RM. 10⁰ x 7⁴

PANTRY

PDR. RM

FOYER

LIVING RM. 17⁰ x 13⁶

GARAGE 21⁴ x 21⁸

COVERED PORCH

59'-8"

44'-0"

BEDROOM / STUDY 11⁰ x 13²

BATH DRESS. RM. VANITY

MASTER BEDROOM 13⁰ x 13²

BATH

BEDROOM 10⁰ x 10⁶

BEDROOM 13⁰ x 10⁶

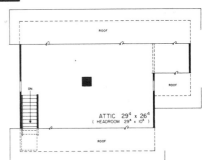

ROOF

ATTIC 29⁴ x 26⁴ (HEADROOM 29⁴ x 10⁴)

ROOF

CUSTOMIZABLE
Custom Alterations? See page 381 for customizing this plan to your specifications.

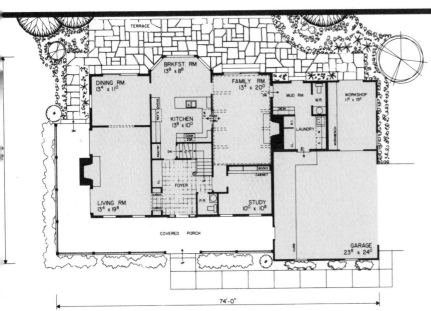

TERRACE

DINING RM. 13⁴ x 11

BRKFST. RM. 13⁸ x 8⁸

FAMILY RM. 13⁴ x 20⁰

MUD RM.

WORKSHOP 11⁰ x 15⁰

KITCHEN 13⁸ x 10⁰

LAUNDRY

W.R.

LIVING RM. 13⁴ x 19⁸

FOYER

P.R.

STUDY 10⁰ x 10⁸

COVERED PORCH

GARAGE 23⁸ x 24⁰

74'-0"

BEDROOM 13⁴ x 14²

BATH

BATH

HIS WALK-IN CLOSET

DRESS. RM.

HER WALK-IN CLOSET

VANITY

RAILING

BEDROOM 13⁴ x 14²

BEDROOM 13⁸ x 10⁰

MASTER BEDROOM 13⁴ x 19⁴

Design Y2946 First Floor: 1,590 square feet
Second Floor: 1,344 square feet; Total: 2,934 square feet

L D

CUSTOMIZABLE
Custom Alterations? See page 381 for customizing this plan to your specifications.

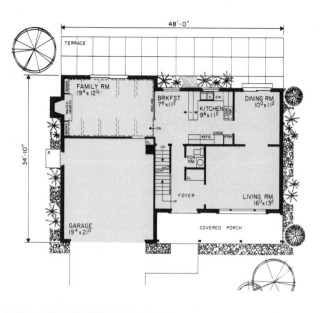

Design Y1956

First Floor: 990 square feet
Second Floor: 728 square feet
Total: 1,718 square feet

D

● The blueprints for this home include details for both the three bedroom and four bedroom options. The first floor livability does not change.

Design Y2908 First Floor: 1,427 square feet

Second Floor: 1,153 square feet; Total: 2,580 square feet

L **D**

● This Early American farmhouse with a covered front porch offers plenty of modern comfort. Inside are fireplaces in both the living room and the family room with bay window.

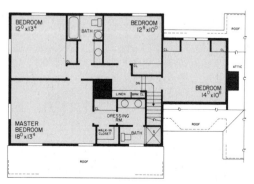

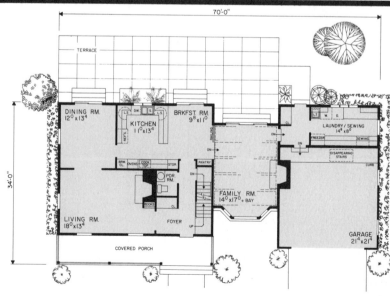

CUSTOMIZABLE

Custom Alterations? See page 381
for customizing this plan to your
specifications.

Design Y2786

Main Level: 871 square feet
Upper Level: 1,132 square feet
Lower Level: 528 square feet
Total: 2,531 square feet

● Here is a Colonial farmhouse
exterior adapted to accommodate a
split-level plan. It is loaded with
three levels of livability, plus a
fourth basement level. The covered
porch, bay windows, projecting
gable roofs, clapboard siding and
pleasing window and door treatment add up to an eye-catching
exterior. Sliding glass doors provide access to the two rear terraces.
The balcony provides a place to
enjoy the outdoors from the master
bedroom.

CUSTOMIZABLE

Custom Alterations? See page 381
for customizing this plan to your
specifications.

Design Y2775

First Floor: 1,317 square feet
Second Floor: 952 square feet; Total: 2,269 square feet

L

● This front-porch farmhouse adaptation is characteristic of the rolling hills of Pennsylvania. Warm summer evenings will be a delight when the outdoors can be enjoyed in such an impressive manner. Double front doors lead the way into this interior. Both the formal and informal areas are outstandingly spacious.

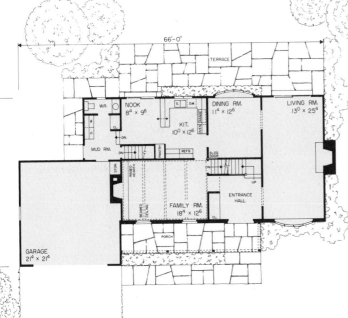

Design Y2223 First Floor: 1,266 square feet
Second Floor: 1,232 square feet; Total: 2,498 square feet

L **D**

● This appealingly proportioned four bedroom Gambrel exudes an aura of coziness. The beauty of the main part of the house is delightfully symmetrical and is enhanced by the attached garage and laundry room.

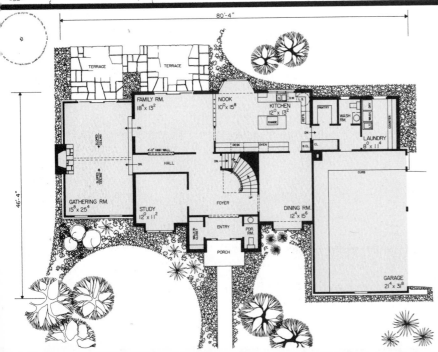

Design Y2599
First Floor: 2,075 square feet
Second Floor: 1,398 square feet
Total: 3,473 square feet

D

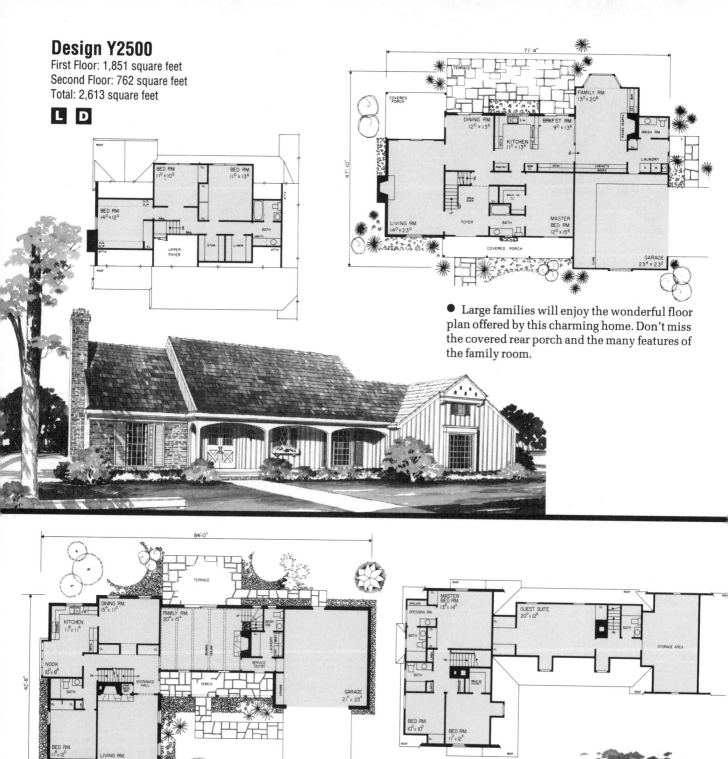

Design Y2500

First Floor: 1,851 square feet
Second Floor: 762 square feet
Total: 2,613 square feet

L **D**

● Large families will enjoy the wonderful floor plan offered by this charming home. Don't miss the covered rear porch and the many features of the family room.

Design Y2614

First Floor: 1,701 square feet
Second Floor: 1,340 square feet
Total: 3,041 square feet

D

● A pleasing appearance and an excellent floor plan. The exceptionally large family room is more than 20′ x 15′ and features a beamed ceiling and a fireplace. Included are four large bedrooms plus a guest suite and 4½ baths.

Design Y2174

First Floor: 1,506 square feet
Second Floor: 1,156 square feet
Total: 2,662 square feet

L **D**

● Your building budget could hardly buy more charm or greater livability. The appeal of the exterior is wrapped up in a myriad of design features. Inside are four bedrooms, three baths and two fireplaces, plus plenty of storage space.

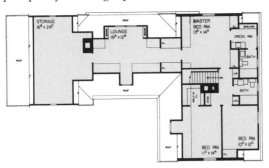

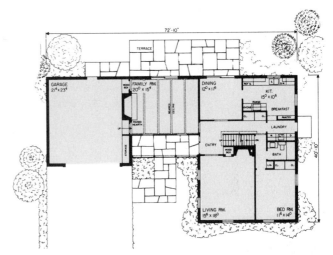

Design Y2865

First Floor: 1,703 square feet
Second Floor: 1,044 square feet
Total: 2,747 square feet

D

● Here's a cozy traditional farmhouse with a big wraparound covered porch. Up front, flanking the entry foyer, are a living room with fireplace and formal dining room. To the rear are a study, that could be used as a guest room, and the family room with another fireplace. The kitchen/breakfast room combination is conveniently located near the service entrance off the garage. Note bedrooms with dormer windows upstairs.

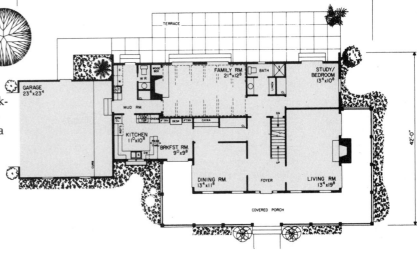

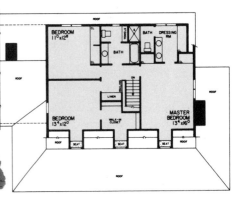

Farmhouses of the Northeast   153

Design Y2963

First Floor: 2,046 square feet
Second Floor: 1,644 square feet
Total: 3,690 square feet

● Featuring a gracious foyer and stairway at the entry, this home in the Colonial tradition is actually a modified version of the center-hall classic. Unlike the classic standard, the entrance here is off-center in the facade, with three windows to the left and two to the right of the entry door. Yet the design offers the dignity and grace so readily associated with its center-hall cousin. In addition, the rambling proportions of the house reflect Colonial precedents—as families grew, so did their houses. Both the dining and living rooms boast large fireplaces. Family meals are likely to be served in the cozy nook attached to the kitchen. Ample cabinet, shelf, and pantry space is provided wherever storage space is most needed. To retreat from the clamor of an active household, family members can read a good book in the study tucked in behind the living room, where generous provision is made for an entire library. Upstairs, four bedrooms provide a comfortable arrangement for each family member.

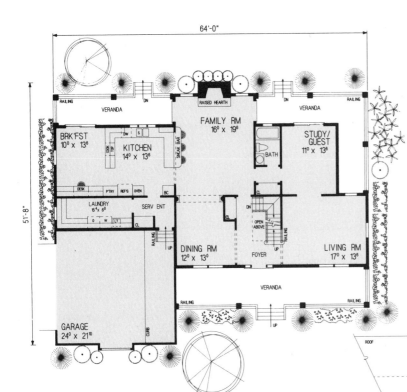

Design Y3307

First Floor: 1,765 square feet
Second Floor: 1,105 square feet
Total: 2,870 square feet

L **D**

● This charming design brings together the best in historical styling and modern floor planning. Inside, the first-floor plan boasts formal living and dining areas on either side of the entry foyer, a study that could double as a guest room, a large family room with raised-hearth fireplace and snack bar pass-through, and a U-shaped kitchen with attached breakfast room. Two family bedrooms on the second floor share a full bath; the master bedroom has a thoughtfully appointed bath and large walk-in closet.

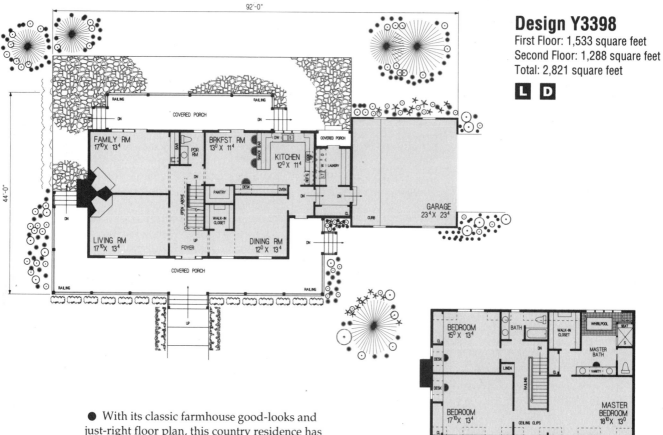

Design Y3398
First Floor: 1,533 square feet
Second Floor: 1,288 square feet
Total: 2,821 square feet

L D

● With its classic farmhouse good-looks and just-right floor plan, this country residence has it all. The wraparound covered porch at the entry gives way to a long foyer with open staircase. To the right and left are the formal dining room and living room. More casual living areas are to the rear: a family room, and U-shaped kitchen with attached breakfast room. The second floor holds sleeping areas — two family bedrooms and a huge master suite with walk-in closet and pampering master bath.

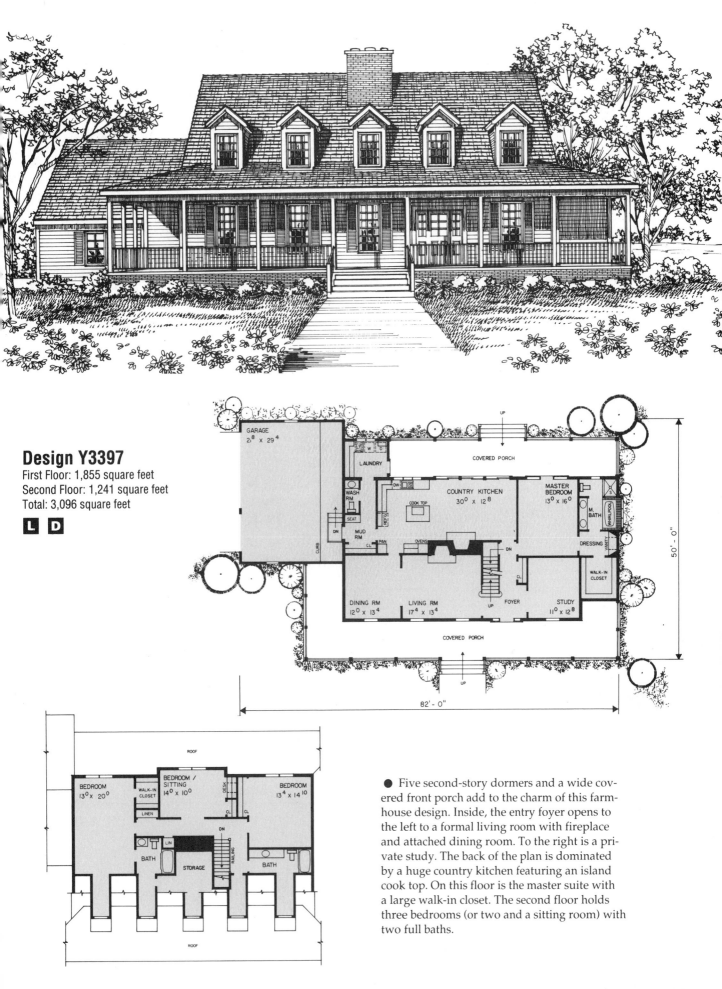

Design Y3397

First Floor: 1,855 square feet
Second Floor: 1,241 square feet
Total: 3,096 square feet

L **D**

GARAGE
2⁸ x 29⁴

COVERED PORCH

UP

LAUNDRY

WASH RM

DW

COOK TOP

COUNTRY KITCHEN
30⁰ x 12⁸

MASTER BEDROOM
13⁰ x 16⁰

M. BATH

WHIRLPOOL

DN

SEAT

MUD RM

CL PAN

OVENS

DN

DRESSING

VANITY

WALK-IN CLOSET

DINING RM
12⁰ x 13⁴

LIVING RM
17⁴ x 13⁴

UP

CL

FOYER

STUDY
11⁰ x 12⁸

COVERED PORCH

UP

50' - 0"

82' - 0"

BEDROOM
13⁰ x 20⁰

WALK-IN CLOSET

LINEN

BEDROOM / SITTING
14⁰ x 10⁰

DESK

CL CL

BEDROOM
13⁴ x 14¹⁰

ROOF

BATH

LIN

DN

RAILING

BATH

STORAGE

ROOF

● Five second-story dormers and a wide covered front porch add to the charm of this farmhouse design. Inside, the entry foyer opens to
the left to a formal living room with fireplace
and attached dining room. To the right is a private study. The back of the plan is dominated
by a huge country kitchen featuring an island
cook top. On this floor is the master suite with
a large walk-in closet. The second floor holds
three bedrooms (or two and a sitting room) with
two full baths.

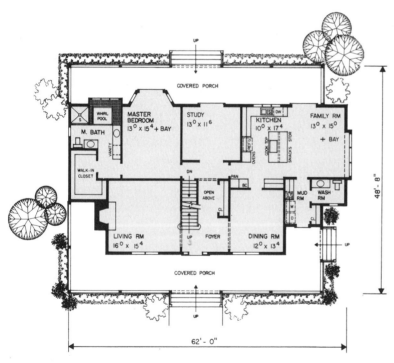

COVERED PORCH

MASTER BEDROOM 13⁰ x 15⁴ + BAY

STUDY 13⁰ x 11⁶

KITCHEN 10⁰ x 17⁴

FAMILY RM 13⁰ x 15⁰

WHIRL POOL

M. BATH

VANITY

WALK-IN CLOSET

+ BAY

DN

PAN

BC

MUD RM

WASH RM

OPEN ABOVE

CL

CL

LIVING RM 16⁰ x 15⁴

UP

FOYER

DINING RM 12⁰ x 13⁴

UP

COVERED PORCH

UP

62' - 0"

48' - 8"

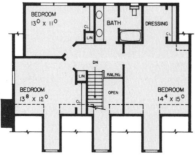

BEDROOM 13⁰ x 11⁰

BATH

DRESSING

LIN

CL

CL

DN

LIN

RAILING

BEDROOM 13⁸ x 12⁰

CL

OPEN

BEDROOM 14⁴ x 15⁰

Design Y3396

First Floor: 1,829 square feet
Second Floor: 947 square feet
Total: 2,776 square feet

L **D**

● Rustic charm abounds in this pleasant farmhouse rendition. Covered porches to the front and rear enclose living potential for the whole family. Flanking the entrance foyer are the living and dining rooms. Each is large enough to handle both casual and formal entertaining. To the rear is the L-shaped kitchen with island cook top and snack bar. A small family room/breakfast nook is attached for very informal activities. A private study is tucked away on this floor next to the master suite. On the second floor are three bedrooms and a full bath. Two of the bedrooms have charming dormer windows.

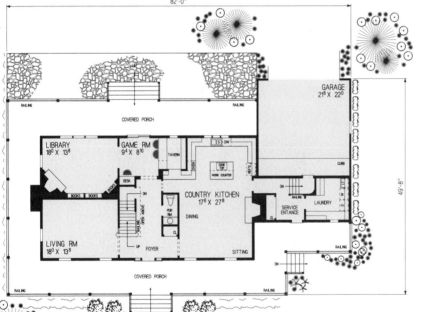

GARAGE
27⁸ X 22⁰

Design Y3399

First Floor: 1,716 square feet
Second Floor: 2,102 square feet
Total: 3,818 square feet

L **D**

● This is the ultimate in farmhouse living — six dormer windows and a porch that stretches essentially around the entire house. Inside, the plan is open and inviting. Besides the large country kitchen with fireplace, there is a small game room with attached tavern, a library with built-in bookshelves and a fireplace, and a formal living room. The second floor has four bedrooms and three full baths. The service entrance features a laundry area conveniently just off the garage.

Formal Living Rooms

For most building budgets, the cost of housing is too expensive to include in the floor plan a room that will be seldom used. The house with a parlor used only for weddings, funerals and infrequent ministerial visits has become an anachronism. But, that does not mean the formal living room does not have a prominent place in contemporary lifestyles. Nor does it mean today's active family has acquired living patterns that are particularly formal in nature and require a separate room. While family living has become more informal and modern technology has led to family-room TV and entertainment centers, there is a demand for a room in the house to cater to quiet conversation, reading and relaxation. The living room provides this haven away from the kitchen and gathering areas. During holidays and special occasions

Design Y2395, page 60.
Raised mouldings add character.

All set for sitting.

Symmetrically formal.

the living room and the family room make vital contributions to the success of get-togethers.

The formal living room can be of many shapes and sizes. It functions best when relatively free of cross-room traffic. The presence of the fireplace provides a focal point and makes a contribution to the room's ambience. Window locations, blank wall spaces and passage openings, like the fireplace, influence and control effective furniture placement. The decoration of the formal living room with appropriate and comfortable furnishing presents a wonderful opportunity to express one's tastes and personality. Wall and floor coverings, as well as drapery, offer an exciting selection challenge. Raised mouldings, wainscoting and fireplace mantels all offer chances to create a distinctive and inviting surrounding.

Design Y2250, page 236.
A charming living room wall.

(Right) Paneled walls make a difference.

Design Y2631, page 57.
A warm, timeless setting.

Formal Living Rooms   161

Formal Living Rooms

Traditionally styled fireplaces serve as the focal points for formal living rooms while raised mouldings, chair rails and mantels set the character. The types and styles of furniture and their groupings around the hearth offer an almost limitless number of possibilities. Whatever the mix, the result will surely produce an inviting and cozy ambience. A careful study of the details of these views will reveal the myriad of elements that flow together to produce a pleasing family living environment.

Design Y2654, page 92.
A mantel and mouldings add appeal.

Design Y2145, page 38.
A setting for conversation.

Design Y2692, page 89.
A hearth for kith and kin.

Design Y2600, page 193.
Corner fireplace commands attention.

Flanking the fireplace with windows.

Formal Living Rooms 163

Formal Living Rooms

The formal living room and its environment can be significantly affected by the style, size, location and treatment of its window areas. Vertically thrusting radial head windows with muntins can be a dramatic addition. These can be particularly effective when high ceilings are possible. Sloping ceilings and long, horizontal expanses of glass assure a spacious atmosphere. A single window, stylishly draped, can achieve a decorative impact. Of course, the placement of pictures, lamps, lighting fixtures and mementos is important to complete a homey picture.

Design Y2699, page 36.
Radial-head windows provide drama.

Design Y2954, page 314.
A high ceiling and high windows.

A pleasant sitting corner.

Sloping ceiling above a windowed wall.

Windowed doors deliver light and access.

Formal Living Rooms 165

Formal Living Rooms

The living room can establish its character in a number of ways, besides its furnishing and decorating, its windows and drapery or its flooring. Simulated beamed ceilings can be either flat or sloping. Fireplace walls may be of brick, stone or paneling. Projecting bays may highlight a built-in seat or bookcase. Consider all the elements that go into making these scenes ones that are warm and inviting. Don't overlook the wood boxes, fireplace screens, clocks or candelabra.

Design Y2656, page 53.
The beamed ceiling is a cozy touch.

Beams and stone go together.

Design Y1719, page 96.
A visually effective brick wall.

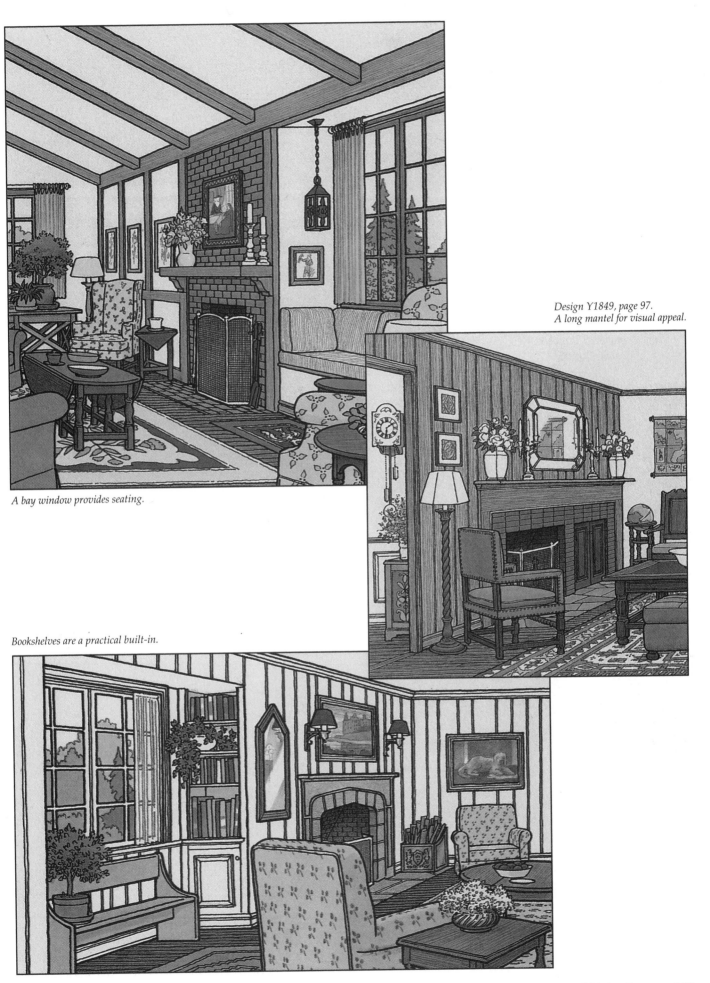

A bay window provides seating.

Design Y1849, page 97.
A long mantel for visual appeal.

Bookshelves are a practical built-in.

Formal Living Rooms

The living room is shown here with more
dramatic fireplaces and interesting
groupings of furniture in front of the
hearths. The mantels offer further opportunities for decorative statements.

A dramatic hooded fireplace.

A most pleasant grouping.

Design Y2963, page 154.
Natural woods set a tone.

Just a few steps from the foyer.

Time for tea.

Formal Living Rooms

Formal living rooms that function with formal dining rooms foster wonderful entertaining patterns. Placing these two rooms adjacent to one another is the result of thoughtful and practical floor planning. The opening between these two functional rooms may be large or small depending upon the amount of common wall space and how each room may utilize it. Placing these two rooms side by side with a generous opening fosters the feeling of spaciousness. Further, the decorating and ambience of one room can serve to enhance the appeal of the other. As these views illustrate, the formal dining room offers an interesting backdrop for the formal living room.

Design Y2907, page 146.
Viewing the dining room.

Design Y2616, page 91.
A sip before dining.

Design Y2786, page 149.
Twin bays and delightful views.

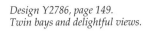

Design Y2658, page 50.
A practical dividing wall.

Design Y2852, page 62.
A matter of spaciousness.

Formal Living Rooms   171

EARLY GEORGIAN HOUSES OF NEW ENGLAND

During the 18th Century, Georgian architecture in New England and surrounding regions became a favorite style for a growing middle class of homeowners. The preferred exterior material was either clapboard or shingles. In some cases a rusticated wood siding was used to simulate masonry. The front doorway of Georgian houses heralded a departure from an unadorned past. Taking advantage of the skills of Yankee carpenters and shipwrights, pilasters and pediments in varied forms resulted in ornamented door enframement. Double-hung windows became universal in Georgian architecture and the Palladian window became popular. Georgian roofs were lower pitched than their earlier Colonial counterparts. Their cornices were more decorative. Cupolas and roof decks were common. The designs on these pages portray a wide range of houses incorporating the variety of Georgian architectural influences. A comparison of Design Y2687 on page 174 and Design Y2980 on page 183, for instance, is interesting.

18th-Century
Connecticut Valley Homestead

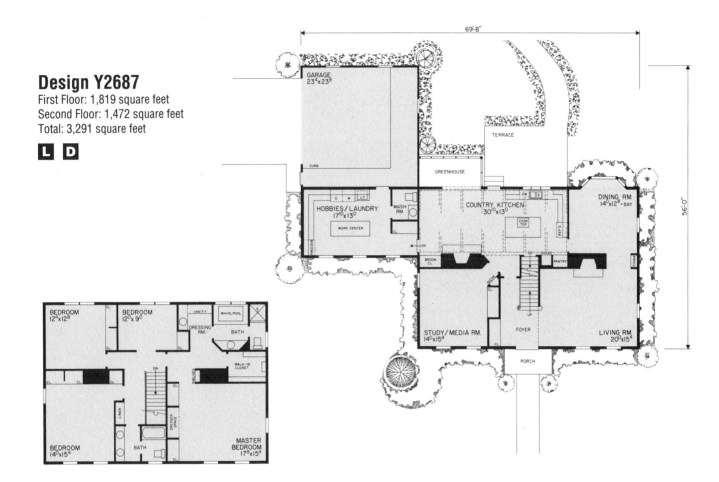

Design Y2687

First Floor: 1,819 square feet
Second Floor: 1,472 square feet
Total: 3,291 square feet

L **D**

● The homes built by prosperous farmers of the Connecticut Valley during the early part of the 18th Century began to reflect the elegance and refinement of Georgian motifs. This stolid house features the most elaborate of doorways with a scroll or "swans neck" pediment and supporting fluted pilasters. The massive twin chimneys, the window placement and the two lanterns flanking the central entrance exemplify the symmetry of this facade. The four-square nature of the structure is complemented by the projecting wing of the utility area and the two-car garage. This home is well-suited for a corner or interior building site. The rear projecting garage provides a sheltered area for the outdoor terrace and the greenhouse. The interior, as contemporary as the exterior is traditional, offers the large, active family an abundance of living potential. The central foyer opens to the large formal living room with its commanding fireplace. A few steps past the china cabinet is the dining room with its delightful bay window. A quiet study or media room is placed privately to the left of the foyer. The second floor offers four bedrooms and plenty of closet space. The master bedroom has a whirlpool, stall shower, two lavatories, a vanity and a walk-in closet.

The family living center is the spacious country kitchen. It opens to the pleasant greenhouse with all its natural light. Looking over the island cooking surface one finds plenty of area for informal dining and lounging. The fireplace will provide a warm and cozy backdrop for a multitude of family-oriented activities.

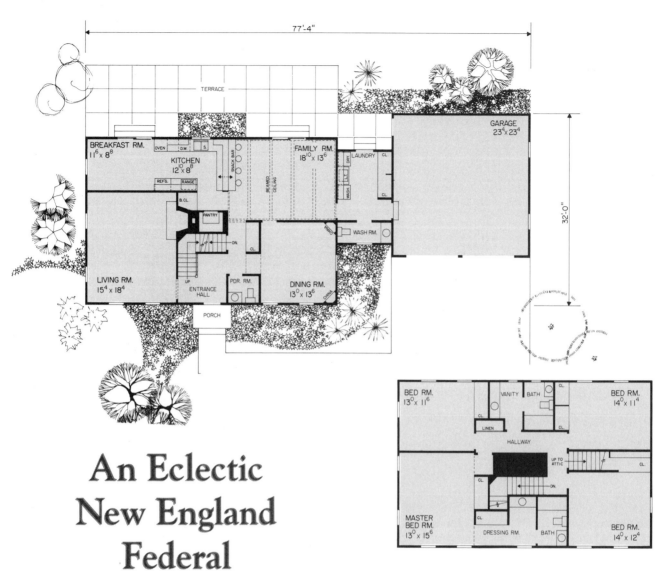

First floor plan labels:
77'-4" | 32'-0"
TERRACE
GARAGE 23⁴ x 23⁴
BREAKFAST RM. 11⁶ x 8⁸
KITCHEN 12¹⁰ x 8⁶
OVEN | D.W. | S.
REF'G. | RANGE
B. CL.
PANTRY
SNACK BAR
FAMILY RM. 18¹⁰ x 13⁶
BEAMED CEILING
LAUNDRY | CL.
WASH | DRY | CL.
DN. | CL.
UP
PIANO
WASH RM.
LIVING RM. 15⁴ x 18⁴
ENTRANCE HALL
PDR. RM.
DINING RM. 13⁰ x 13⁶
CHINA
PORCH

Second floor plan labels:
BED RM. 13⁰ x 11⁶
CL. | VANITY | BATH | CL.
LINEN
CL. | CL.
HALLWAY
BED RM. 14⁰ x 11⁴
CL.
UP TO ATTIC
DN.
MASTER BED RM. 13⁰ x 15⁶
CL.
DRESSING RM. | BATH
BED RM. 14⁰ x 12⁴

An Eclectic New England Federal

Design Y2640 First Floor: 1,386 square feet; Second Floor: 1,232 square feet; Total: 2,618 square feet

D

● Southeastern Massachusetts was a populous and prosperous section of Federal America. Here is an example of the blending of architectural forms common to both the 17th and 18th Centuries. This design recalls the Deane-Barstow House actually built in 1807. Its symmetrical Georgian-styled exterior includes all the classical elements plus the decorative motifs and finer detailing of the Federal style. The floor plan features formal living and dining rooms located to the front of the house. To the rear, functioning with the huge outdoor terrace, are the informal living areas. The efficient L-shaped kitchen opens to the sizable breakfast room. A pass-through opens the kitchen to the snack bar in the family room with beamed ceiling. The appendage connecting the house and garage accommodates the laundry and wash room. Note its direct access to the terrace as well as that of the garage. The second floor includes four bedrooms and two compartmented baths. Don't miss the stairs to the third-floor attic area—a great place to develop additional livability.

The central entrance hall with its fanlight window, fluted pilasters, paneled door, wide crown molding and wainscot is elegant indeed. An open staircase with finely detailed balusters completes the picture. This richly detailed area has a handy cloak closet and a powder room. A centrally located stairway provides access to the basement, another place to develop extra hobby, recreational and storage space.

An Historic House from Rhode Island

Design Y2659 First Floor: 1,023 square feet; Second Floor: 1,008 square feet; Third Floor: 476 square feet; Total: 2,507 square feet

L **D**

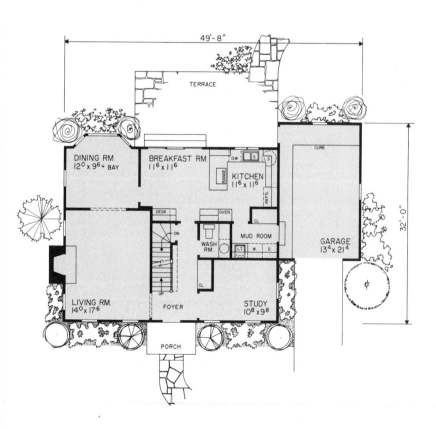

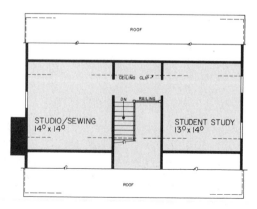

In 1770, Nathaniel Greene, who became George Washington's second-in-command wartime general, built his home in Anthony, Rhode Island. Here is a Georgian-styled house modeled after the general's homestead. The central entrance, with its pilasters and bracketed pediment, is flanked by twin carriage lamps. The symmetry of the shuttered windows with appealing muntins sets the character. While this version has an attached one-car garage, your preference for a two- or three-car appurtenance would be equally complementary. The rectangular structure will be economical to build and will deliver three stories of family livability. The compact plan is extremely practical and highly efficient. The study may serve as just that or function as a TV or media room. The U-shaped kitchen works well with the breakfast room and adjacent formal dining room. A mud room with laundry equipment and coat closet provides passage to the garage. Bonus space for the three-bedroom, two-bath second floor is available on the third floor. This large area can be developed into a couple of family areas for hobbies and studying.

The formal dining room will provide a particularly enjoyable environment. In addition to the side double-hung window, there is an expansive bay window. At mealtime there will be no lack of natural light or views of the surrounding landscape.

A Stately New Hampshire Georgian

● Portsmouth, New Hampshire was a bustling seaport throughout the 18th and into the 19th Century. The growth of shipbuilding and trade produced a period of prosperity that led to the building of homes that reflected a classical dignity and refinement in design and furnishing. Here is a design whose facade recalls the home built in 1730 by a sea captain whose wife, upon his death, counted John Paul Jones as one of her illustrious boarders. The gambrel roof caps the third floor with its pedimented dormer windows. Massive twin chimneys make a stolid statement. The centered classical doorway has a segmental pediment and pilasters. Efficient and flexible traffic patterns develop from

the rectangular floor plan. Separating the formal living room from the informal family room is the common fireplace wall. The dining room is large and has a fireplace of its own. The L-shaped kitchen has an island cooking counter and opens into the breakfast nook area with beamed ceiling. Two sets of sliding glass doors provide ample access to the raised terrace. Other highlights of the first floor include the powder room, pantry and roomy laundry. The second floor may function with four bedrooms, or three plus a sitting room for the master bedroom. Don't miss the stairway to the third floor with plenty of bonus space.

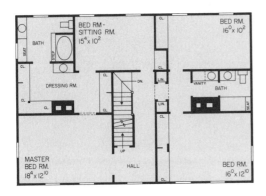

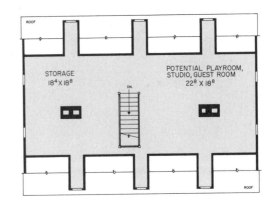

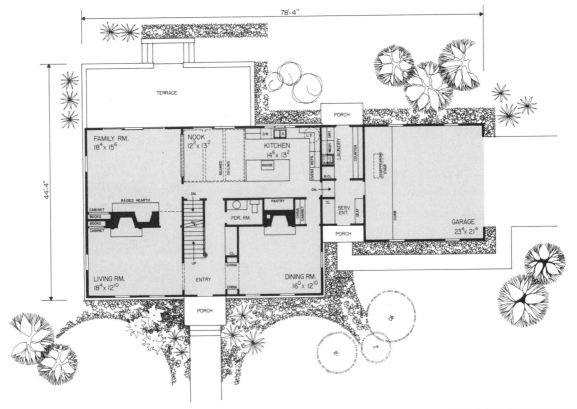

Design Y2556

First Floor: 1,675 square feet
Second Floor: 1,472 square feet
Third Floor: 1,016 square feet
Total: 4,163 square feet

The elegance of the formal living room is captured by the finely detailed decorative woodwork. As in the family room, a built-in bookcase with cabinets below is located adjacent to the fireplace.

Late-Georgian Elegance

Design Y2980

First Floor: 1,648 square feet
Second Floor: 1,368 square feet
Third Floor: 567 square feet
Total: 3,583 square feet

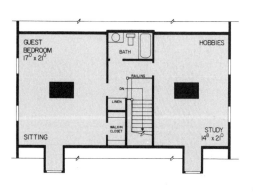

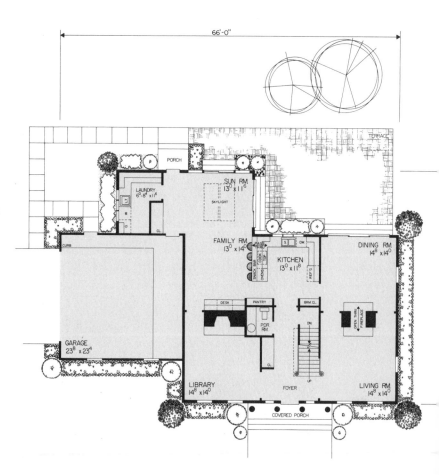

● This late-Georgian adaptation is reminiscent of the Cowles house built in Farmington, Connecticut around 1786. The formal symmetry and rich ornamentation are typical of houses of this period. Until around 1750 the facades of Georgian houses were "flat". Following that date came the introduction of a projecting central pavilion, topped by a gable in the form of a classic pediment. Other classical elements included Ionic columns and a Palladian window. This design has a gambrel roof with two pedimented gables and massive twin chimneys. Dentils, wooden quoins, bracketed cornices and

crossetted window lintels complete the picture of elegance. Projecting from the rear is a shed-type roof which encloses the sun room. A skylight and sliding glass doors guarantee plenty of natural light. Inside are three floors of livability. The central foyer leads to the formal living room, the library, or straight ahead to the U-shaped kitchen. The family room area with handy snack bar opens to the spacious sun room. The highlight of the second floor is the master bedroom with fireplace and spacious bath with whirlpool, stall shower, twin lavatories, vanity and a walk-in closet.

The living room has as its focal point a striking fireplace with a bracketed pediment and fluted pilasters above the classic mantel. This is a through-fireplace which can also be enjoyed from the formal dining room located behind the paneled doors flanking the fireplace.

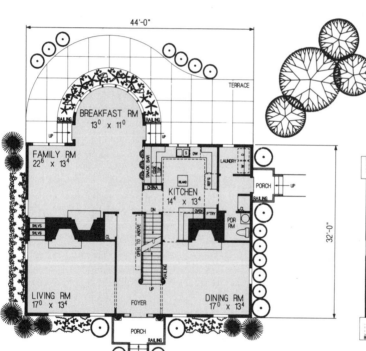

Design Y2992
First Floor: 1,541 square feet
Second Floor: 1,541 square feet
Third Floor: 1,016 square feet
Total: 4,098 square feet

L **D**

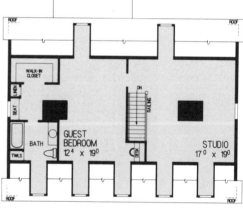

● The Dalton house, built between 1750 and 1760 in Newburyport, Massachusetts, inspired our plan shown here. Its lovely proportion and graceful exterior give way to a floor plan designed for the times. Left of the entry foyer is the formal living room; to the right formal dining. Both rooms have warming hearths. A family room to the rear of the plan connects with a unique glass-enclosed breakfast room. Nearby is the kitchen with pass-through snack bar. The second floor holds three bedrooms — the master suite and two family bedrooms. On the third floor is a guest bedroom with private bath and studio.

Design Y2998

First Floor: 2,243 square feet
Second Floor: 1,532 square feet
Total: 3,775 square feet

L **D**

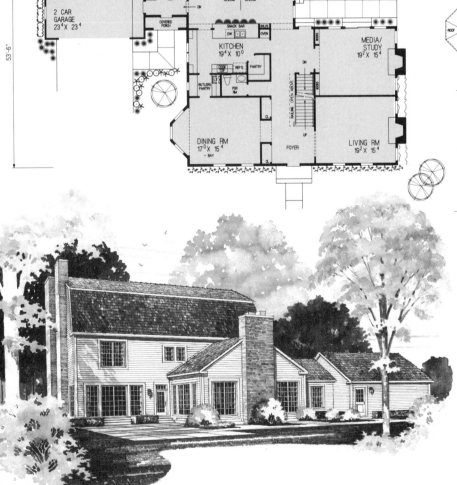

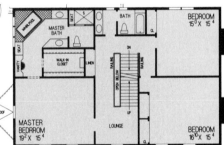

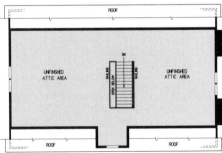

● This gambrel-roofed three-story house recalls the home fondly known as "Old Manse," located in Concord, Massachusetts. History reports that the grandfather of Ralph Waldo Emerson built the original dwelling around 1769 and it later became home for the famous philosopher. The floor plan incorporates all the elements that ensure fine family livability into the 21st Century. Don't miss the media room, large family room, master bath, lounge area, three fireplaces and the bonus space on the third floor.

Design Y2641

First Floor: 1,672 square feet
Second Floor: 1,248 square feet
Total: 2,920 square feet

● This Georgian adaptation is from the early 18th-Century and has plenty of historical background. The classical details are sedately stated. The plan promises up-to-date livability. The size of your site need not be large, either.

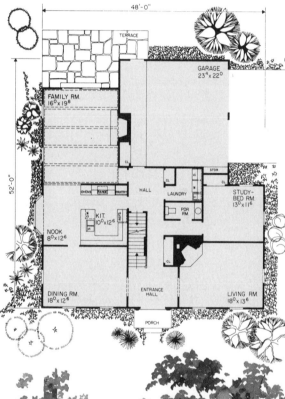

Design Y2994

First Floor: 1,736 square feet
Second Floor: 1,472 square feet
Total: 3,208 square feet

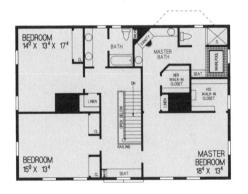

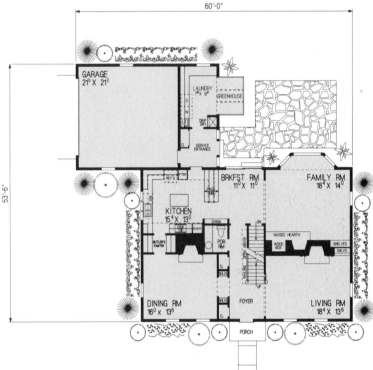

● Modeled after the homes of successful merchants in Amherst, New Hampshire, this lovely two-story plan presents an historical facade. Two chimney stacks, fluted pilasters and a bracketed pediment add their distinctive details. The floor plan is equally as classic with center hall separating living and dining rooms and leading back to the family room. All three living spaces have fireplaces. The second floor holds three bedrooms including a gracious master suite with two walk-in closets and whirlpool tub. Secondary bedrooms share a full bath with dual lavatories.

Design Y2989 First Floor: 1,972 square feet
Second Floor: 1,533 square feet; Total: 3,505 square feet

L

● This dramatic residence, patterned after one built in 1759 by Major John Vassall in Cambridge, offers a floor plan that is intriguing in its wealth of amenities. On the first floor are the formal living and dining rooms, each with a fireplace.

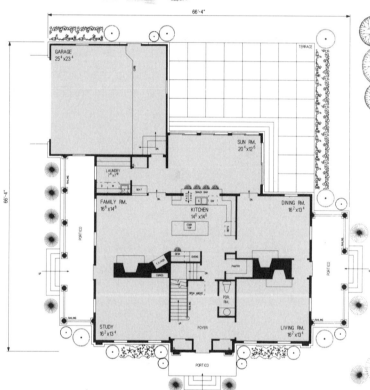

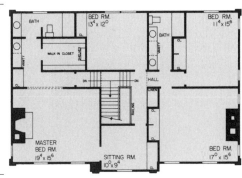

Design Y2522

First Floor: 1,835 square feet
Second Floor: 1,625 square feet
Total: 3,460 square feet

● This wood frame Georgian adaptation revives the architecture of an earlier period in New England. Its formal facade houses an abundance of spacious livability.

First Floor Plan

85'-8"

TERRACE

GARAGE 23⁴ x 23⁴

LAUNDRY RM.

KITCHEN 12' x 12'

NOOK 9⁰ x 12⁰

DINING RM. 15⁰ x 12⁰

WALK-IN CLOSET

STUDY 12⁰ x 15⁶

PDR. RM.

WASH RM.

SERVICE ENTRANCE

PORCH

HALL

FAMILY RM. 19⁴ x 19⁰

FOYER

LIVING RM. 19⁴ x 15⁶

PORCH

35'-8"

Second Floor Plan

BATH

BED RM. 13⁴ x 12⁰

BED RM. 11⁴ x 15⁶

WALK-IN CLOSET

BATH

VANITY

HALL

MASTER BED RM. 19⁴ x 15⁶

SITTING RM. 10⁰ x 9⁴

BED RM. 17⁰ x 15⁶

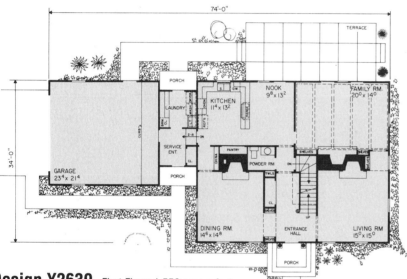

74'-0"

TERRACE

PORCH

LAUNDRY

KITCHEN
11⁴ x 13²

NOOK
9⁸ x 13²

FAMILY RM.
20⁰ x 14⁰

GARAGE
23⁴ x 21⁴

34'-0"

SERVICE
ENT.

CHINA

PANTRY

POWDER RM.

TWLS.

SHELVES

PORCH

DINING RM.
14⁶ x 14⁸

ENTRANCE
HALL

UP

LIVING RM.
15⁰ x 15⁰

PORCH

● Here is a New England Georgian adaptation with an elevated doorway highlighted by pilasters and a pediment. It gives way to a second-story Palladian window, capped in turn by a pediment projecting from the hipped roof. The interior is decidely up-to-date with even an upstairs lounge.

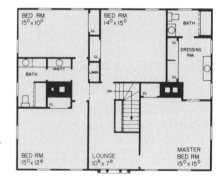

BED RM.
15⁰ x 10⁰

BED RM.
14⁰ x 15⁰

BATH

CL

CL

DRESSING
RM.

BATH

VANITY

LINEN

DN

CL

BED RM.
15⁰ x 12⁸

LOUNGE
10⁸ x 7⁸

MASTER
BED RM.
15⁰ x 15⁰

Design Y2639 First Floor: 1,556 square feet
Second Floor: 1,428 square feet; Total: 2,984 square feet

● This Cape Cod Georgian recalls the Julia Wood House built approximately 1790 in Falmouth, Mass. Such homes generally featured a balustraded roof deck or "widow's walk" where wives of captains looked to sea for signs of returning ships. Our updated floor plans include four bedrooms including master suite on the second floor and country kitchen, study, dining room, and living room on the first floor. A third floor makes a fine 15 x 10 studio, with ladder leading up to the widow's walk.

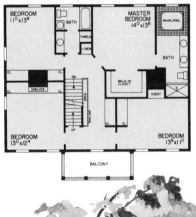

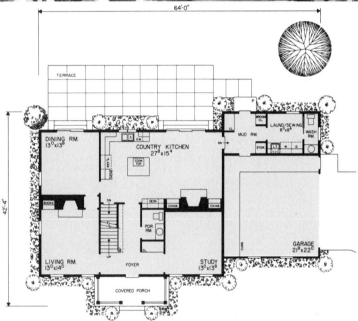

Design Y2690

First Floor: 1,559 square feet
Second Floor: 1,344 square feet; Third Floor: 176 square feet
Total: 3,079 square feet

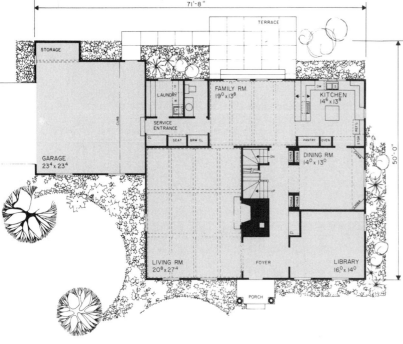

Design Y2653

First Floor: 2,016 square feet
Second Floor: 1,656 square feet
Total: 3,672 square feet

● Livability and special features are absolutely outstanding in this Colonial design. Imagine a living room with beamed ceiling and fireplace that measures more than 20 x 27 feet. And the second fireplace in the luxurious master suite. Make a special note about all the built-ins featured in the dining room.

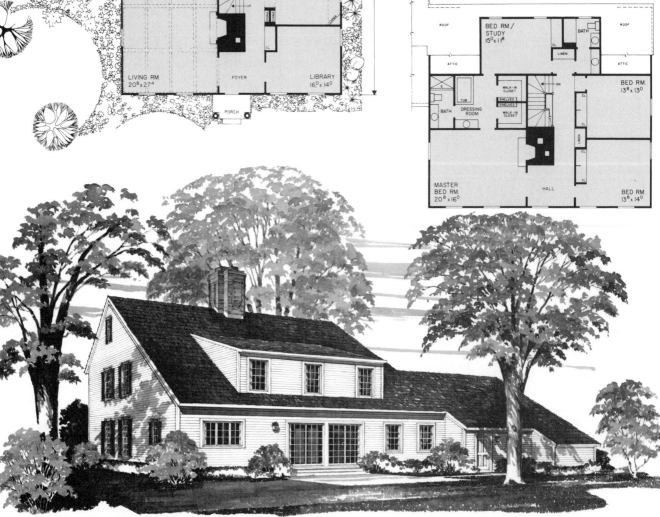

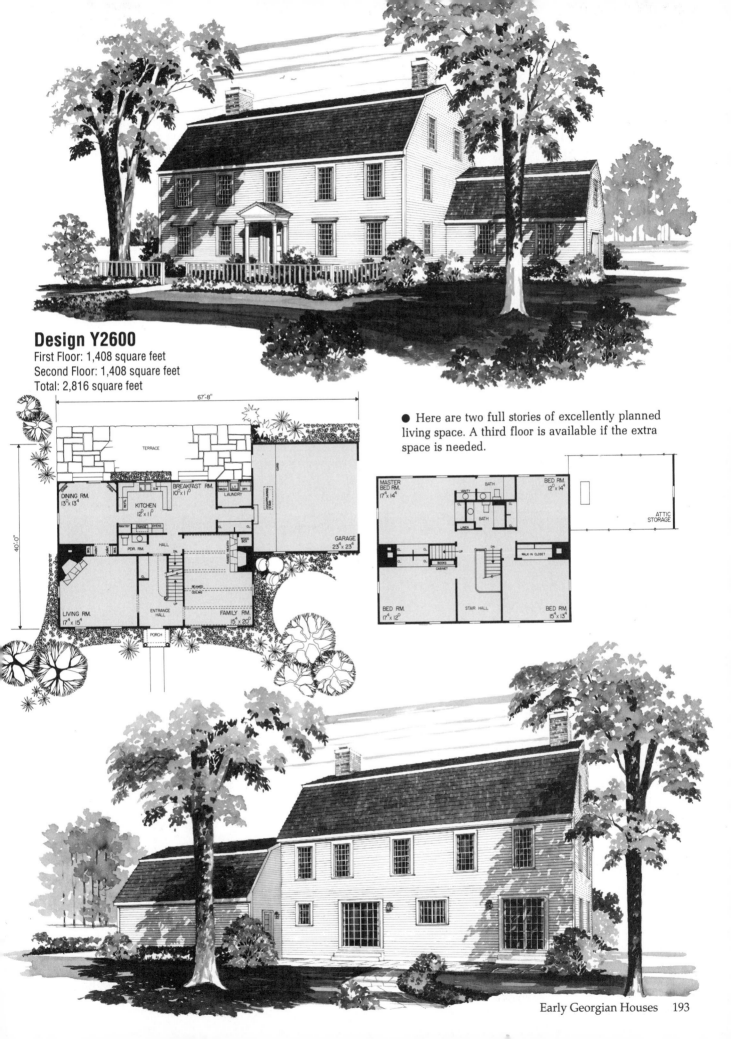

Design Y2600

First Floor: 1,408 square feet
Second Floor: 1,408 square feet
Total: 2,816 square feet

● Here are two full stories of excellently planned living space. A third floor is available if the extra space is needed.

Design Y2221 First Floor: 1,726 square feet
Second Floor: 1,440 square feet; Total: 3,166 square feet

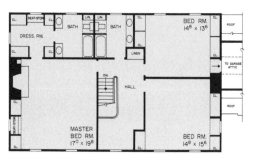

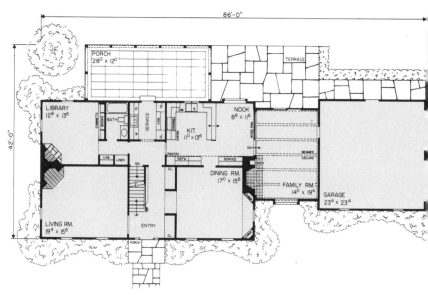

● A Georgian Colonial adaptation on the grand scale. The authentic front entrance is delightfully detailed. Two massive end chimneys, housing four fireplaces, are in keeping with the architecture of its day.

Design Y2840 First Floor: 1,529 square feet
Second Floor: 1,344 square feet; Total: 2,873 square feet

● Designed with energy efficiency in mind, this design has two air locks to control the flow of cold air, double exterior walls and super insulation.

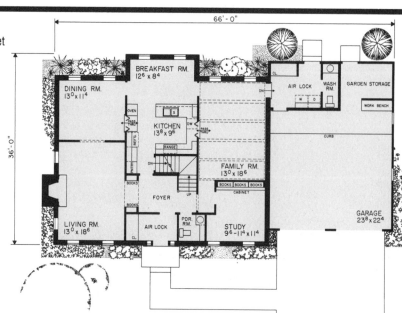

Design Y2188

First Floor: 1,440 square feet
Second Floor: 1,280 square feet
Total: 2,720 square feet

● This design is characteristic of early America and its presence will create an atmosphere of that time in our heritage. However, it will be right at home wherever located. Along with exterior charm, this design has outstanding livability to offer its occupants.

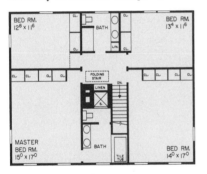

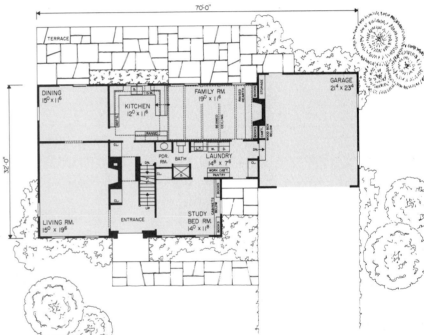

Design Y2102

First Floor: 1,682 square feet
Second Floor: 1,344 square feet
Total: 3,026 square feet

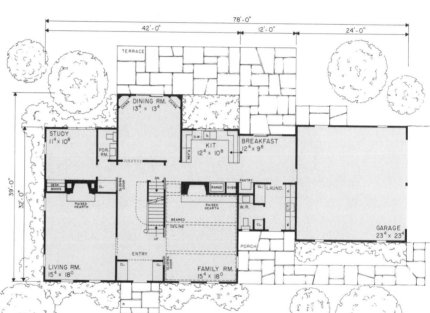

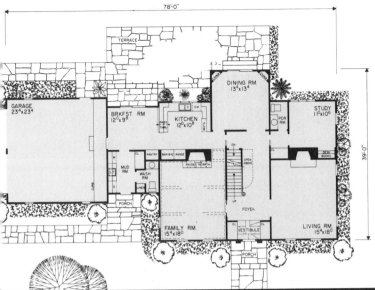

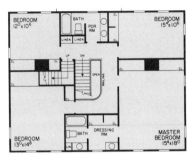

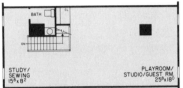

Design Y2100 First Floor: 1,682 square feet
Second Floor: 1,344 square feet; Third Floor: 780 square feet
Total: 3,806 square feet

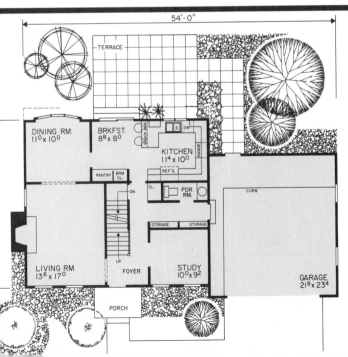

Design Y2870 First Floor: 900 square feet
Second Floor Left Suite: 467 square feet
Second Floor Right Suite: 493 square feet
Total: 1,860 square feet

● This colonial home was designed to provide comfortable living space for two families. The first floor is the common living area, with all of the necessary living areas; the second floor has two two-bedroom-one-bath suites.

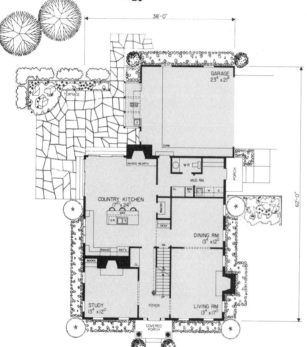

● The memory of Noah Webster's house, built in 1823, in New Hampshire is recalled by this Greek Revival adaptation. A picture home for a narrow site, it delivers big-house livability. In addition to the formal living and dining rooms, there is the huge country kitchen and handy mud room. There is also a study. Upstairs, four bedrooms and three full baths. Don't miss the four fireplaces or the outdoor balcony of the master bedroom. A basement provides additional space for recreation and the pursuit of hobbies.

Design Y2979 First Floor: 1,440 square feet
Second Floor: 1,394 square feet; Total: 2,834 square feet

Design Y3504

First Floor: 2,124 square feet
Second Floor: 1,658 square feet
Total: 3,782 square feet

● Following the Revolutionary War, many New Englanders settled in New York near the Catskill Mountains. In Rensselaerville a number of quietly dignified houses were built. They had clapboard siding, symmetrically placed windows and a central motif of wide pedimented doorways below graceful Palladian windows. Here is an appealing rendition of the simple, straightforward character of these houses. This present-day version will adapt well to a relatively narrow interior site or a corner lot. The dramatic foyer has a curving, open staircase to the second floor, which in turn has a stairway to the bonus space of the third floor. In addition to the sunken family room there is a large library. Notice the fine master suite.

ATTIC

S. SEAT WHIRLPOOL SEAT

MASTER BATH

WALK-IN CLOSET

WALK-IN CLOSET

VANITY

LIN.

BEDROOM
12⁰ x 14⁴+ BAY

BATH

UP TO ATTIC

LINEN

DN

OPEN TO BELOW

LIN.

BEDROOM
14¹⁰ x 12⁰

RAILING

MASTER BEDROOM
15⁰ x 21⁸

READING AREA

GARAGE
23⁴ x 23⁴

VERANDA

LT W D
LAUNDRY

FAMILY ROOM
17⁸ x 1⁸

KITCHEN/BRKFST
15⁴ x 29⁴

DN

PANTRY

DN

TAVERN

PANTRY

DW

C.T.

LIBRARY
12⁸ x 13²+ BAY

PDR. RM.

OPEN TO ABOVE

B.C. DN

REF'G

DN

LIVING ROOM
18⁴ x 15⁶

FOYER

DINING ROOM
15⁰ x 13²

WIDTH 53'
DEPTH 75'-6"

Formal Dining Areas

The primary function of any house is to provide shelter for its occupants. As we know, early structures had but a single room to take care of the many activities involved in family living. As houses grew in size and sophistication, areas began to be defined. By the 18th Century, the consumption of meals solely at a trestle table in the multi-purpose hall had progressed to more spacious and comfortable accommodations—the separate dining room. The changing lifestyles of prosperous farmers and merchants hastened the growth in popularity of this important room. As exteriors of houses became more stylish, so did their interiors. The dining room and its decoration and furnishings took no back seat to any other part of the house. In fact, it became a room of exquisite beauty. With the availability of crown mouldings, chair rails, wainscotings and wood casings, along with drapery, wall, floor and ceiling treatments, the decoration of the dining room became a pleasing challenge.

Design Y2623, page 102.
Ready for dinner to begin.

Design Y2301, page 238.
Setting the mood.

Fine formal living and dining.

Adjacent to the foyer.

Design Y2320, page 127.
Corner china cabinet adds appeal.

Design Y2211, page 105.
Two windows provide double enjoyment.

Formal Dining Areas

Formal dining rooms with large glass areas can have a bright and cheerful atmosphere and provide a pleasant view of the surrounding landscape. This fenestration can take many sizes and shapes. Here are some examples of larger glass areas and the impact they have on the dining environment. Incorporating window bays not only provides an inordinate amount of natural light and a larger view of the outdoor scenery, but also delivers several extra livable square feet. Additionally, windows, whether large or small, make a vital contribution to the room's decor when tastefully draped.

Design Y2685, page 142.
A charming and practical wall.

A sliding glass door provides outdoor access.

Design Y2225, page 41.
Window bay with a seat.

Design Y2571, page 62.
A bay window adds space.

Design Y2185, page 259.
Appealing china cabinets and window walls.

Bringing the outdoors in.

Formal Dining Areas

Dining areas, in lieu of separate and distinct dining rooms, can have a full measure of appeal and utility. They can enjoy the advantages of open planning, including a feeling of spaciousness, added convenience and a continuity of ambience and decoration. Sometimes formal living and dining areas may flow together with no walls, dividers or barriers of any kind. Or, they may be partially separated by open room dividers of short walls with spindles and planters. An effective, decorative and practical room divider can be the through-fireplace, which can be enjoyed from both the living and dining areas. Formal dining can be successfully provided for in a corner of the living room. This can work well when such space is located close to the kitchen, thus facilitating the serving of meals.

Seeing through the fireplace.

Spaciousness is the byword.

A divider with utility and decor.

A half wall provides full enjoyment.

Design Y2565, page 334.
A formal, open area.

Formal Dining Areas

Dining formally in a separate room planned, furnished and decorated toward that end enhances and enriches the family's living patterns. The environment is key. Here are several scenes that illustrate how all the elements can come together to produce a pleasant atmosphere for family dining. Consider the windows—their sizes, shapes and decoration. Notice the surface treatments and decor of the walls.

Sliding doors to the dining terrace.

Design Y2398, page 86.
Awaiting the family arrival.

Adjacent to the foyer.

A bright depository for plants.

(Right) A picture window backdrop.

A bay adds floor space.

The Study

T he study is hardly a phenomenon of 20th-Century floor planning. Whether referred to as a study or library, its roots are deep in our architectural heritage. Reproductions of floor plans dating back into the 18th Century frequently carried the legend "study" or "library." The Thomas Hancock House (c.1737), in Boston, Shirley Place (c.1747), in Roxbury and the Jeremiah Lee House (c.1768) in Marblehead are such examples. And, of course, George Washington's Mt. Vernon and Thomas Jefferson's Monticello had their libraries. As the name implies, the study provides the family with a room for quiet pursuits away from the hubbub

Functioning with other rooms.

The bibliophile's retreat.

of family activity. It is, naturally, the household's book depository. It can also be a room planned around its fenestration, fireplace and access to other rooms. It offers no less of a decorating and furnishing challenge than rooms in the sleeping, dining or living areas of the house. The arrival of the age of technology, with its high-tech TV, VCR and sound equipment, has found many families turning the study/library into a media room—hardly a place of peace and quiet.

A study within an open area.

Design Y2616, page 91.
A study desk before the fireplace.

Design Y1900, page 78.
Study overlooking the great room.

A quiet desk for homework.

The Study

The study and its functions can be found in many parts of the plan. It may be upstairs or down. It may or may not have access to the outdoors. It may also serve as a lounge area on an indoor balcony. The study lends itself to providing a guest room on occasion. As a dual-use room, it may be just the place to pursue one's hobby, take a cat nap or ruminate on the week's busy schedule. The study lends itself to functioning as a lounge or a small, secondary living room. However you and your family use, decorate or furnish your study or library, it will surely serve all members well.

Design Y2188, page 195.
Curling up with a good book.

Design Y2951, page 366.
The study as a mariner's lookout.

Design Y2899, page 236.
A study desk and a reading chair.

Design Y2221, page 194.
Serious study before the fireplace.

A cozy secondary living room.

Design Y2157, page 137.
Another study use—setting up the easel.

GEORGIAN HOUSES OF THE SOUTHERN COLONIES

Georgian houses in the South were different from their counterparts in the North. Brick was the most used exterior material in the Southern Colonies as compared to clapboard and shingles in the North, although there were many examples of rusticated boards of pine grooved to simulate stone masonry. Mount Vernon had such an exterior. Hipped roofs were popular in the South while side-gabled and gambrel roofs were more common in the North. Paired end chimneys were more prevalent in the South than in the North where the central chimney predominated. Generally, Georgian houses of the South were larger than those in the North. Beginning on page 239 is a section of houses identified as "Southern Colonial." Because of their porticos and two-story columns, they are a highly recognizable group. However, the projecting portico was not a common feature of Georgian architecture. The widespread use of the "giant portico" with its high, graceful columns characterized the Federal and Greek Revival style of the late 18th and early 19th Centuries. In the context of this section, the sobriquet, Southern Colonial, is more of a contemporary term to identify these stately and dramatic dwellings. Of interest is the contrast of the charm of small frame Williamsburg-type houses, such as Design Y2520 and Design Y2695, with the luxurious manor houses, exemplified by designs Y2230 and Y2683.

Georgian Elegance from the Past

BEDROOM 15⁰ x 11⁴

BEDROOM 10⁴ x 13⁴

BATH

TUB

UP

DRESSING RM.

VANITY

WALK-IN CLOSET

LINEN

ATTIC STORAGE

ROOF

UP BATH

VANITY

LINEN

DN

OPEN STAIR WELL

CL

LOUNGE 21⁰ x 11⁸

RAILING

BEDROOM 15⁰ x 11⁴

ROOF

MASTER BEDROOM 14⁰ x 18⁰

ROOF

Design Y2683
First Floor: 2,126 square feet
Second Floor: 1,882 square feet
Total: 4,008 square feet

L **D**

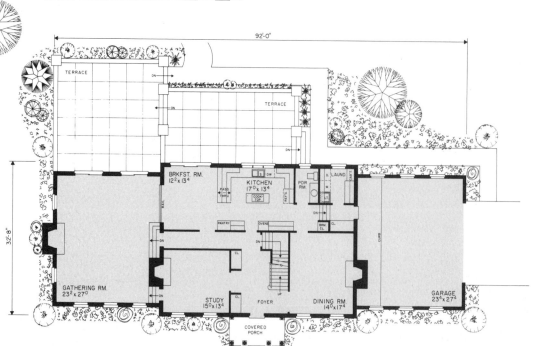

92'-0"

TERRACE

DN

TERRACE

DN

DN

32'-8"

BRKFST. RM. 12² x 13⁴

KITCHEN 17⁰ x 13⁴

COOK TOP

PDR RM

LAUND

PASS THRU

RAIL

PANTRY

OVEN

REFG.

BRM CL

DN

GATHERING RM. 23² x 27⁰

CL

STUDY 15⁰ x 13⁴

CL

FOYER

DN

DINING RM. 14⁰ x 17⁴

GARAGE 23⁴ x 27⁴

CURB

COVERED PORCH

● This historical Georgian home has its roots in the 18th Century. Dignified symmetry is a hallmark of both front and rear elevations. The full two-story center section is delightfully complemented by the 1½-story wings. Interior livability has been planned to serve today's active family. The elegant gathering room (below), three steps down from the rest of the house, has ample space for entertaining on a grand scale. It fills an entire wing and is dead ended so that traffic does not pass through it. Guests and family alike will enjoy the two rooms flanking the foyer, the study and formal dining room. Each of these rooms has a fireplace as its highlight. The breakfast room, kitchen, powder room and laundry are arranged for maximum efficiency. This area will always have that desired light and airy atmosphere with the sliding glass door and the triple window over the kitchen sink. The second floor houses the family bedrooms. Take special note of the spacious master bedroom suite. It has a deluxe bath, fireplace and sunken lounge with dressing room and walk-in closet. Surely an area to be appreciated.

Georgian Architecture Comes to Life

Design Y2192 First Floor: 1,884 square feet; Second Floor: 1,521 square feet; Third Floor: 808 square feet; Total: 4,213 square feet

L **D**

● You'll not need a curving front drive or formal gardens to insure an impressive setting for this house. The mere stateliness of its facade will command the complete and extraordinary attention of even the most casual of passers-by. The authentic detailing centers around the fine proportions, the dentils, the window symmetry, the front door and entranceway, the massive chimneys and the masonry work. The rear elevation retains all the grandeur exemplary of exquisite architecture. The projecting wing adds to the breadth of the overall design. This provides for the inclusion of the oversize garage and the family room with its view of both front and rear yards. Surely a fine adaptation from the 18th Century when formality and elegance were bywords.

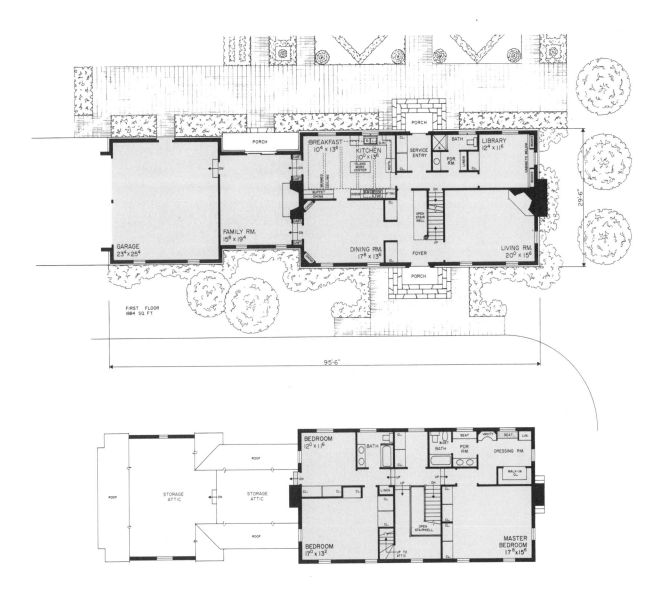

FIRST FLOOR
1884 SQ. FT.

GARAGE
23⁴ x 25⁴

FAMILY RM.
15⁸ x 19⁴

PORCH

BREAKFAST
10⁴ x 13⁶

KITCHEN
10⁰ x 13⁶

ISLAND WORK CENTER

BEAMED CEILING

BUFFET CHINA

DINING RM.
17⁸ x 13⁶

SERVICE ENTRY

PDR. RM.

BATH

LIBRARY
12⁴ x 11⁶

LINEN

PORCH

OPEN STAIR WELL

FOYER

LIVING RM.
20⁰ x 15⁶

PORCH

29'-6"

95'-6"

ROOF

STORAGE ATTIC

STORAGE ATTIC

ROOF

BEDROOM
12⁰ x 11⁶

BATH

BEDROOM
17⁰ x 13²

LINEN

OPEN STAIRWELL

UP TO ATTIC

BIDET

BATH

PDR. RM.

SEAT

VANITY

SEAT

LIN.

DRESSING RM.

WALK-IN CL.

MASTER BEDROOM
17⁸ x 15⁶

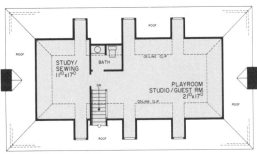

ROOF

STUDY/ SEWING
11⁰ x 17⁰

BATH

PLAYROOM STUDIO/GUEST RM.
21⁰ x 17⁰

ROOF

The delightfully spacious and dramatic second-floor hallway area features an open stairwell and provides extra storage space.

● The appeal of this outstanding home does not end with its exterior elevations. Consider the formal living room with its corner fireplace and the library with a wall of bookshelves and cabinets. Two corner china cabinets highlight the dining room. The two entrances to the sunken family room feature storage niches. The second floor has three big bedrooms, including a master suite with dressing room and compartmented bath.

Georgian Houses of the Southern Colonies   217

A Tidewater Virginia Manor

Design Y2990

First Floor: 2,615 square feet
Second Floor: 1,726 square feet
Third Floor: 437 square feet
Total: 4,778 square feet

● This finely proportioned dwelling brings to mind the St. George Tucker house in Williamsburg. Reflected here is the "Roman Country House" style of Palladio which was exemplified in a number of late Georgian houses. It is identified by its central two-story structure and the lower attached dependencies. This sprawling configuration results in the main living areas being on the first floor and enjoying good cross-ventilation. This was surely an important factor in the South during the period. Today, air conditioning makes such room placement less important. However, with contemporary living patterns putting such emphasis on convenient indoor/outdoor relationships, this plan has much to recommend it. Notice how the raised terrace with its wood railing is directly accessible from most first-floor areas.

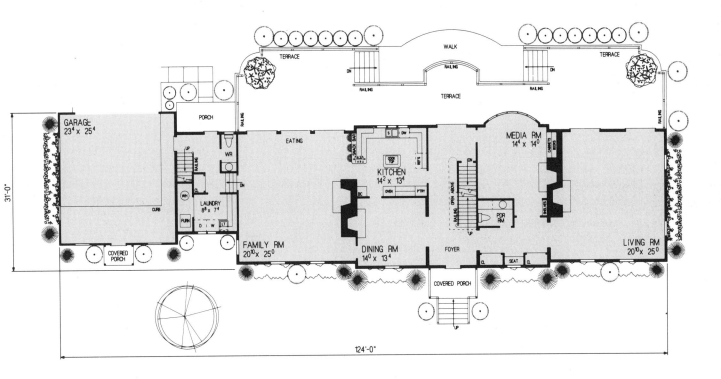

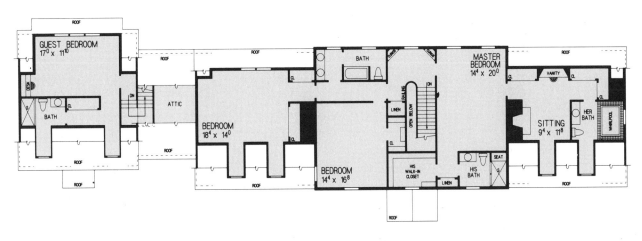

● As appealing as the rambling nature of this exterior is, the interior also offers great livability. The end living room is sure to offer privacy. The media room with built-in units will be a favorite spot. But a step or two from the informal and formal eating areas, the U-shaped kitchen functions wonderfully. The family room provides plenty of space for a variety of activities. A one-story connector links house to garage and serves as the laundry, utility and mud room area. A flight of stairs leads to the guest room with full bath over the garage. The central foyer runs straight through to the rear terrace and has an open staircase to the second floor. Here there are two family bedrooms, plus an enormous master suite with His and Hers baths and a sitting room complete with fireplace. Altogether there are five fireplaces in this house.

A Late Georgian Classic

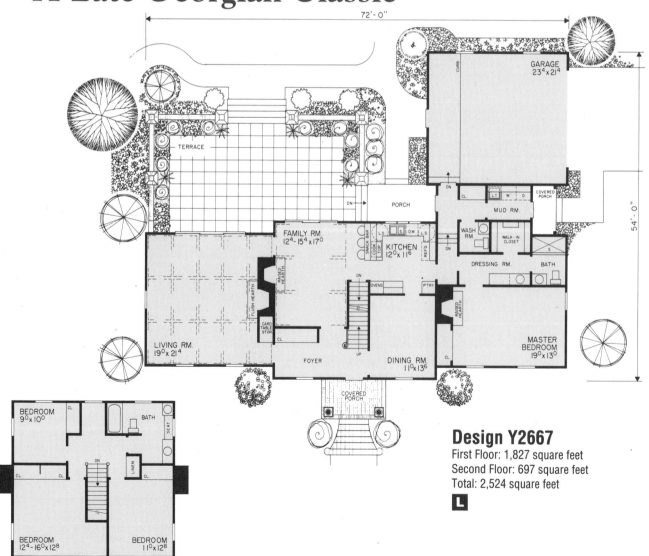

Design Y2667
First Floor: 1,827 square feet
Second Floor: 697 square feet
Total: 2,524 square feet

● This 18th-Century late Georgian house has a heritage that goes back to the work of noted 16th-Century Italian Renaissance architect Andrea Palladio. Its configuration of a high, pedimented center section flanked by lower wings was reflected in numerous Anglo-Palladian structures. An example of this form is the James Semple House in Williamsburg, believed to have been built around 1780. The rich detailing of the flat pediment gable and the portico is carried through at the roof lines on all four sides of the house. With its rear projecting garage, this house will adapt to a corner building site as well as an interior site. Well-zoned, the floor plan will serve the large, active family admirably. The spacious living room is effectively balanced by a wing that accommodates the outstanding master bedroom suite. The kitchen is efficient and serves the formal dining room and the family room with beamed ceiling outstandingly. Note the three fireplaces, two of which have raised hearths. A second floor with three bedrooms (make one a study if you wish) and a bath with two lavatories caters to the younger family members.

The spacious living room is highlighted by a beamed ceiling, an appealing fireplace and an expanse of sliding glass doors providing access to outdoor living. This is a room that will be fun to decorate and furnish.

Georgian Houses of the Southern Colonies   221

Dignified Federal Manor

Design Y2662

First Floor: 1,735 square feet
Second Floor: 1,075 square feet
Third Floor: 746 square feet
Total: 3,556 square feet

● Influences from both Georgian and Federal architecture are apparent in the design of this home. The exterior is highlighted with multi-lite windows, two classic chimneys and well-proportioned dormers. A curved window is visible in each wing. The interior of this design has been planned just as carefully as the exterior. Study each area carefully and imagine how your family would utilize the space. You'll find a study, parlor, gathering room, U-shaped kitchen, formal and informal dining rooms plus a powder room and laundry. Three bedrooms and two baths are on the second floor. Two additional bedrooms and another bath are on the third floor. Lack of space will never be a problem in this house.

The fine-functioning, U-shaped kitchen features built-in cooking equipment and, in addition, an alcove specially designed to hold a barbecue unit. A pass-through opens up the area and facilitates work patterns. The pantry is strategically located. Adjacent to the barbecue unit is the doorway to the sunken breakfast room. Enjoyable hours will be spent in this room with its beamed ceiling, fireplace and large bowed window.

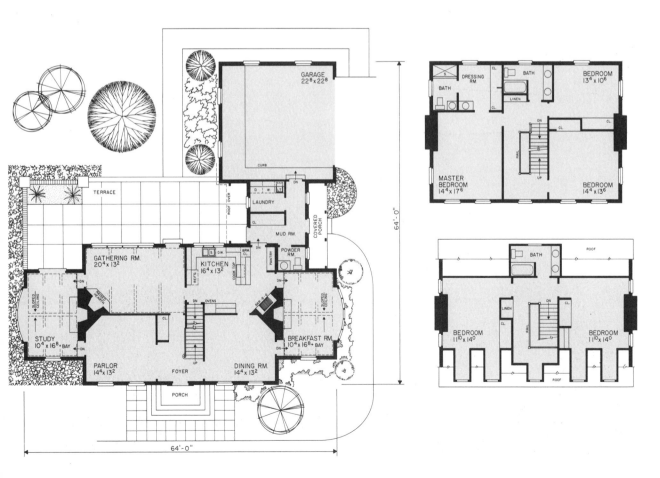

Echoes of a Maryland Past

● Prosperous merchants along Maryland's eastern shore built Georgian-style houses during the 18th Century that rivaled those found throughout the Colonies. The main portion of this graceful facade is faithful to its ancestors. The hipped roof, so common in the South, supports stylish dormers on each of its four sides. The symmetry of the windows with their louvered shutters and keystoned lintels is pleasing. The recessed front doorway is classic with its architrave, pediment and Greek columns. Three massive chimneys provide further linkage to the past. The raised terrace at the rear is enclosed by a brick wall. Wide steps lead down to the rear yard. The interior of this modern-day manor is equally as impressive. The central foyer is spa-cious and dramatic as it provides views past raised columns into the stair hall. The angular, open staircase leads to the expansive second floor. The living room, dining room and library provide havens for formal living. The L-shaped kitchen looks down into an informal, sunken breakfast/family room area. The utility area includes a big laundry room, a handy wash room and an open staircase to an apartment over the garage—perfect for a live-in relative. Don't miss the small office adjacent to the family bedroom area. Each of the children's rooms is of good size. The master suite has two walk-in closets, a whirlpool and stall shower, twin lavatories and a vanity. A third floor is available for storage or future expansion.

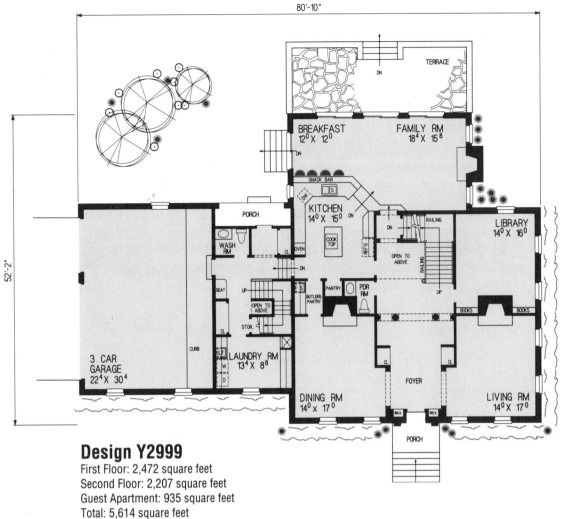

Design Y2999

First Floor: 2,472 square feet
Second Floor: 2,207 square feet
Guest Apartment: 935 square feet
Total: 5,614 square feet

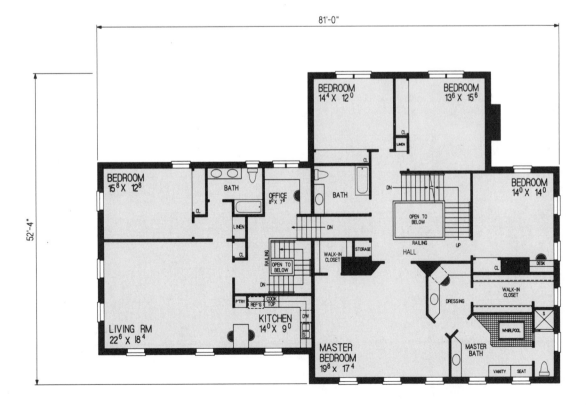

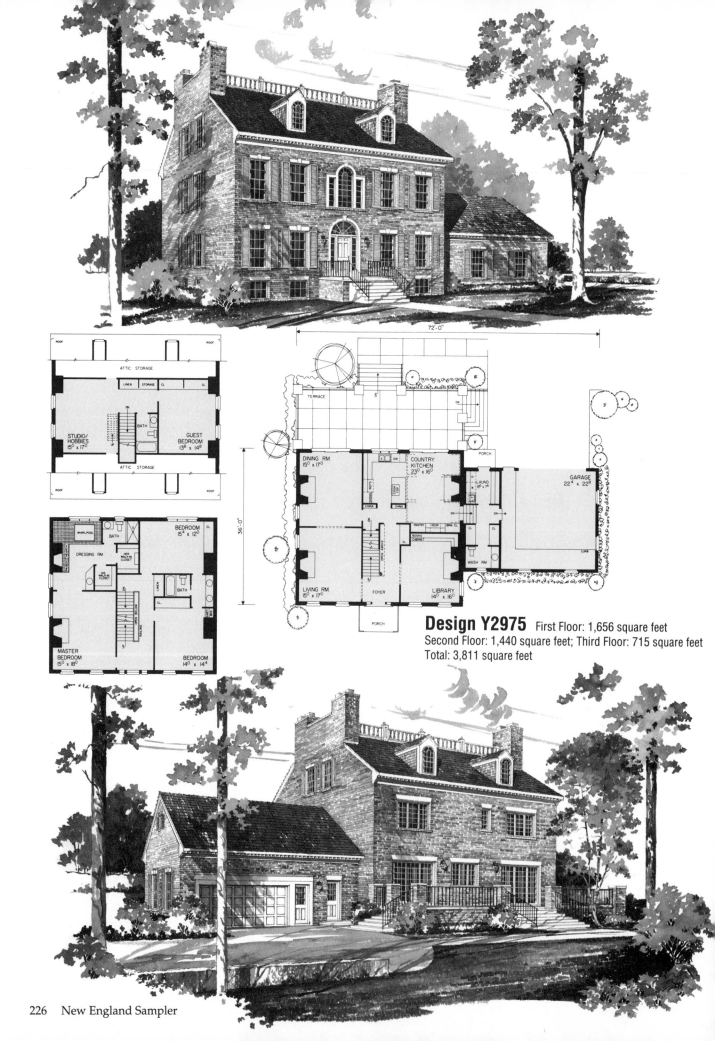

Design Y2975 First Floor: 1,656 square feet
Second Floor: 1,440 square feet; Third Floor: 715 square feet
Total: 3,811 square feet

Design Y3349

First Floor: 2,807 square feet
Second Floor: 1,363 square feet
Total: 4,170 square feet

L **D**

● Grand traditional design comes to the forefront in this elegant two-story. From the dramatic front entry with curving double stairs to the less formal gathering room with fireplace and terrace access, this plan accommodates family lifestyles. Notice the split-bedroom plan with the master suite on the first floor and family bedrooms upstairs. A four-car garage handles the largest of family fleets.

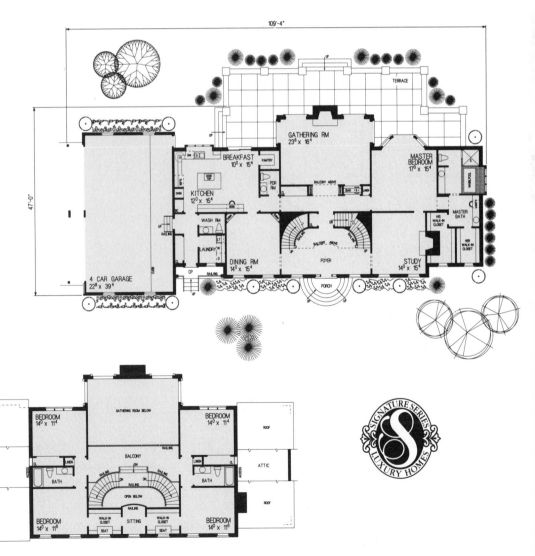

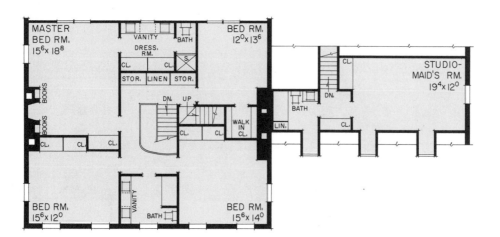

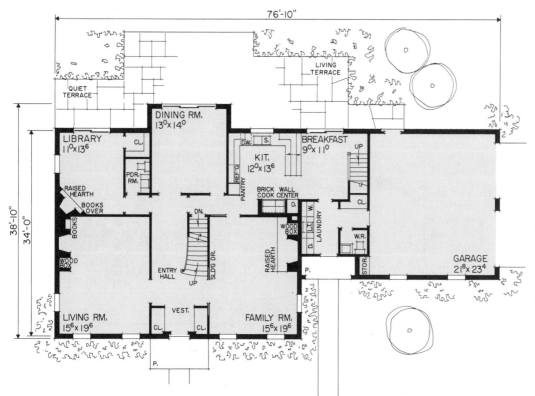

76'-10"

38'-10"
34'-0"

Design Y1858

First Floor: 1,794 square feet
Second Floor: 1,474 square feet
Studio: 424 square feet
Total: 3,692 square feet

● You'll never regret your
choice of this Georgian design. Its stately façade seems
to foretell all of the exceptional features to be found
inside. From the delightful
spacious front entry hall, to
the studio or maid's room
over the garage, this home is
unique all along the way.
Imagine four fireplaces,
three full baths, two extra
washrooms, a family room,
plus a quiet library. Don't
miss the first floor laundry.
Note the separate set of
stairs to the studio or maid's
room. The center entrance
leads to the vestibule and
entry hall. All the major
areas are but a step or two
from this formal hall. The
kitchen is well planned and
strategically located between
the separate dining room
and the breakfast room. Sliding glass doors permit easy
access to the functional rear
terraces.

Design Y2982

First Floor: 1,584 square feet
Second Floor: 1,513 square feet
Total: 3,097 square feet

● An early 18th Century Georgian so common to Williamsburg, Va. and environs. Observe the massive twin chimneys, the cornice ornamentation, and the wrought iron balcony sheltering the front panelled door. The rectangular shape of this house will lead to economical construction costs. The 30 foot, beamed-ceiling country kitchen with its commanding corner fireplace and rear yard access is outstanding. Notice the fireplaces for the country kitchen, living, dining and master bedrooms.

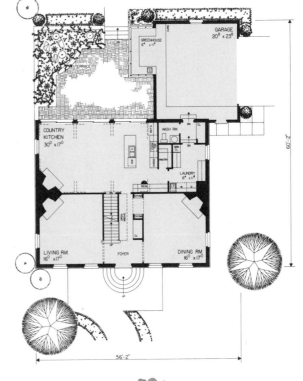

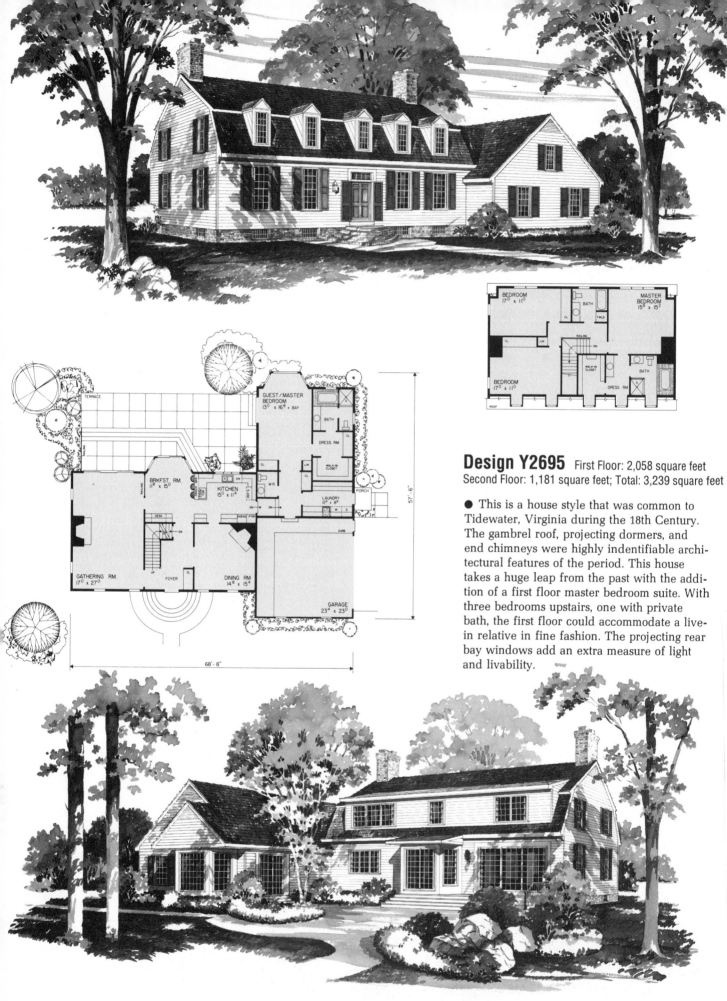

Design Y2695 First Floor: 2,058 square feet
Second Floor: 1,181 square feet; Total: 3,239 square feet

● This is a house style that was common to Tidewater, Virginia during the 18th Century. The gambrel roof, projecting dormers, and end chimneys were highly indentifiable architectural features of the period. This house takes a huge leap from the past with the addition of a first floor master bedroom suite. With three bedrooms upstairs, one with private bath, the first floor could accommodate a live-in relative in fine fashion. The projecting rear bay windows add an extra measure of light and livability.

Design Y2520

First Floor: 1,419 square feet
Second Floor: 1,040 square feet
Total: 2,459 square feet

L **D**

● Another historic adaptation from Tidewater, Virginia. The center entrance gives way to fine traffic circulation. Note the two corner fireplaces, wet bar, built-in desk and walk-in coat closet.

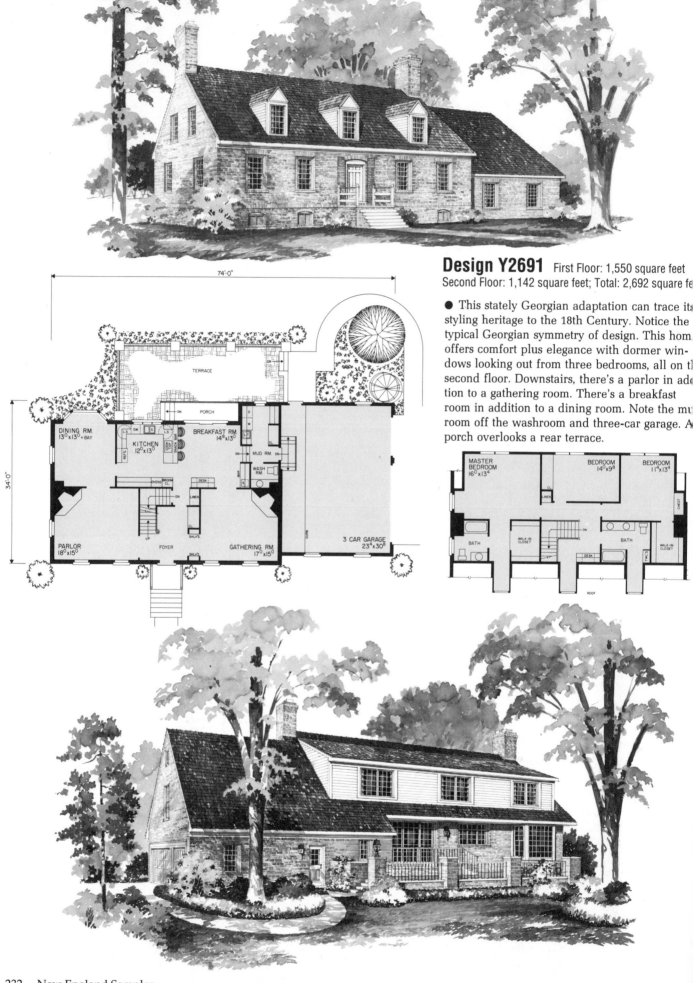

Design Y2691 First Floor: 1,550 square feet
Second Floor: 1,142 square feet; Total: 2,692 square fe

● This stately Georgian adaptation can trace its
styling heritage to the 18th Century. Notice the
typical Georgian symmetry of design. This hom
offers comfort plus elegance with dormer windows looking out from three bedrooms, all on th
second floor. Downstairs, there's a parlor in add
tion to a gathering room. There's a breakfast
room in addition to a dining room. Note the mu
room off the washroom and three-car garage. A
porch overlooks a rear terrace.

Design Y2132

First Floor: 1,958 square feet
Second Floor: 1,305 square feet
Total: 3,263 square feet

L

● Another Georgian adaptation with a great heritage dating back to 18th-Century America. Exquisite and symmetrical detailing set the character of this impressive home. Don't overlook such features as the two fireplaces, the laundry, the beamed ceiling, the built-in china cabinets and the oversized garage.

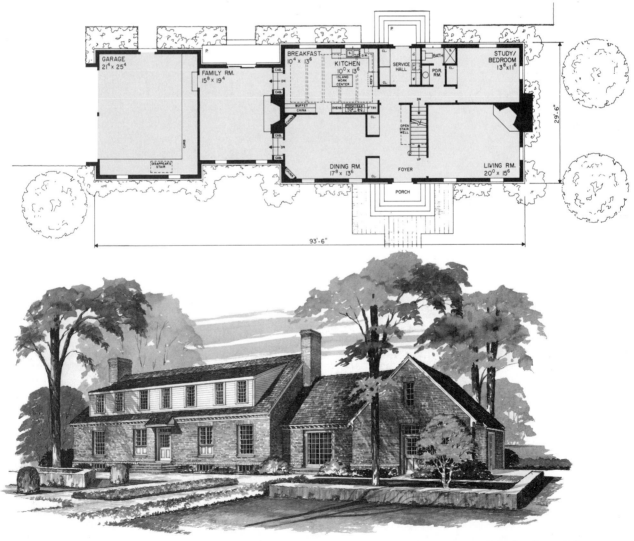

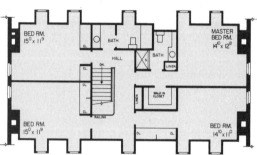

BED RM.
15⁰ x 11⁹

BATH

HALL

BATH

LINEN

MASTER
BED RM.
14¹⁰ x 12⁸

DN.

CL

WALK IN
CLOSET

LINEN

RAILING

BED RM.
15⁰ x 11⁹

BED RM.
14¹⁰ x 11⁰

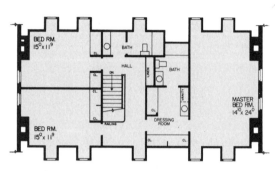

BED RM.
15⁰ x 11⁹

BATH

HALL

LINEN

BATH

DN.

VANITY

MASTER
BED RM.
14¹⁰ x 24⁰

BED RM.
15⁰ x 11⁹

RAILING

DRESSING
ROOM

84'-6"

TERRACE

TERRACE

PORCH

COUNTRY KITCHEN
21⁸ x 15⁶

EATING

RANGE

LAUNDRY

FAMILY RM.
18⁸ x 15⁶

PDR.
RM.

SHELVES

CAB'T

REF'S.

CAB'T

SHELVES

BOOKS

BOOKS

B. CL.

CABINET

PANTRY

OVEN

GARAGE
23⁴ x 23⁴

CHINA
CABINET

UP

CL

SHELVES

CL

33'-6"

DINING RM.
17⁴ x 15⁶

ENTRANCE HALL

LIVING RM.
20⁰ x 15⁶

BOOKS

CHINA
CABINET

PORCH

Design Y2638

First Floor: 1,836 square feet
Second Floor: 1,323 square feet
Total: 3,159 square feet

● The brick facade of this two-story represents the mid-18th-Century design concept. Examine its fine exterior. It has a steeply pitched roof which is broken by two large chimneys at each end and by pedimented dormers. Inside Georgian details lend elegance. Turned balusters and a curved banister ornament the formal staircase. Blueprints include details for both three and four bedroom options.

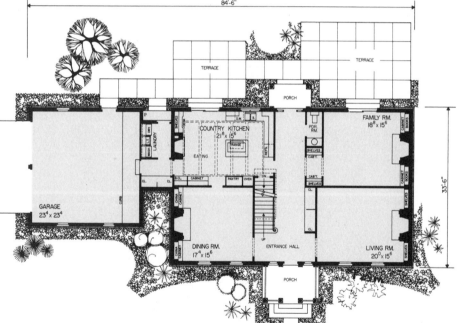

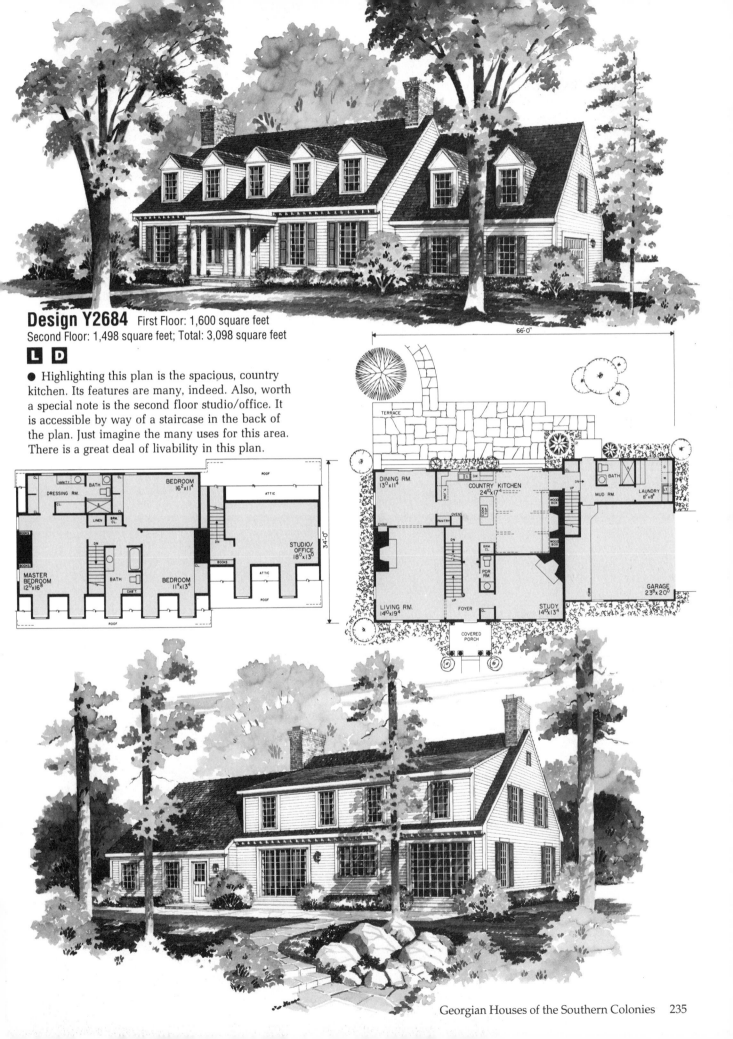

Design Y2684 First Floor: 1,600 square feet
Second Floor: 1,498 square feet; Total: 3,098 square feet

L D

● Highlighting this plan is the spacious, country kitchen. Its features are many, indeed. Also, worth a special note is the second floor studio/office. It is accessible by way of a staircase in the back of the plan. Just imagine the many uses for this area. There is a great deal of livability in this plan.

Design Y2899

First Floor: 1,685 square feet
Second Floor: 1,437 square feet
Total: 3,122 square feet

● This impressive Georgian home with massive twin chimneys and slender Roman doric columns is authentic in its 18th-Century detailing. Inside, the home offers comfort and elegance with living room, study, large formal dining room, breakfast room and even a butler's pantry. Upstairs is thoughtfully zoned, too, with three family bedrooms and a master suite.

Design Y2250

First Floor: 1,442 square feet
Second Floor: 1,404 square feet
Total: 2,846 square feet

● This stately home, which has roots that go back to an earlier period in American architecture, will forever retain its aura of distinction. The spacious front entry effectively separates the formal and informal living zones. Four bedrooms and three full baths are on the second floor.

Design Y2139

First Floor: 1,581 square feet
Second Floor: 991 square feet
Total: 2,572 square feet

● Four bedrooms and
two baths make-up the
second floor of this two-
story design. The first
floor has all of the living
areas and work center.
Note the convenience of
the powder room.

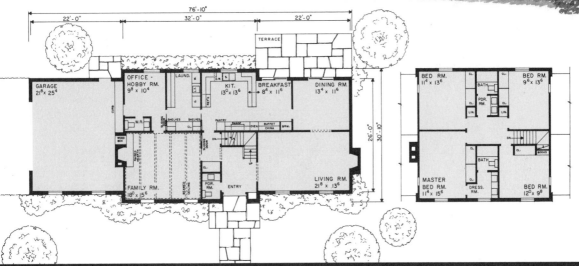

Design Y2176

First Floor: 1,485 square feet
Second Floor: 1,175 square feet
Total: 2,660 square feet

L D

● A big, end living room
featuring a fireplace and
sliding glass doors is the
focal point of this Georgian
design. Adjacent is the formal dining room strategi-
cally located but a couple
of steps from the efficient
kitchen. Functioning
closely with the kitchen is
the family room.

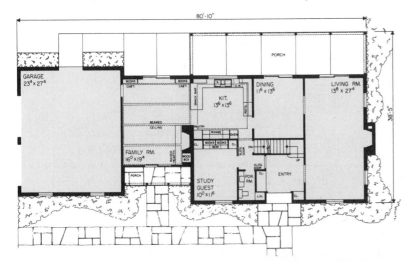

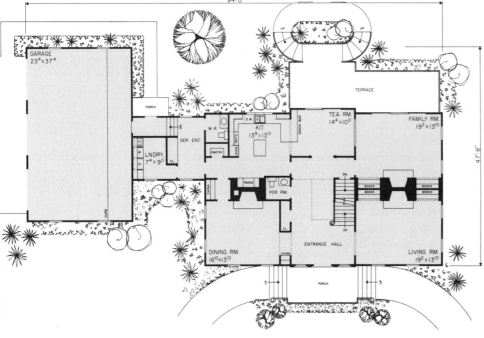

Design Y2301

First Floor: 2,044 square feet
Second Floor: 1,815 square feet
Total: 3,859 square feet

● This delicately detailed clapboard late Georgian echoes the facade of the William Gibbes House of Charleston, South Carolina, circa 1779. The modern floor plan has all the elements to cater to the demands of a large family.

Southern Colonial Homes

As a generalized term of reference, Southern Colonial may include examples of the broad spectrum of architectural styling in the South during the 17th and 18th Centuries. However, in today's vernacular "Southern Colonial" has come to be identified with houses of the late Georgian and Federal period which reflect the influences of Greek architecture. These houses are identifiable by the graceful elegance of their impressive Greek columns. The designs in this section are a varied lot, but their common inheritance makes them an appealing and popular group of houses.

Design Y2889

First Floor: 2,529 square feet
Second Floor: 1,872 square feet
Total: 4,401 square feet

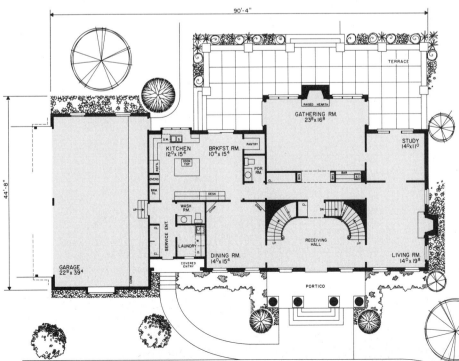

● This is truly a classic design. Some of the exterior highlights of this two-story include the pediment gable with cornice work and dentils, the beautifully proportioned columns, the front door detailing and the window treatment. Behind the facade of this design is an equally elegant interior. Imagine greeting your guests in the large receiving hall. It is graced by two curving staircases and opens to the formal living and dining rooms. Beyond the living room is the study. It has access to the rear terrace. Those large, informal occasions for family get-togethers or entertaining will be enjoyed in the spacious gathering room. It has a centered fireplace flanked by windows on each side, access to the terrace and a wet bar. The work center is efficient: a kitchen with island cooktop, breakfast room, washroom, laundry and service entrance. The second floor also is outstanding. Three family bedrooms and two full baths are joined by the feature-filled master bedroom suite.

A Mount Vernon Reminiscence

● This magnificent manor's streetview illustrates a centralized mansion connected by curving galleries to matching wings. What a grand presentation this home will make! The origin of this house dates back to 1787 and George Washington's stately Mount Vernon. The underlying aesthetics for this design come from the rational balancing of porticoes, fenestration and chimneys. The rear elevation of this home also deserves mention. Six two-story columns, along with four sets of French doors, highlight this view. Study all of the intricate detailing that is featured all around these exteriors.

The flanking wings create a large formal courtyard where guests of today can park their cars. This home, designed from architecture of the past, is efficient and compact enough to fit many suburban lots. Its interior has been well planned and is ready to serve a family of any size.

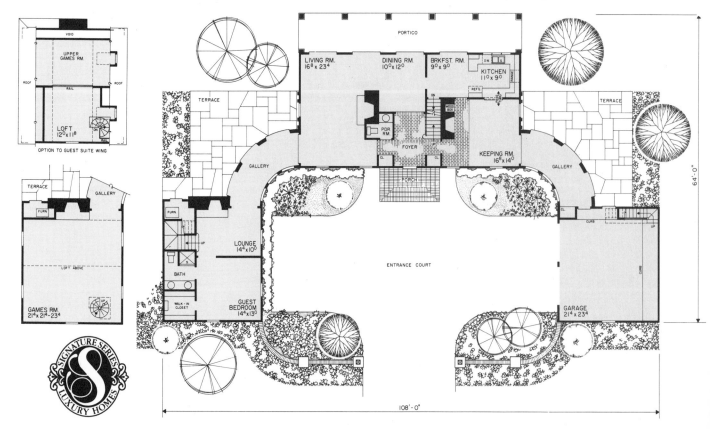

Design Y2665 First Floor: 1,152 square feet
Second Floor: 1,152 square feet; Total: 2,304 square feet (Excludes Guest Suite and Galleries)

● The main, two-story section of this home houses the living areas. First - there is the large, tiled foyer with two closets and powder room. Then there is the living room which is the entire width of the house. This room has a fireplace and leads into the formal dining room. Three sets of double French doors lead to the rear portico from this formal area. The kitchen and breakfast room will function together. There is a pass-thru from the kitchen to the keeping room. All of the sleeping facilities, four bedrooms, are on the second floor. The gallery on the right leads to the garage; the one on the left, to a lounge and guest suite with studio above. The square footage quoted above does not include the guest suite or gallery areas. The first floor of the guest suite contains 688 sq. ft.; the second floor studio, 306 sq. ft. The optional plan shows a game room with a loft above having 162 sq. ft.

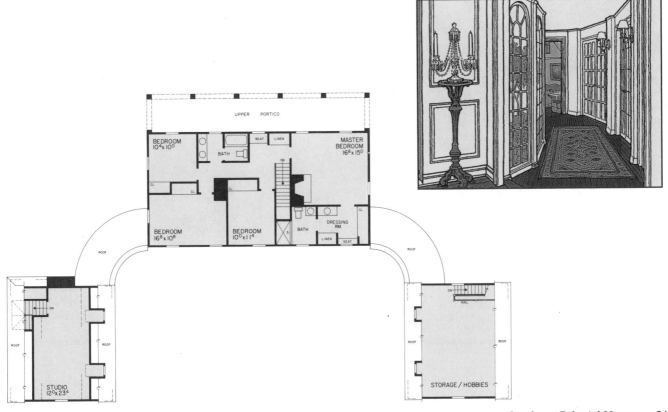

Greek Revival Manor

● This classic design with its portico and six Doric columns recalls an Alabama mansion, Belle Mina, built in 1820. The stately facade is also reminiscent of other plantation manors throughout the South. The six columns support a molded entablature which is surmounted by a hipped roof. Wide cornices surround the house and attached garage with its appealing columned porch. The

delicate detail work surrounding the central entrance is complemented by the symmetry of the muntined double-hung windows. While the exterior is mostly brick, an attractive large frame bay projects from the rear exterior. The raised terrace and its wrought iron railing add a nice touch. A lower terrace paved with flagstones provides additional outdoor living space.

Here is one of the two fireplaces serving the master suite. It is flanked by accommodating bookshelves and a cabinet plus a chest in a window alcove.

Design Y2696

First Floor: 2,217 square feet
Second Floor: 1,962 square feet
Total: 4,179 square feet

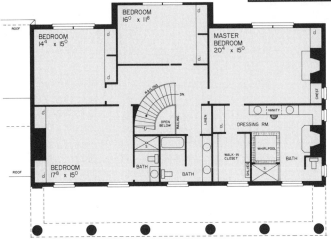

BEDROOM
16⁰ x 11⁸

BEDROOM
14⁴ x 15⁰

MASTER BEDROOM
20⁴ x 15⁰

BEDROOM
17⁸ x 15⁰

OPEN BELOW   RAILING   DN.   RAILING

LINEN   VANITY

DRESSING RM.

WALK-IN CLOSET   WHIRLPOOL

BATH   BATH   BATH

SHELVES

CHEST

ROOF

● Even the most casual visitor will be taken with this dramatic foyer and its curving, open staircase to the equally spacious second-floor hall. Both the formal living and dining rooms flanking the foyer have commanding fireplaces centered on their far walls. The media room, which may also function as a library, has another fireplace. The U-shaped kitchen with abundant counter and cupboard space functions with the snack bar and cheerful morning room via a pass-through. Past the pantry and flanking the passageway to the garage are the laundry and wash rooms. Upstairs, three bedrooms and two full baths serve the children. The master bedroom is also spacious and has an outstanding private bath.

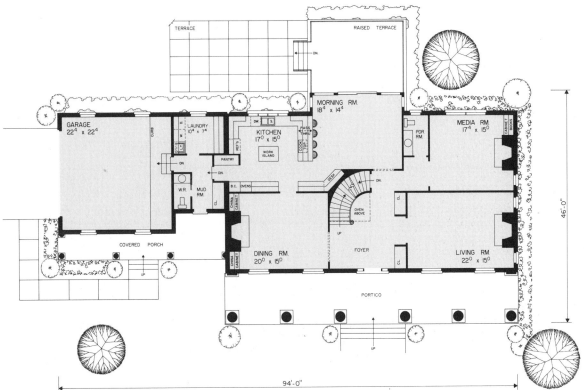

TERRACE   RAISED TERRACE

MORNING RM.
18⁴ x 14⁴

GARAGE
22⁴ x 22⁴

LAUNDRY
10⁴ x 7⁴

KITCHEN
17⁰ x 15⁰

PASS THRU

MEDIA RM.
17⁴ x 15⁰

POR. RM.

WORK ISLAND

PANTRY

B.C. OVENS

OVEN ABOVE

MUD RM.

W.R.

CHINA CABINET

DINING RM.
20⁰ x 15⁰

FOYER

LIVING RM.
22⁰ x 15⁰

COVERED PORCH

PORTICO

46'-0"

94'-0"

An Antebellum Manor

Design Y2668

First Floor: 1,206 square feet
Second Floor: 1,254 square feet
Total: 2,460 square feet

● Here is a frame house whose clap-boards, wide corner boards, center entrance and symmetrically placed shuttered windows give it a distinctly Georgian ambience, until its Greek Revival elements are added. The portico with its four soaring columns and denticulated pediment gives this house an identity common to the estates of the Deep South in the 1820s. However, this is a house that is designed not to require a large building site. A two-car garage is integrated within the perimeter of the basic structure. The house lends itself to orientation on a corner, as well as an interior, lot. An interior view from the top of the stairs looks across to the balcony of the master bedroom and the window above the paneled front door. A decidedly dramatic view—whether looking down or looking up!

● Highlighting the rear elevation are a bay of two-story windows, a projecting shed-like structure for garage storage space and a big, raised brick terrace with an attractive railing. Inside, to the right of the foyer, are a coat closet, powder room and a private library. To the left is the spacious country kitchen with plenty of space for informal eating, an island cooking unit and a pass-through to the dining room. Between the flanking pantry and broom closet is a built-in desk. The great room is outstanding. It has a high ceiling, a wall of windows and a fireplace. Upstairs, in addition to the pleasant lounge, there are four bedrooms and two full baths, including laundry facilities.

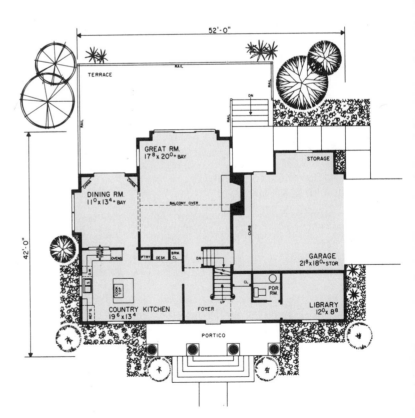

An Aristocratic Federal Motif

● The gracefulness and appeal of this southern adaptation will be everlasting. The imposing, two-story portico is truly dramatic. Notice the authentic detailing of the tapered Doric columns, balustraded roof deck, denticulated cornice, front entrance and shuttered windows. The architecture of the rear is no less appealing with its formal symmetry and smaller Doric portico. The spacious, formal entrance hall provides a fitting introduction to the scale and elegance of the interior. Observe the openness of the stairwell which provides a view of the curving balusters above. The large living room with a colonial fireplace enjoys a full measure of privacy. Across the hall is the formal dining room with built-in china cabinets. Beamed ceilings and plenty of space produce a country-style kitchen. A compartmented full bath is handy to the service entrance and the isolated library, which may double as a guest room when the occasion demands it. Functioning between the house and the garage is the sunken family room. It stretches the full width of the house. Two family bedrooms are on the second floor with the master bedroom suite. This outstanding area includes an enormous dressing room, His and Hers baths and an abundance of closet space.

Design Y2230
First Floor: 2,288 square feet
Second Floor: 1,863 square feet
Total: 4,151 square feet

The sunken family room, here decorated and furnished to reflect all the formality of the living room, has an aura of elegance all its own. The raised moulding, the fluted pilaster, the columned and arched opening, the crown moulding and the wainscoting carry out the motif established by the classic refinement of the exterior. Notice the built-in bookshelves in the passageway.

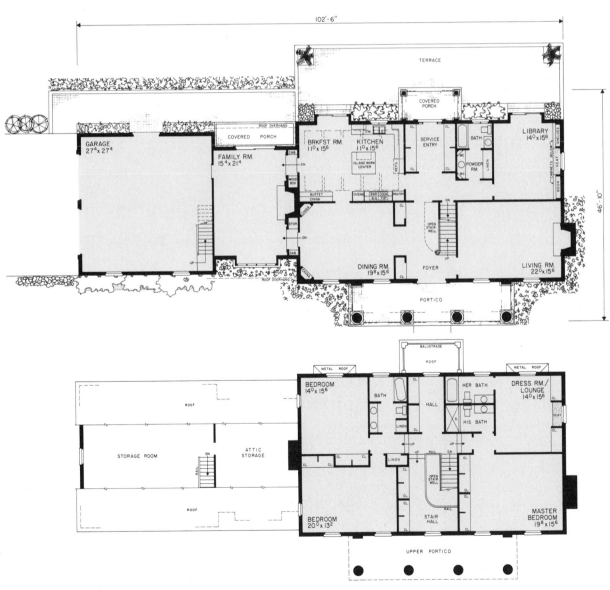

A Classic Kentucky One-Story

Design Y2693 Square Footage: 3,462

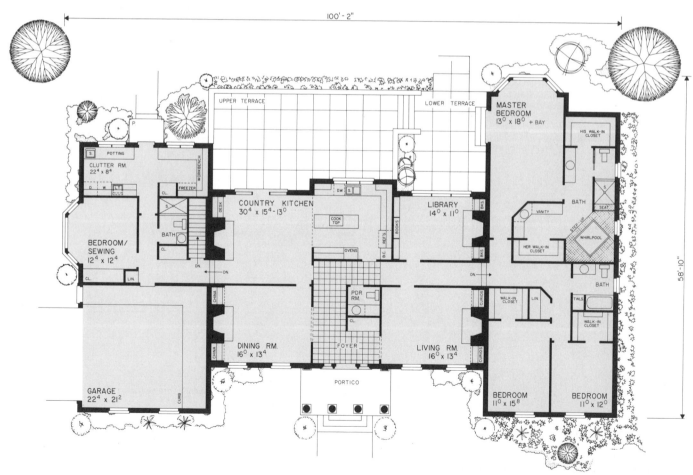

The white-pillared one-story house is a significant Kentucky contribution to the architectural heritage of the South. This imposing design recalls Rose Hill, built near Lexington, Kentucky around 1820. The exterior is of brick with shuttered windows and a classical portico with four Ionic columns. A hipped roof fosters interesting roof lines while four large chimneys rise impressively above. The detailing of the front doorway is exquisite with its paneled door, elliptical fanlight and flanking sidelights. The rear of the home features upper and lower terraces enclosed by a low brick wall. The modified H-shaped floor plan of this home is truly unique. The central portion of the plan is the living zone. It features formal living and dining rooms, each with a fireplace flanked by built-in curio shelves or china cabinets. To the rear is the large country kitchen with its island cooking counter, fireplace, desk and access to the terrace. The library has an additional fireplace flanked by bookshelves. The sleeping zone is sunken down two steps. The two front bedrooms have walk-in closets. The rear master suite has a nice bay window and many personal care facilities. Don't miss the Hers and His walk-in closets, two lavatories, vanity, whirlpool, stall shower and compartmented water closet. At the opposite end of the house is the utility zone with a 22-foot all-purpose clutter room . and laundry. Observe the potting area, work bench and freezer space. There is also an extra room which may function as a sewing room or guest bedroom.

The delicately detailed doorway of the foyer makes a style statement for the interior as well as the exterior. The door enframement is beautiful, indeed. Backing up to the coat closet of this spacious welcoming area is the strategically placed powder room.

A Federal Adaptation of the Middle Colonies

● The central portion of this rambling Federal-styled house accommodates second-floor livability. Here there are two large bedrooms, each with excellent blank wall space for flexible and effective furniture placement. In addition, each room has its own private bath, two walk-in closets and large windows overlooking the rear yard. There is also access to attic storage.

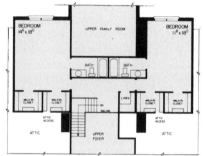

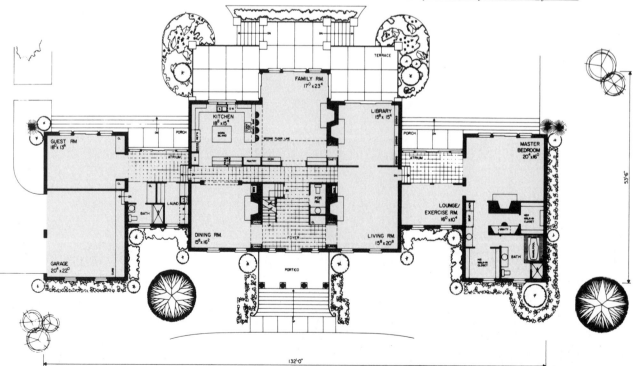

Design Y2977 First Floor: 4,104 square feet; Second Floor: 979 square feet; Total: 5,083 square feet

L

● The Federal style has been referred to as one of the most sophisticated and nearly perfect of American architectural achievements. It developed from the Georgian style and prospered after the Revolutionary War from around 1785 to 1820. Here is an adaptation that is reminiscent of Homewood, circa 1809, near Baltimore, Maryland. The inviting raised portico provides a sheltered approach to the fanlight entranceway. To each side of the foyer there is a formal room—one for dining, the other for quiet conversation. To the rear of the plan are the kitchen and family room. The kitchen has an island counter and cabinets with a pass-through to facilitate serving meals to the dining room. The high-ceilinged family room (above) has a

dramatic array of windows and three sets of sliding glass doors for easy access to the raised terrace. Back-to-back fireplaces serve the family room and neighboring library with its full wall of bookshelves. Connecting the main portion of the house and master bedroom wing are a sunken lounge/exercise room and atrium. The master suite has a centered fireplace and a fine array of windows. The personal care facilities include two walk-in closets, a vanity and a whirlpool plus stall shower. At the far end of the plan there is another glass-enclosed atrium. It provides passage to the guest room, a full bath, laundry and the two-car garage.

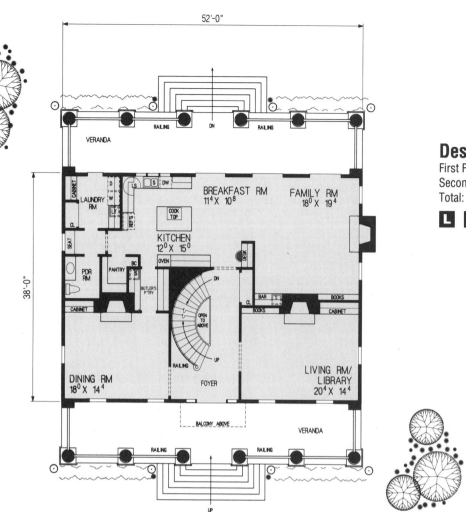

Design Y3500

First Floor: 1,968 square feet
Second Floor: 1,901 square feet
Total: 3,869 square feet

● Stepping into the foyer the dramatic impact of the open, curving staircase to the second floor and its spacious hall is a delight to behold. The size, shape and location of the family room present the option of either a living room or library as a secondary living area. Notice the fireplace flanked by bookshelves and cabinets. Across the foyer is the dining room which also has a fireplace and cabinetry. A butler's pantry is a nice, practical feature and facilitates access to the kitchen. This L-shaped work center has an island cooking surface and opens to the breakfast area. A built-in planning desk is a bonus feature. Just a few steps away are the pantry, powder room and laundry. Upstairs there are four large bedrooms and three full baths. Two of the bedrooms share a common bath with twin lavatories, while the third bedroom has a private bath. Down the hall and past the doors to the balcony is the master bedroom. The outstanding master bath is filled with amenities.

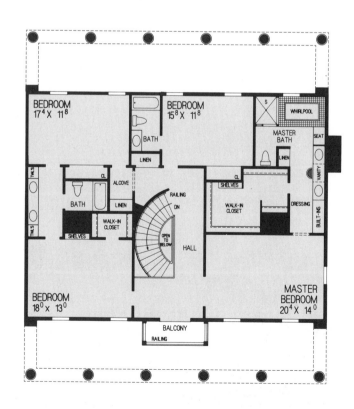

The Grandeur of Greek Revival

● Here is a stately antebellum manor in the Greek Revival tradition. It recalls many such houses that can be seen even today in Macon, Georgia and other sections of the South. Of particular interest is the charm of both the front and rear elevations. The low-pitched, hipped roof and six Doric columns produce a portico that runs the width of the house—both front and rear. The balustrades result in two enclosed verandas. Massive twin chimneys, a fanlight double-door entry, a second-floor balcony and symmetrical window treatment enhance the appeal of this clapboard-sided two-story house. The rectangular shape of this structure will translate into relatively economical construction and efficient functionality.

The Hermitage Revisited

Design Y2987 First Floor: 2,822 square feet; Second Floor: 1,335 square feet; Total: 4,157 square feet

● Andrew Jackson's dream of white-pillared splendor resulted in the building of his pride, The Hermitage, from 1819 to 1834 near Nashville, Tennessee. The essence of that grand dream is recaptured in this modern variation. Like its forebear, this home has six soaring Corinthian columns on both the front and rear. Sheltered by the long porticos are balconies accessible from the second floor. Two sets of twin chimneys along with the two projecting wings effectively balance the central portion of the house. The delicate detailing of the cornices, the door enframements, the windows with their fanlights and shutters and the balustrades is exquisite. The large glass areas and projecting bays add their measure of exterior appeal and interior light. The low roof lines and masses of brick make fine contributions, too.

● The central foyer routes traffic past doorways to the living and dining rooms, past
the open staircase to the spacious informal
family room and the bright and cheerful
gallery. The outdoor ambience of this area
can be viewed through the columns of the
living room. Three sliding glass doors provide direct access to the covered porch.
Two etageres flank the passageway to the
18 x 17-foot family room with sliding
glass doors to the porch, plus a fireplace
and two bookcases. The country kitchen
offers a through-fireplace to the dining
room. The bay window provides extra
floor space for a cheerful breakfast setting. The island counter accommodates
the cooktop and snack bar. On the
way to the garage are the pantry, complete laundry, wash room, coat closet
and built-in seat. The second floor features three bedrooms and two baths—
one with extra vanity space and both
tub and stall shower.

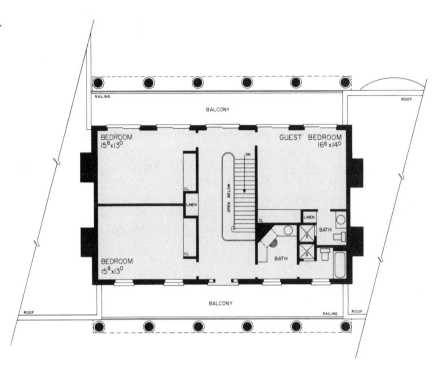

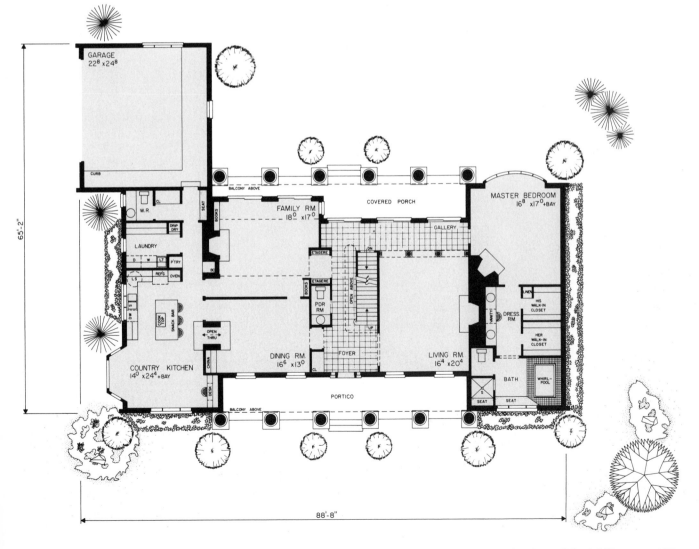

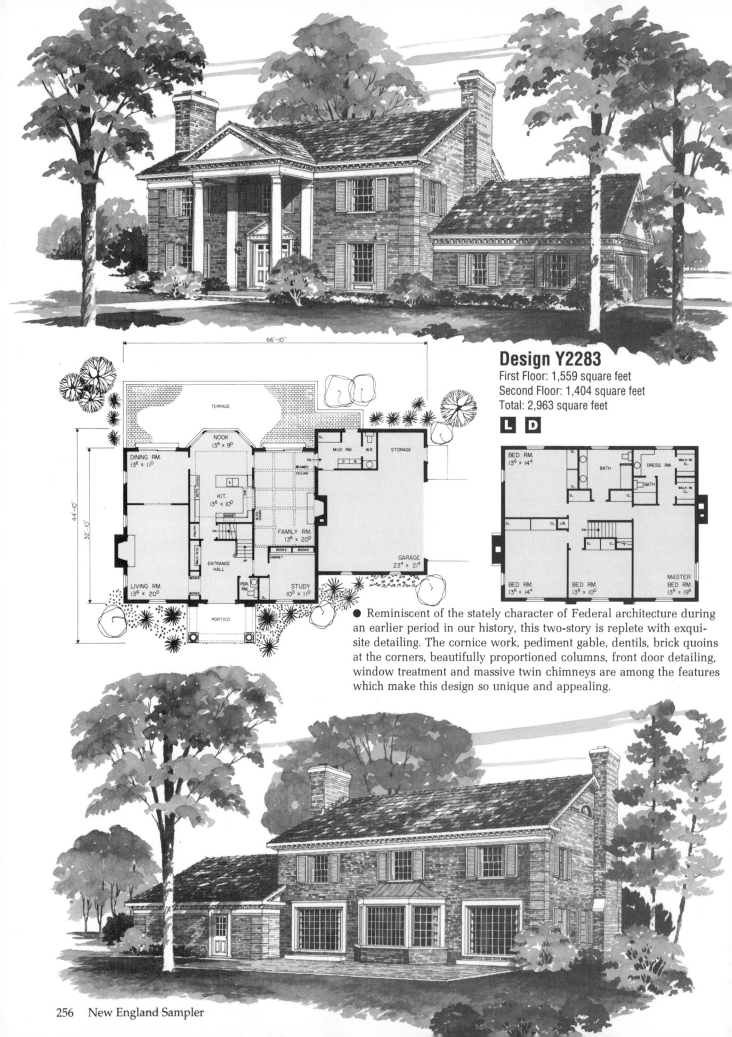

Design Y2283

First Floor: 1,559 square feet
Second Floor: 1,404 square feet
Total: 2,963 square feet

L **D**

● Reminiscent of the stately character of Federal architecture during an earlier period in our history, this two-story is replete with exquisite detailing. The cornice work, pediment gable, dentils, brick quoins at the corners, beautifully proportioned columns, front door detailing, window treatment and massive twin chimneys are among the features which make this design so unique and appealing.

Design Y2984

First Floor: 3,116 square feet
Second Floor: 1,997 square feet
Total: 5,113 square feet

● An echo of Whitehall, built in
1765 in Anne Arundel County,
Maryland, resounds in this home.
Its classic symmetry and columned
facade herald a grand interior.
There's no lack of space whether
entertaining formally or just enjoying a family get-together, and all
are kept cozy with fireplaces in
the gathering room, study, and
family room. An island kitchen
with attached breakfast room
handily serves the nearby dining
room. Four second floor bedrooms
include a large master suite with
another fireplace, a whirlpool,
and His and Hers closets in
the bath. Three more full baths
are found on this floor.

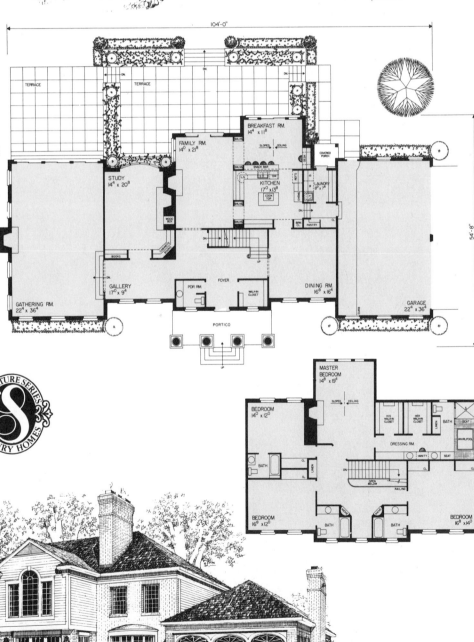

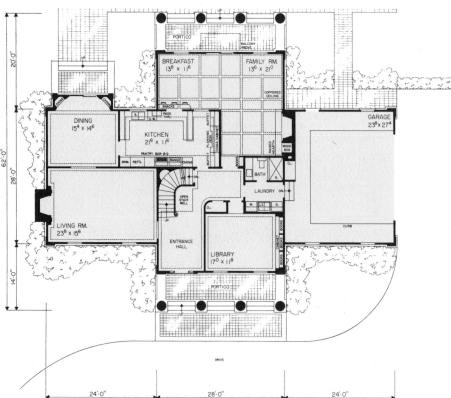

Design Y2184

First Floor: 1,999 square feet
Second Floor: 1,288 square feet
Total: 3,287 square feet

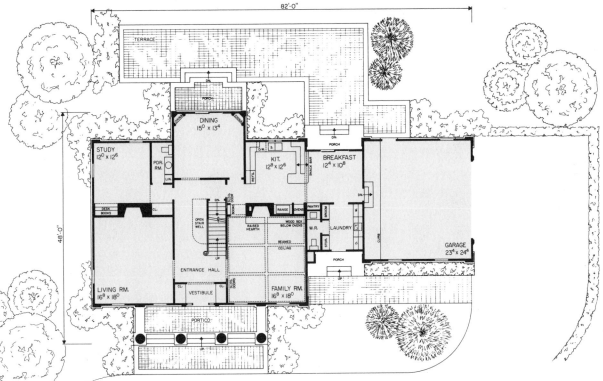

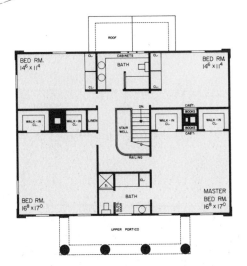

Design Y2185 First Floor: 1,916 square feet
Second Floor: 1,564 square feet; Total: 3,480 square feet

● The elements of Greek Revival architecture when adapted to present day standards can be impressive, indeed. A study of this floor plan will reveal its similarity to that on the opposite page. There is a vestibule which leads to a wonderfully spacious entrance hall. The open stairwell is most dramatic. As it affords a view of the four bedroom, two bath second floor. The study and family room will be favorite spots for family relaxation. Both the dining and living rooms can be made to function as formally as you wish.

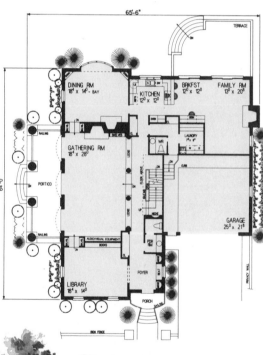

Design Y2993

First Floor: 2,440 square feet
Second Floor: 2,250 square feet
Total: 4,690 square feet

L **D**

● 18th-Century Charleston, South Carolina, with its long, narrow sites, was known for the "single house." This type of house was situated with the narrow end to the street. This variation shows an impressive two-story portico and an attached garage with the family room located behind it. The sunken gathering room is open to the hall through its colonnade. Upstairs are four bedrooms and three baths. Don't overlook the through-fireplace of the master bedroom and bath.

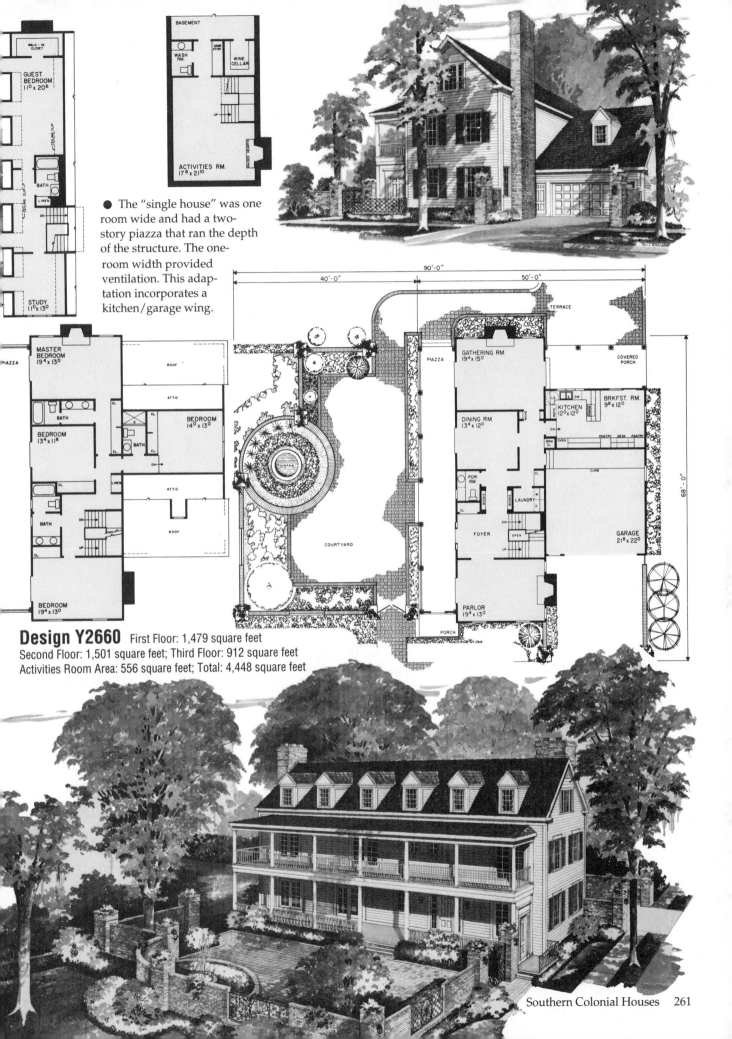

GUEST BEDROOM 11⁰ x 20⁶

WALK-IN CLOSET

BATH

LINEN

DN

STUDY 11⁰ x 13⁰

BASEMENT

WASH RM.

GAME STOR

WINE CELLAR

UP

ACTIVITIES RM. 17⁸ x 21¹⁰

● The "single house" was one room wide and had a two-story piazza that ran the depth of the structure. The one-room width provided ventilation. This adaptation incorporates a kitchen/garage wing.

MASTER BEDROOM 19⁴ x 13⁰

PIAZZA

ROOF

ATTIC

BATH

BEDROOM 13⁴ x 11⁸

BEDROOM 14⁰ x 13⁰

BATH

ATTIC

LINEN

DN

BATH

ROOF

UP

BEDROOM 19⁴ x 13⁰

90'-0"

40'-0"

50'-0"

TERRACE

FOUNTAIN

COURTYARD

PIAZZA

GATHERING RM. 19⁴ x 15⁰

COVERED PORCH

DINING RM. 13⁴ x 12⁰

KITCHEN 12⁰ x 12⁰

BRKFST. RM. 9⁸ x 12⁰

NICHE

PANTRY DESK PANTRY

OVEN

PDR RM.

BOOKS

BOOKS

CURB

LAUNDRY

68'-0"

FOYER

OPEN

UP

GARAGE 21⁸ x 22⁰

PARLOR 19⁴ x 13⁰

PORCH

Design Y2660 First Floor: 1,479 square feet
Second Floor: 1,501 square feet; Third Floor: 912 square feet
Activities Room Area: 556 square feet; Total: 4,448 square feet

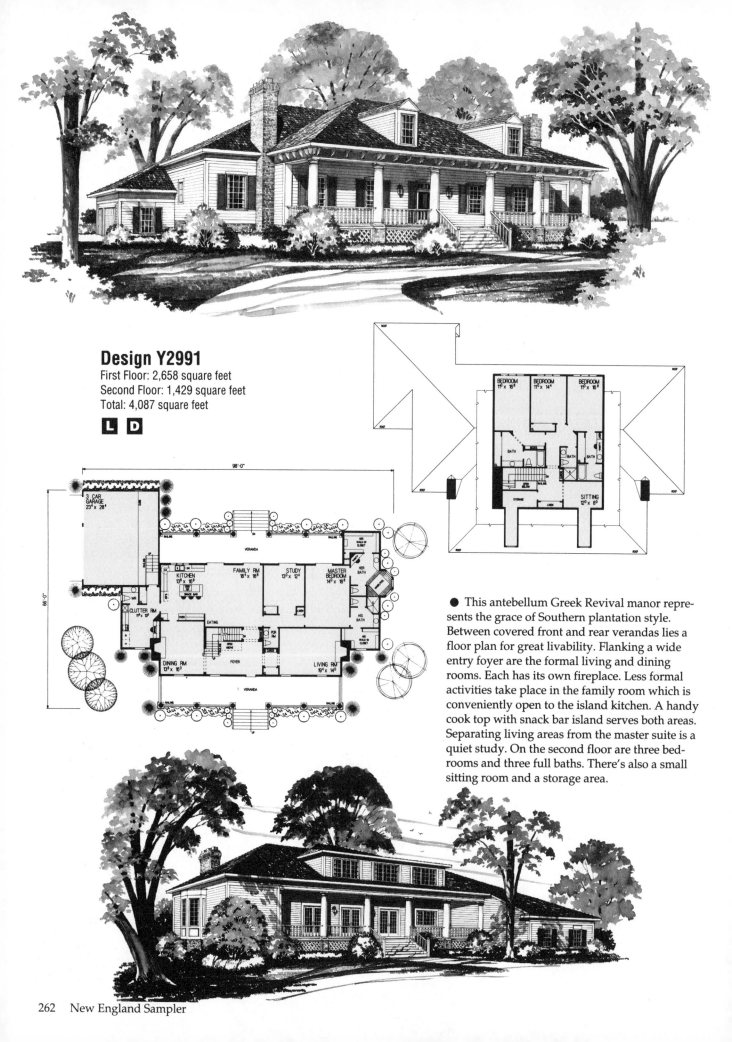

Design Y2991

First Floor: 2,658 square feet
Second Floor: 1,429 square feet
Total: 4,087 square feet

L D

● This antebellum Greek Revival manor represents the grace of Southern plantation style. Between covered front and rear verandas lies a floor plan for great livability. Flanking a wide entry foyer are the formal living and dining rooms. Each has its own fireplace. Less formal activities take place in the family room which is conveniently open to the island kitchen. A handy cook top with snack bar island serves both areas. Separating living areas from the master suite is a quiet study. On the second floor are three bedrooms and three full baths. There's also a small sitting room and a storage area.

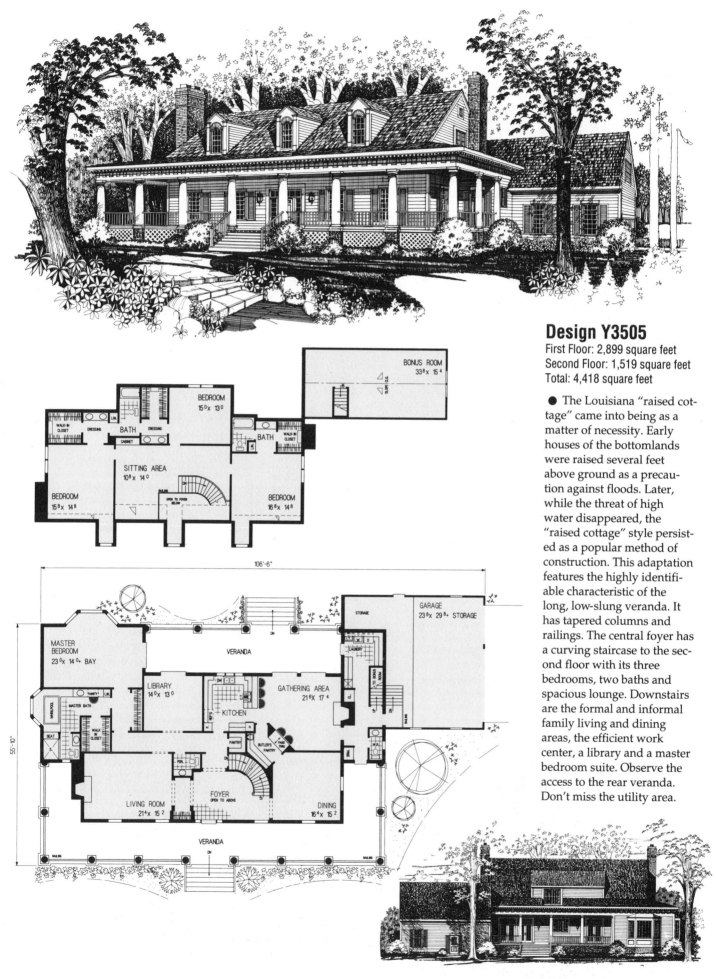

Design Y3505

First Floor: 2,899 square feet
Second Floor: 1,519 square feet
Total: 4,418 square feet

● The Louisiana "raised cottage" came into being as a matter of necessity. Early houses of the bottomlands were raised several feet above ground as a precaution against floods. Later, while the threat of high water disappeared, the "raised cottage" style persisted as a popular method of construction. This adaptation features the highly identifiable characteristic of the long, low-slung veranda. It has tapered columns and railings. The central foyer has a curving staircase to the second floor with its three bedrooms, two baths and spacious lounge. Downstairs are the formal and informal family living and dining areas, the efficient work center, a library and a master bedroom suite. Observe the access to the rear veranda. Don't miss the utility area.

Floor plan labels

BONUS ROOM
33⁸ x 15⁴

BEDROOM
15⁰ x 13⁰

BATH

BATH

WALK-IN CLOSET

DRESSING

DRESSING

LIN.

CABINET

WALK-IN CLOSET

SITTING AREA
10⁸ x 14⁰

OPEN TO FOYER BELOW

BEDROOM
15⁸ x 14⁸

BEDROOM
16⁸ x 14⁸

106'-6"

55'-10"

MASTER BEDROOM
23⁰ x 14⁰+ BAY

VERANDA

STORAGE

GARAGE
23⁸ x 29⁸+ STORAGE

LAUNDRY

LIBRARY
14⁰ x 13⁰

GATHERING AREA
21⁶ x 17⁴

KITCHEN

MASTER BATH

WHIRLPOOL

VANITY

LIN.

WALK IN CLOSET

SEAT

PANTRY

BUTLER'S PANTRY

PASS THRU

POR.

LIVING ROOM
21⁴ x 15²

FOYER
OPEN TO ABOVE

DINING
16⁴ x 15²

VERANDA

DN

RAILING

RAILING

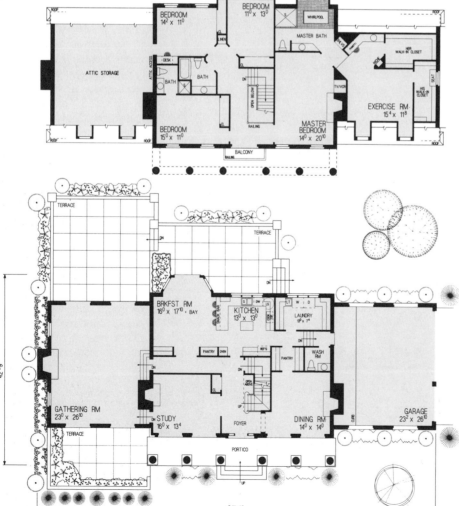

Design Y3337

First Floor: 2,167 square feet
Second Floor: 1,992 square feet
Total: 4,159 square feet

● The elegant facade of this design with its columned portico, fanlights, and dormers houses an amenity-filled interior. The gathering room, study and dining room, each with fireplace, provide plenty of room for relaxing and entertaining. A large work area contains a kitchen with breakfast room and snack bar, laundry room and pantry. The four-bedroom upstairs includes a master suite with a sumptuous bath and an exercise room.

Design Y3303

First Floor: 2,563 square feet
Second Floor: 1,496 square feet
Total: 4,059 square feet

● With its stately columns and one-story wings, this design is a fine representation of 18th Century adaptations. Formal living and dining areas flank the entry foyer at the front of the home. Look for a fireplace in the living room, china cabinet built-ins in the dining room. More casual living dominates the back section in a family room and kitchen/breakfast room combination that features access to the rear terrace and plenty of space for cooking and informal dining. The left wing garage is connected to the main structure by a service entrance adjacent to the laundry. The right wing contains the private master suite. Four second floor bedrooms share two full baths and each has its own walk-in closet.

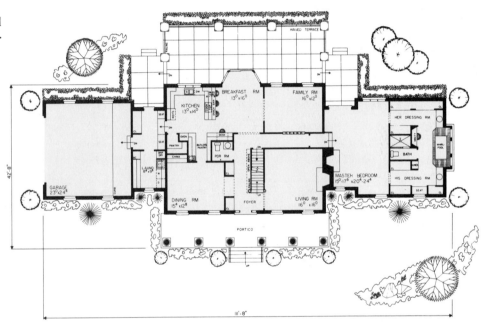

Design Y3320

First Floor: 2,337 square feet
Second Floor: 1,232 square feet
Total: 3,569 square feet

● What a grand impression this home makes! A spacious two-story foyer with circular staircase greets visitors and leads to the dining room, media room and two-story gathering room with fireplace. The well-equipped kitchen includes a snack bar for informal meals. A luxurious master suite downstairs and four bedrooms upstairs complete this impressive plan.

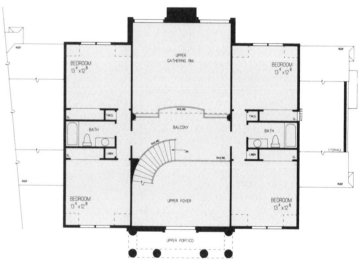

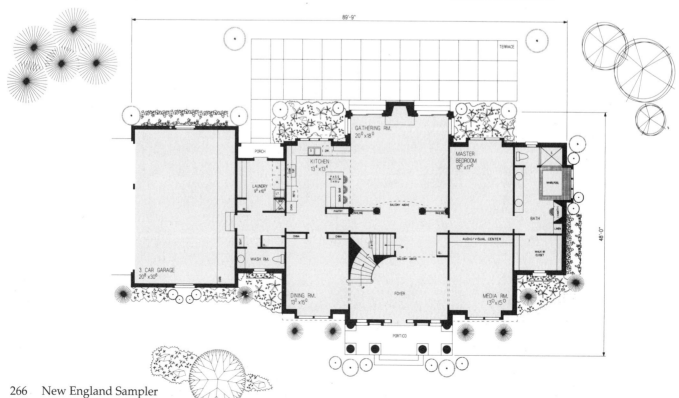

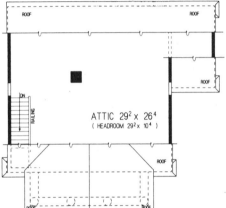

ATTIC 29² x 26⁴
(HEADROOM 29² x 10⁴)

BEDROOM
11⁰ x 10⁸

BATH   DRESS RM

VANITY

MASTER
BEDROOM
13⁴ x 13⁴

BATH

LINEN

BEDROOM
10⁸ x 9²

BEDROOM
12⁰ x 10⁶

UPPER PORTICO

Design Y3339

First Floor: 1,460 square feet
Second Floor: 1,014 square feet
Total: 2,474 square feet

● This Colonial four-bedroom features the livable kind of plan you're looking for. A formal living room extends from the front foyer and leads to the formal dining area and nearby kitchen. A sunken family room has a raised-hearth fireplace. Three family bedrooms share a bath and are joined by the master bedroom with its own full bath.

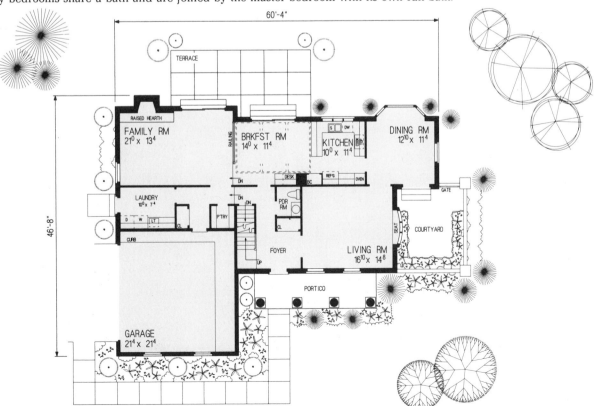

60'-4"

46'-8"

TERRACE

RAISED HEARTH

FAMILY RM
21⁰ x 13⁴

BRKFST RM
14⁰ x 11⁴

KITCHEN
10⁰ x 11⁴

DINING RM
12¹⁰ x 11⁴

LAUNDRY
10⁰ x 7⁴

PDR RM

REF'G

OVEN

DESK

COURTYARD

SEAT

GATE

FOYER

LIVING RM
16¹⁰ x 14⁸

PORTICO

GARAGE
21⁴ x 21⁴

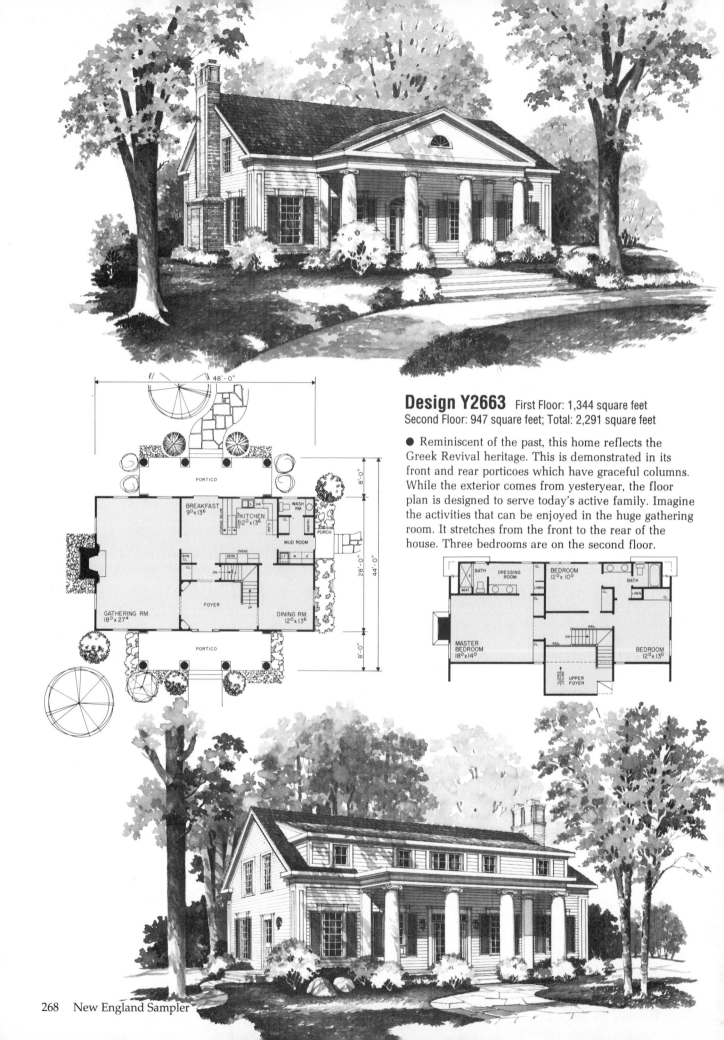

Design Y2663 First Floor: 1,344 square feet
Second Floor: 947 square feet; Total: 2,291 square feet

● Reminiscent of the past, this home reflects the Greek Revival heritage. This is demonstrated in its front and rear porticoes which have graceful columns. While the exterior comes from yesteryear, the floor plan is designed to serve today's active family. Imagine the activities that can be enjoyed in the huge gathering room. It stretches from the front to the rear of the house. Three bedrooms are on the second floor.

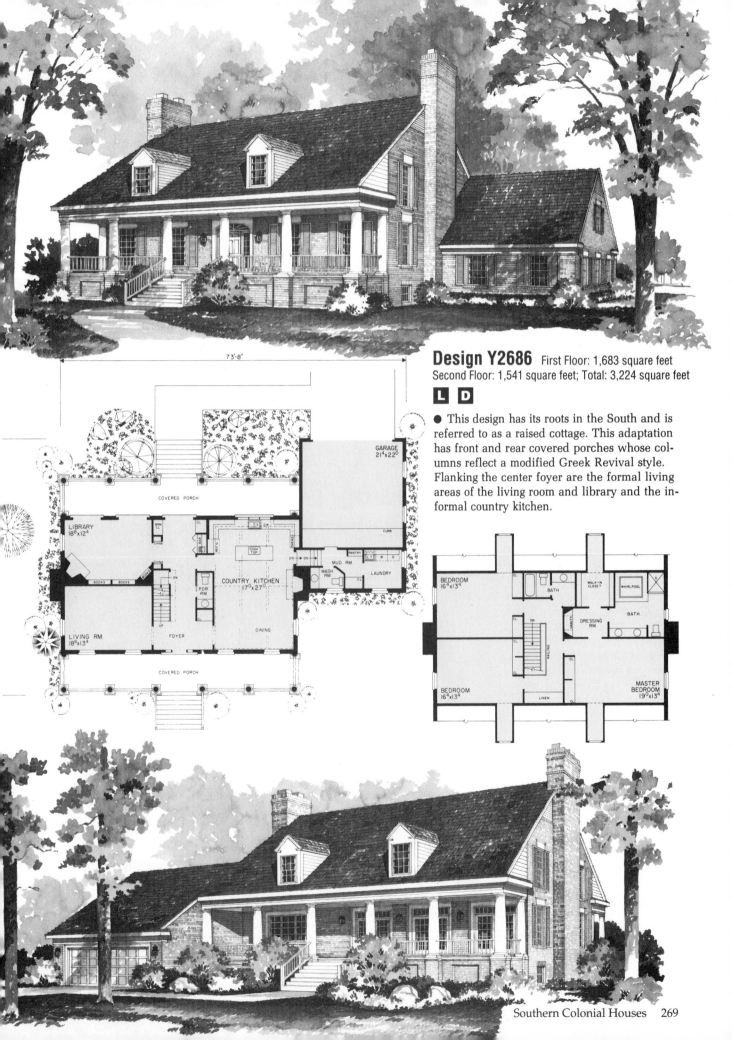

Design Y2686 First Floor: 1,683 square feet
Second Floor: 1,541 square feet; Total: 3,224 square feet

L D

● This design has its roots in the South and is referred to as a raised cottage. This adaptation has front and rear covered porches whose columns reflect a modified Greek Revival style. Flanking the center foyer are the formal living areas of the living room and library and the informal country kitchen.

Design Y2997

Square Footage: 3,442

L **D**

● Here is a Greek Revival home that is a reminder of similar houses in the South after 1820. While many were of stucco or clapboard, this is of brick. The fine features include five fireplaces. One fireplace warms the master bedroom with expansive bath and dressing area, plus access to a private rear terrace. Two additional bedrooms each adjoin a full bath. Large living areas include the living room, dining room and family room with snack bar. A library with fireplace, sloped ceiling and built-in shelves is tucked away in the rear of the home.

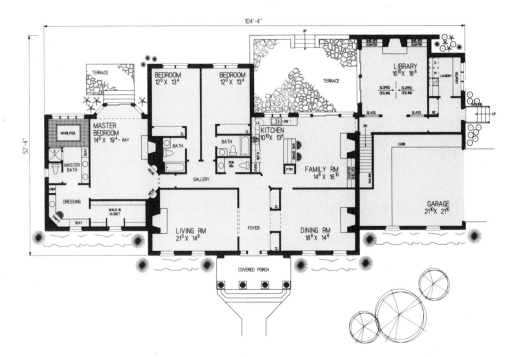

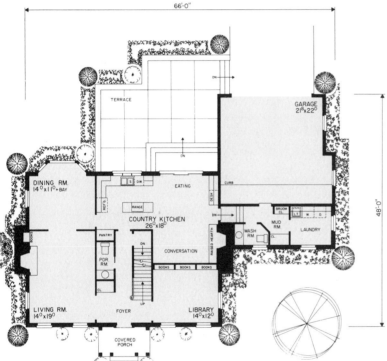

66'-0"

TERRACE

DN

DN

GARAGE
21⁸x22⁰

DINING RM.
14⁰x11⁰+BAY

EATING

REF'G.

RANGE

COUNTRY KITCHEN
26⁰x18⁰

DN

CURB

DESK

BROOM CL.

MUD RM.

WASH RM.

LT

W

D

LAUNDRY

48'-0"

PANTRY

CONVERSATION

RAISED HEARTH

PDR. RM.

DN

BOOKS BOOKS BOOKS

CL.

UP

LIVING RM.
14⁰x19⁰

FOYER

LIBRARY
14⁰x12⁰

COVERED PORCH

Design Y2688 First Floor: 1,588 square feet
Second Floor: 1,101 square feet; Total: 2,689 square feet

● Here are two floors of excellent livability. Start at the country kitchen. It will be the center for family activities. It has an island, desk, raised hearth fireplace, conversation area and sliding glass doors to the terrace. Adjacent to this area is the washroom and laundry. Quieter areas are available in the living room and library. Three bedrooms are housed on the second floor.

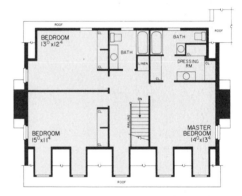

ROOF

BEDROOM
13⁰x12⁴

BATH

BATH

LINEN

DRESSING RM.

ROOF

CL

DN

RAILING

BEDROOM
15⁰x11⁴

MASTER BEDROOM
14⁰x13⁴

ROOF

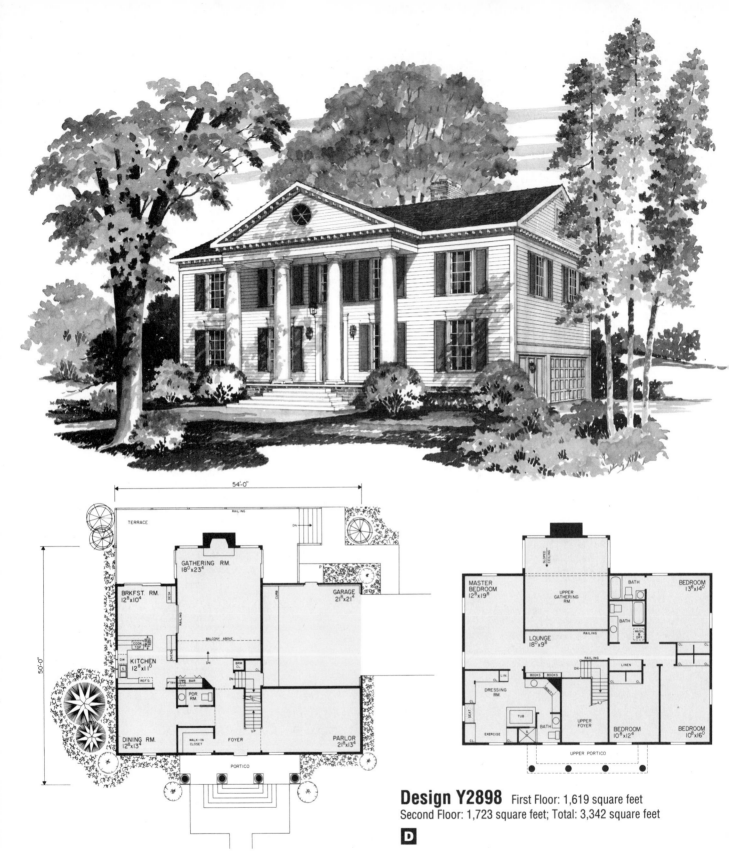

Design Y2898 First Floor: 1,619 square feet
Second Floor: 1,723 square feet; Total: 3,342 square feet

D

● Four soaring Doric columns highlight the exterior of this Greek Revival dwelling. The elevation reflects a balanced design that incorporates four bedrooms and a two-car garage in one central unit. The stylish heart of this dwelling is a two-story gathering room. A balcony lounge on the second floor offers a quiet aerie overlooking this living area. Both of these areas will have sunlight streaming through the high windows. A second living area is the parlor. It could serve as the formal area whereas the gathering room could be considered informal. Entrance to all of these areas will be through the foyer. It has an adjacent powder room and spacious walk-in closet. The U-shaped kitchen will conveniently serve the breakfast and dining rooms. Second floor livability is outstanding. Study all of the features in the master bedroom: dressing room, tub and shower, large vanity and exercise area. Three more bedrooms, another has a private bath which would make it an ideal guest room.

Design Y4305 First Floor: 2,841 square feet; Second Floor: 2,019 square feet; Total: 4,860 square feet

● Two-story columns and an air of gentility dominate the facade of this classic Greek Revival home. The view from the large, formal foyer includes the grand stair hall and a spectacular circular staircase. To the left of the foyer is a living room or parlor and to the right is a magnificent oval-shaped dining room. A sunny breakfast room opens to the rear porch and family room. The deep, U-shaped kitchen is designed with ample space for preparing family meals as well as entertaining. Each of the first-floor living areas, including the master bedroom, has a fireplace. The master suite features convenient His and Hers baths (His with a shower, Hers with a tub) and three walk-in closets. Five bedrooms, including one for guests, and four full baths are located on the second floor.

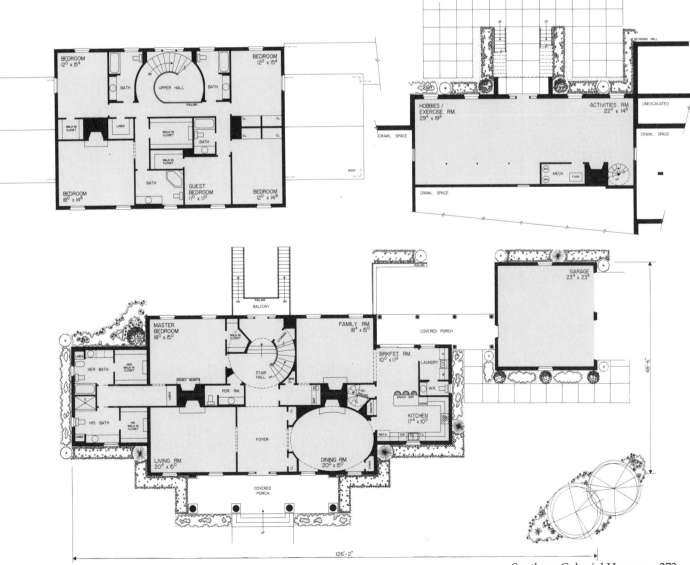

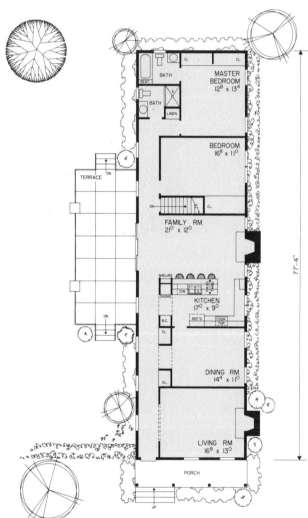

Design Y2698
Square Footage: 1,700

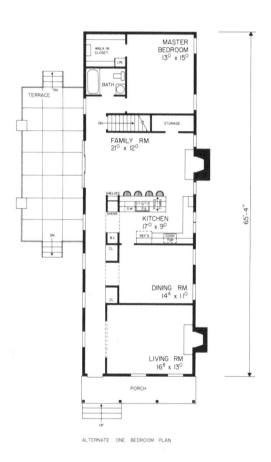

ALTERNATE ONE BEDROOM PLAN

● Here is the quintessential narrow lot house. It was found in 19th Century New Orleans and many other southern towns. Its origins go back to the West Indies and Africa and has been called, the "shotgun house". A name derived from the fact that a bullet could travel through the front door and exit the rear without striking a partition. For the sake of contemporary floor planning this version forsakes the rear door in favor of two full baths. Despite its small size, the facade with its projecting gable and columned front porch is charming, indeed. As a starter home, or even as a retirement home, this unique house will serve its occupants well. An alternate one bedroom version contains 1,436 sq. ft. Notice that all of the amenities to be found in the other rooms remain the same.

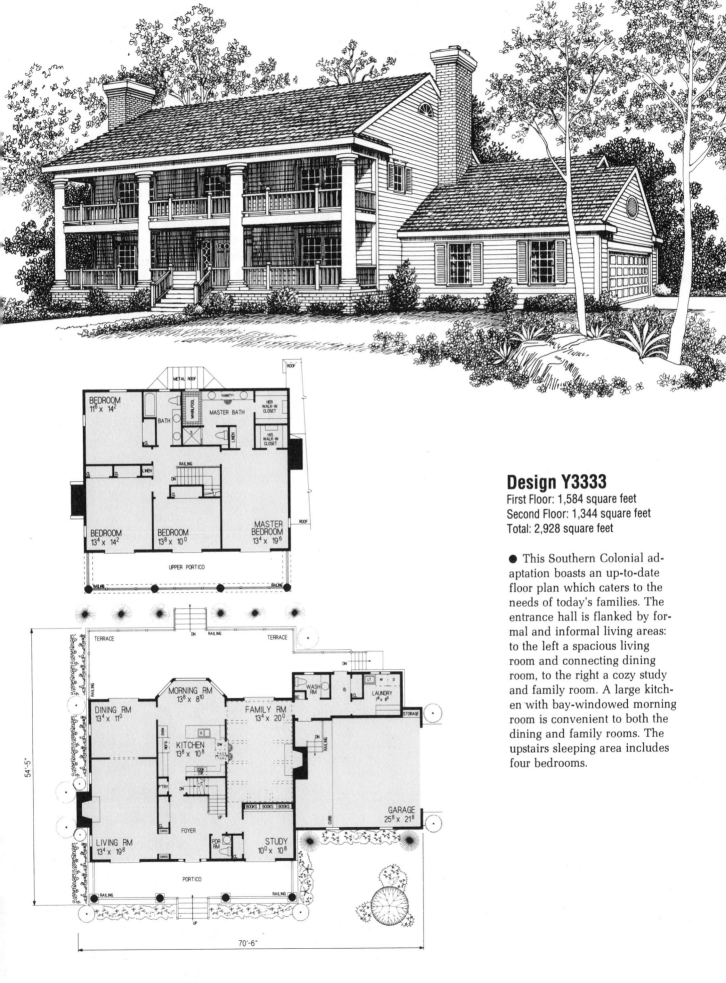

Design Y3333

First Floor: 1,584 square feet
Second Floor: 1,344 square feet
Total: 2,928 square feet

● This Southern Colonial adaptation boasts an up-to-date floor plan which caters to the needs of today's families. The entrance hall is flanked by formal and informal living areas: to the left a spacious living room and connecting dining room, to the right a cozy study and family room. A large kitchen with bay-windowed morning room is convenient to both the dining and family rooms. The upstairs sleeping area includes four bedrooms.

The Formal Foyer

The formal foyer of a residence can serve as the introduction to the interior of the home. Just as the front entranceway detailing of the exterior extends a welcoming call to visitors, the foyer makes an introductory statement about the interior. Passing through the front door, the foyer is the first impression a visitor gets of the interior. The statement it makes can often tell much about the decor of the home and the tastes of its occupants.

Whether the term of reference be hall, entry, entrance hall, receiving hall, vestibule or foyer, this area is also important because of its contribution to the floor plan's traffic patterns. Foyers can be large or small, but whatever their size and configuration, they must be able to accommodate staircases, doorways, open archways and accesses to secondary hallways leading to living and sleeping areas.

A foyer as a reception room.

A timeless formal entry.

Design Y2521, page 47.
Traffic leads left, right or straight ahead.

Design Y2538, page 99.
A dramatic curving staircase.

Open planning equals spaciousness.

The Formal Foyer

Often, the most dramatic feature of the foyer is the stairway to the second floor or an upper level. Of course, some foyers usher traffic to open lower levels of livability too. These can be equally eye-catching as they lead downward to recreational areas. As shown on these pages, staircases have many configurations. They may be straight, angular or curving. Some foyers even have twin staircases rising to the second floor. Staircases can be enclosed or they can be open. However, a common feature of Georgian-styled houses was the open stairwell. These were found in foyers, or entrance halls, that were well-lit and high-ceilinged. Foyers gained natural light in varying degrees from the treatment of its exterior doorways and fenestration. Doorways with transom lights, sidelights and fanlights provided at least a minimal amount of light. Two-story foyers had graceful Palladian windows above the doorway, and some foyers received extra light from windows located on staircase landings. Larger foyers even accommodated larger windows to each side of the doorway enframement.

Design Y2638, page 234.
Like a picture frame.

Design Y1987, page 56.
A peek at fireside livability.

Design Y1956, page 148.
An efficient double-door foyer.

A view from the living room.

Design Y2571, page 62.
Open on two sides.

Making a decorative statement.

The Formal Foyer

Foyers achieve an exquisite decor with the prudent application of woodworking. Staircases, with their fancy balusters, handrails and newel posts, have decorative appeal as well as utilitarian function. Wainscotings, crown mouldings, casings, pilasters and pediments around doorways and openings make significant contributions to the ambience of the foyer. Not to be overlooked are the chandeliers, lighting fixtures, pictures, wall and floor coverings and furniture as they add to the environment just inside the front doorway.

Design Y2663, page 268.
Inviting, arched openings.

Design Y1700, page 100.
Up the circular staircase.

Design Y2636, page 43.
A spacious foyer leads the way.

Design Y2521, page 47.
An open, angular stairway.

Design Y2599, page 151.
Curvilinear wall and stairs.

Design Y2693, page 249.
Inside an exquisite doorway.

The Formal Foyer

The foyer frequently offers a most tantalizing glimpse of an immediately adjacent room or of a somewhat distant one. This emphasizes the introductory nature of the foyer as it extends to visitors a warm greeting and an inviting welcome to the remainder of the house.

Design Y2610, page 102.
Appealing window enframement.

A circular entrance viewed from the dining room.

Fanlight and double doors.

A spacious two-story foyer.

An octagonal receiving hall.

Open room dividers in the foyer.

The Formal Foyer

Ideally the foyer routes traffic efficiently to the main areas of the house. The center-hall Colonial of our architectural past endures. From this basic idea of placing the entrance and foyer at the center of the facade emerge innumerable floor planning variations. The most popular basic concept is to create a plan which allows traffic to flow from the foyer directly to a house's three main zones: the living zone, the work zone and the sleeping zone. A varied combination of rooms may comprise each of these zones. However, family living convenience is best served when all the rooms in a given zone cater to the same function.

Design Y2668, page 244.
Two stories of grandeur.

Design Y1858, page 228.
A grand descent to the foyer.

Design Y2569, page 60.
Viewed from up on high.

A coat closet is nearby.

Design Y2399, page 90.
Providing space for furnishings.

View from across the banister.

Master Bedrooms

Master bedrooms are hardly a feature copied from Colonial times when sleeping areas were often shared between parents and children. It is interesting to note, however, that at Monticello, Thomas Jefferson uniquely designed his bed alcove to be flanked on one side by his angular study and on the other by a larger room with a fireplace. Of course, in the late 18th Century, fireplaces were the primary source of heat and were found in all major rooms of the house. In today's houses with central heating, fireplaces are hardly a necessity. But, they are an amenity that need not be relegated solely to the living and dining rooms. Locating a fireplace in the master bedroom can be considered a well-deserved amenity for home owners in the 20th Century.

Design Y2652, page 44.
A bedroom focal point.

A cozy bedroom fireplace.

Design Y2522, page 189.
Decorative mouldings create character.

Design Y2696, page 243.
A setting for quiet conversation.

Design Y2649, page 93.
Tea time by firelight.

Ready for a good read.

Master Bedrooms

With or without a fireplace, the master bedroom provides the parents in an active, and frequently noisy, family with a haven in which to escape the clamor. In addition to serving its primary function of providing a place for undisturbed sleep, with thoughtful planning the master bedroom can be just the place for reading, writing, conversing and meditating in private. While much can be said in favor of contemporary floor planning and its challenge to provide open planning, dual-use spaces, family activity areas and high-tech media rooms, the need for developing a private refuge is worthy of fulfillment.

A bedroom music bay.

A cheerful correspondence corner.

A comfortable window seat.

Inviting the outdoors in.

A bedroom study corner.

A quiet haven for tea.

Master Bedrooms

Like any other room in the house, the master bedroom offers its decorating and furnishing opportunities. There is the choice of windows with their variety of sizes, styles and shapes to be considered. How should they be draped, curtained or even shuttered on the inside? What kinds of mouldings, mantels and wall and floor coverings should be selected?

Some master bedrooms are adjoined to a separate sitting room or lounge area through spacious openings. This can really be fun to fix up with panache. Or the master bedroom may function with an outdoor living area. This may be in the form of a balcony, deck or terrace and there are innumerable ways for these indoor/outdoor areas to be furnished and interact.

Design Y2146, page 39.
A master bedroom library corner.

An adjacent sitting room.

An appealing window ledge.

Houses have two major living areas—living and family rooms. They have two eating areas—breakfast and formal dining rooms. They also have two or more baths. But, houses usually have only one master bedroom. Therefore, be sure it gets all the attention and thought it deserves.

All set for outdoor breakfast.

Design Y2636, page 43.
A niche with built-in utility.

Solariums

Solariums, sun rooms and enclosed porches can offer much of the fun of outdoor living indoors. Providing an abundance of natural light to these areas makes them cheerful, uplifting areas. Maximum enjoyment of the surrounding landscape can be achieved through the use of skylights, expanses of fixed glass doors and bay windows. An extra measure of spaciousness may be attained by employing sloped ceilings where possible. Regional differences in weather and climate conditions may influence the orientation of the house upon its site. This, of course, may determine the location of sun-oriented rooms. Whatever the desired relationship of the house and its rooms to various points of the compass, sun rooms can function well with many other rooms of a house. Functioning with the living room, they become an alternative area for sitting and conversing.

Design Y2615, page 37.
A bright indoor setting.

Design Y2689, page 45.
An enclosed porch for living.

Through sliding glass doors.

The outdoors brought in.

Along with the dining room, it provides a secondary spot for informal eating. The solarium can represent another area to gather informally, or a location in which to enjoy privacy. The solarium effect can be achieved in a corner of a room by proper orientation, the use of windows and the imaginative use of decoration and furnishings. The solarium would fall short of its mission if it did not reflect the touch of a gardener. The profusion of plants and flowers may vary with the tastes and talents of the occupants.

A pleasant corner for relaxation.

On the way to the greenhouse.

VICTORIANA & BUNGALOWS

Today, a traveller through the small towns of New England could not help but notice the presence of Victorian-styled houses. By their very numbers they have claimed their lofty place in our architectural heritage. Consequently, any presentation of home designs of New England, and the larger northeastern region of the country, would be remiss should it overlook the distinct charm of the Victorian style. The Victorian era flourished from 1840 to 1910. It took its name from Queen Victoria of England, whose long reign (1837-1901) influenced so much of the period. With its roots planted in the earlier Gothic Revival period, Victorian architecture, in its various forms, broke from the Classical styles of its antecedents. It embraced a freedom of expression and became known for its liveliness and whimsical nature. When reviewing the designs on the following pages, note the asymmetrical configurations of the structures. Observe the dramatic rooflines with their cross gables and turrets. Other style points include the massive chimneys, the variety of covered porches, the contrasting exterior wall materials, the window treatments and the often exquisite architectural detailing of the cornices, gables and balustrades. Victorian designs show a significant range in size, as exemplified by Design Y2974 at 1,772 square feet and Design Y3395 with 5,385 square feet.

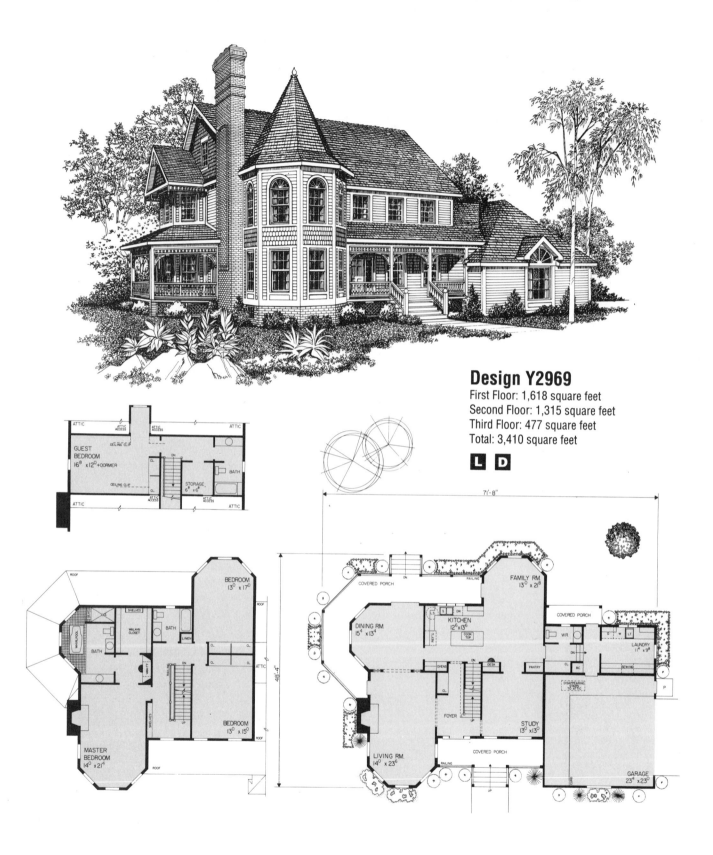

Design Y2969

First Floor: 1,618 square feet
Second Floor: 1,315 square feet
Third Floor: 477 square feet
Total: 3,410 square feet

L **D**

● What could beat the charm of a turreted Victorian with covered porches to the front, side and rear? This delicately detailed exterior houses an outstanding family oriented floor plan. Projecting bays make their contribution to the exterior styling. In addition, they provide an extra measure of livability

to the living, dining and family rooms, plus two of the bedrooms. The efficient kitchen, with its island cooking station, functions well with the dining and family rooms. A study provides a quiet first floor haven for the family's less active pursuits. Upstairs there are three big bedrooms and a fine master bath.

The third floor provides a guest suite and huge bulk storage area (make it a cedar closet if you wish). This house has a basement for the development of further recreational and storage facilities. Don't miss the two fireplaces, large laundry and attached two-car garage. A great investment.

Design Y2971 First Floor: 1,766 square feet
Second Floor: 1,519 square feet; Total: 3,285 square feet

L

● The stately proportions and the exquisite detailing of Victorian styling are exciting, indeed. Like so many Victorian houses, interesting roof lines set the character with this design. Observe the delightful mixture of gable roof, hip roof, and the dramatic turret. Horizontal siding, wood shingling, wide fascia, rake and corner boards make a strong statement. Of course, the delicate detailing of the windows, railings, cornices and front entry is most appealing to the eye. Inside, a great four-bedroom family living plan.

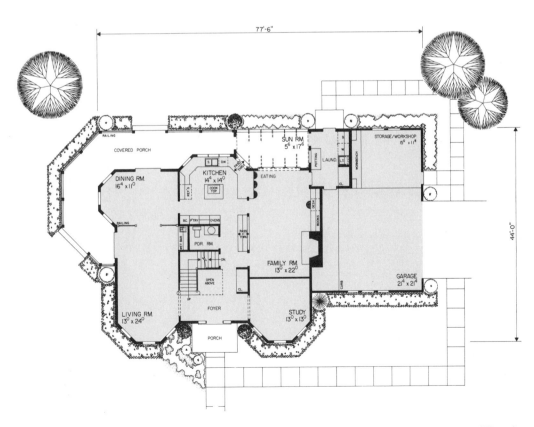

Design Y3309

First Floor: 1,375 square feet
Second Floor: 1,016 square feet
Total: 2,391 square feet

● Covered porches, front and back, are a fine preview to the livable nature of this Victorian. Living areas are defined in a family room with fireplace, formal living and dining rooms, and a kitchen with breakfast room. An ample laundry room, garage with storage area, and powder room round out the first floor. Three second floor bedrooms are joined by a study and two full baths.

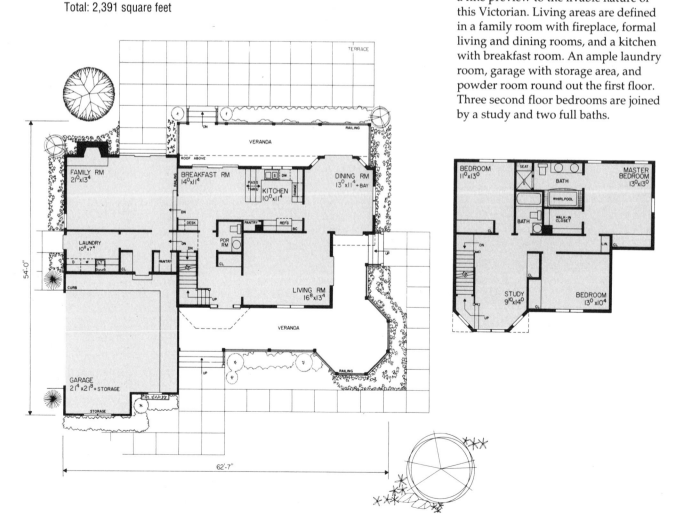

Design Y2970 First Floor: 1,538 square feet
Second Floor: 1,526 square feet; Third Floor: 658 square feet
Total: 3,722 square feet

L

● A porch, is a porch, is a porch. But, when it wraps around to a side, or even two sides, of the house, we have called it a veranda. This charming Victorian features a covered outdoor living area on all four sides! It even ends at a screened porch which features a sun deck above. This interesting plan offers three floors of livability. And what livability it is! Plenty of formal and informal living facilities to go along with the potential of five bedrooms. The master suite is just that. It is adjacent to an interesting sitting room. It has a sun deck and excellent bath/personal care facilities. The third floor will make a wonderful haven for the family's student members.

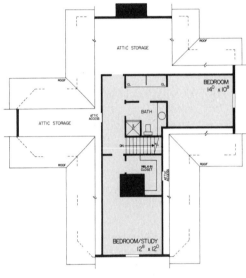

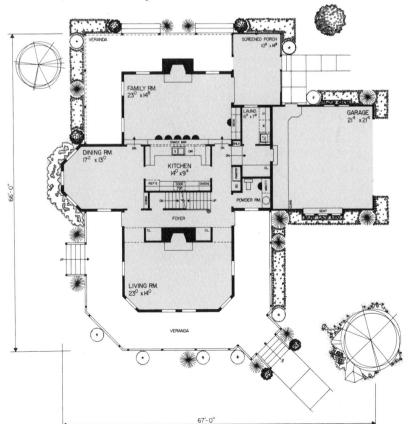

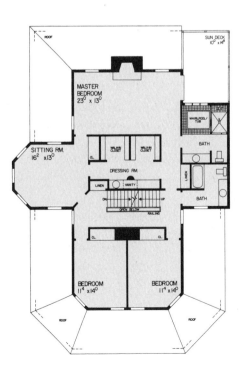

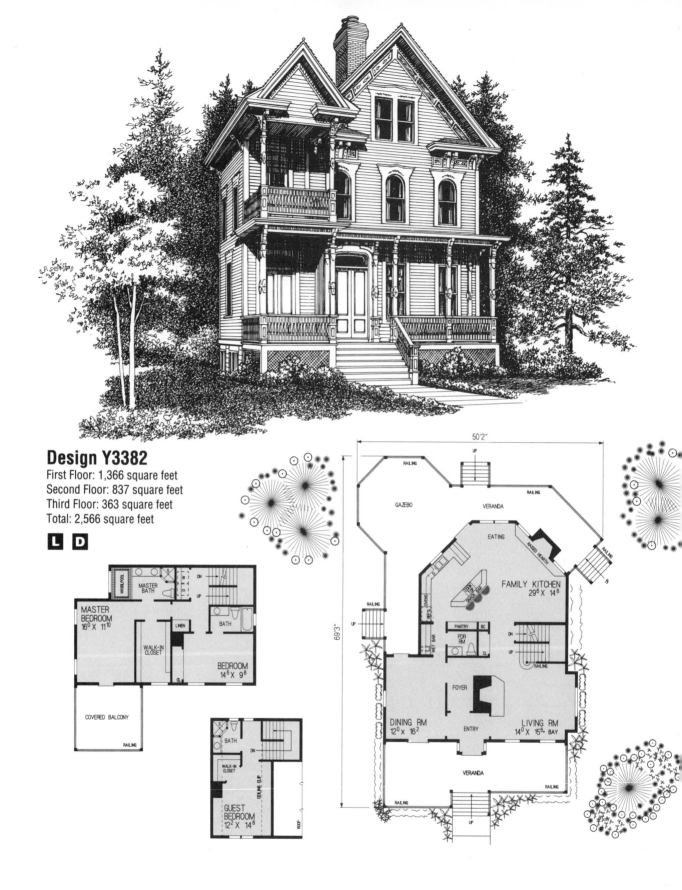

Design Y3382

First Floor: 1,366 square feet
Second Floor: 837 square feet
Third Floor: 363 square feet
Total: 2,566 square feet

● A simple but charming Queen Anne Victorian, this enchanting three-story home boasts delicately turned rails and decorated columns on its covered front porch. Inside is a floor plan that includes a living room with fireplace and dining room that connects to the kitchen via a wet bar. The adjoining family room contains another fireplace. The second floor holds two bedrooms, one a master suite with grand bath. A tucked-away guest suite on the third floor has a private bath.

Design Y2974 First Floor: 911 square feet
Second Floor: 861 square feet; Total: 1,772 square feet

L

● Victorian houses are well known for their orientation on narrow building sites. And when this occurs nothing is lost to captivating exterior styling. This house is but 38 feet wide. Its narrow width belies the tremendous amount of livability found inside. And, of course, the ubiquitous porch/veranda contributes mightily to style as well as livability. The efficient, U-shape kitchen is flanked by the informal breakfast room and formal dining room. The rear living area is spacious and functions in an exciting manner with the outdoor areas. Bonus recreational, hobby and storage space is offered by the basement and the attic.

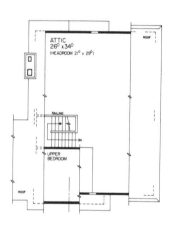

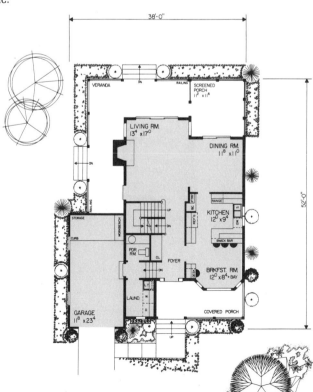

Design Y3391

First Floor: 1,230 square feet
Second Floor: 991 square feet
Total: 2,221 square feet

● Detailing is one of the characteristic features of Queen Anne Victorians and this home has no lack of it. Interior rooms add special living patterns. Features include a powder room for guests in the front hallway, a through-fireplace between the ample gathering room and cozy study, an efficient U-shaped kitchen with pantry, and a full-width terrace to the rear. On the second floor are three bedrooms — one a master suite with walk-in closet and amenity-filled bath. An open balcony overlooks the gathering room.

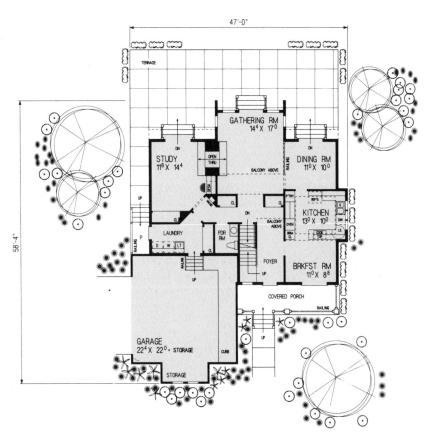

● This two-story farmhouse will be a delight for those who work at home. The second floor has a secluded master bedroom and a studio. A U-shaped kitchen with snack bar and breakfast area with bay window are only the first of the eating areas, which extend to a formal dining room and a covered rear porch for dining al fresco. The two-story living room features a cozy fireplace. A versatile room to the back could serve as a media room or a third bedroom.

Design Y3390

First Floor: 1,508 square feet
Second Floor: 760 square feet
Total: 2,268 square feet

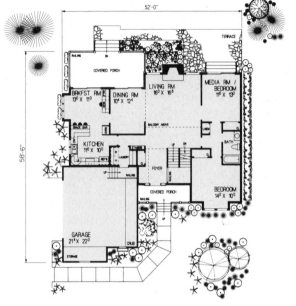

Design Y3385

First Floor: 1,096 square feet
Second Floor: 900 square feet
Total: 1,996 square feet

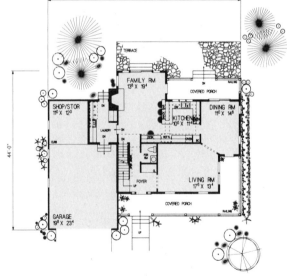

● Covered porches front and rear are complemented by a grand plan for family living. A formal living room and attached dining room provide space for entertaining guests. The large family room with fireplace is a gathering room for everyday use. Four bedrooms occupy the second floor. The master suite features two lavatories, a window seat and three closets. One of the family bedrooms has its own private balcony and could be used as a study.

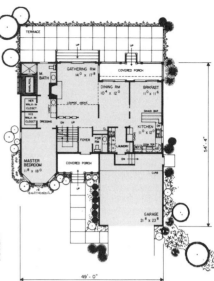

● A grand facade makes this Victorian stand out. Inside, guests and family are well accommodated: gathering room with terrace access, fireplace and attached formal dining room; split-bedroom sleeping arrangements. The master suite contains His and Hers walk-in closets, a separate shower and whirlpool tub and a delightful bay-windowed area. Upstairs there are three more bedrooms (one could serve as a study, one as a media room), a full bath and an open lounge area overlooking the gathering room.

Design Y3393
First Floor: 1,449 square feet
Second Floor: 902 square feet
Total: 2,351 square feet

L **D**

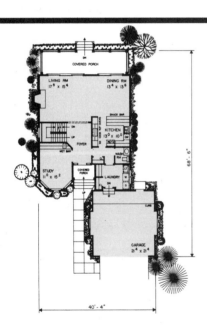

Design Y3389
First Floor: 1,161 square feet
Second Floor: 1,090 square feet
Third Floor: 488 square feet
Total: 2,739 square feet

L **D**

● A Victorian turret accents the facade of this compact three-story. Downstairs rooms include a grand-sized living room/dining room combination. The U-shaped kitchen has a snack-bar pass-through to the dining room. Just to the left of the entry foyer is a private study. On the second floor are three bedrooms and two full baths. The master bedroom has a whirlpool spa and large walk-in closet. The third floor is a perfect location for a guest bedroom with private bath.

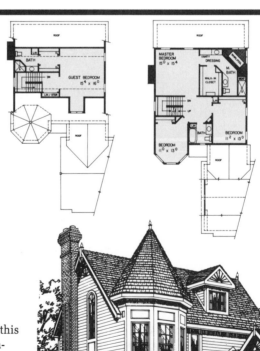

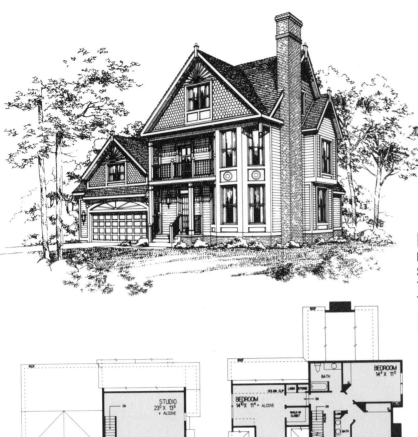

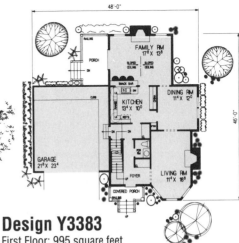

Design Y3383

First Floor: 995 square feet
Second Floor: 1,064 square feet
Third Floor: 425 square feet
Total: 2,484 square feet

L **D**

● This delightful Victorian cottage features exterior details that perfectly complement the convenient plan inside. Note the central placement of the kitchen, near to the dining room and the family room. Two fireplaces keep things warm and cozy. Three second-floor bedrooms include a master suite with bay window and two family bedrooms, one with an alcove and walk-in closet. Use the third-floor studio as a study, office or playroom for the children.

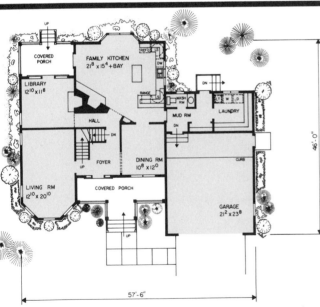

Design Y3384

First Floor: 1,399 square feet
Second Floor: 1,123 square feet
Total: 2,522 square feet

L **D**

● Classic Victorian styling comes to the forefront in this Queen Anne. The interior boasts comfortable living quarters for the entire family. On opposite sides of the foyer are the formal dining and living rooms. To the rear is a country-style island kitchen with attached family room. A small library shares a covered porch with this informal gathering area and also has its own fireplace. Three bedrooms on the second floor include a master suite with grand bath. The two family bathrooms share a full bath.

Design Y2973

First Floor: 1,269 square feet
Second Floor: 1,227 square feet
Total: 2,496 square feet

WIDTH 70'
DEPTH 44'-4"

L

● A most popular feature of the Victorian house has always been its covered porches. In addition to being an appealing exterior design feature, covered porches have their practical side, too. They provide wonderful indoor-outdoor living relationships. Notice sheltered outdoor living facilities for the various formal and informal living and dining areas of the plan. This home has a myriad of features to cater to the living requirements of the growing, active family.

CUSTOMIZABLE

Custom Alterations? See page 381 for customizing this plan to your specifications.

Design Y2972

First Floor: 1,432 square feet
Second Floor: 1,108 square feet
Total: 2,540 square feet

L

● The spacious foyer of this Victorian is prelude to a practical and efficient interior. The formal living and dining area is located to one side of the plan. The more informal area of the plan includes the fine U-shaped kitchen which opens to the big family room. Just inside the entrance from the garage is the laundry; a closet and the powder room are a few steps away. The library will enjoy its full measure of privacy. Upstairs is the three-bedroom sleeping zone with a fireplace.

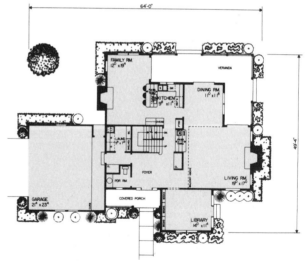

Design Y3388

First Floor: 1,517 square feet
Second Floor: 1,267 square feet
Third Floor: 480 square feet
Total: 3,264 square feet

L D

● This delightful home offers the best in thoughtful floor planning. The home opens to a well-executed entry foyer. To the left is the casual family room with fireplace. To the right is the formal living room which connects to the formal dining area. The kitchen/breakfast room combination features an island cook top and large pantry. Second-floor bedrooms include a master suite and two family bedrooms served by a full bath. A guest room dominates the third floor.

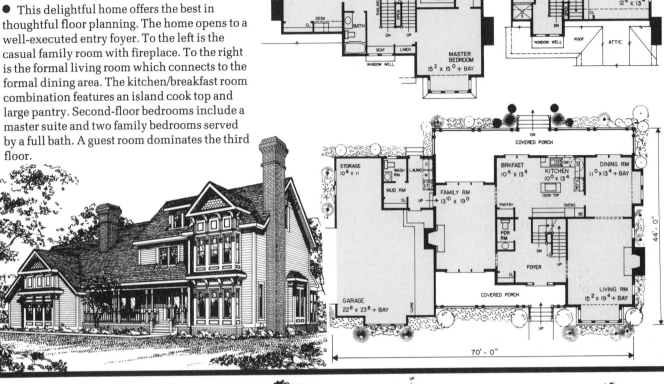

Design Y3394

First Floor: 1,531 square feet
Second Floor: 1,307 square feet
Third Floor: 664 square feet
Total: 3,502 square feet

L D

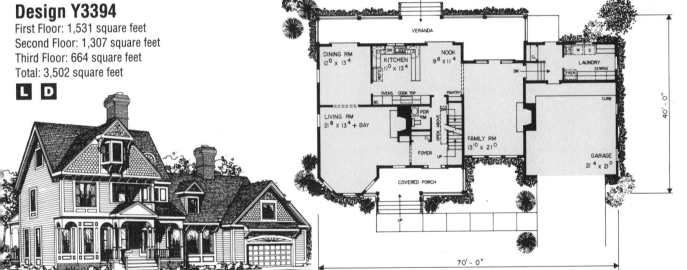

● The Folk Victorian is an important and delightful interpretation. And this version offers the finest in modern floor plans. The formal living areas are set off by a family room which connects the main house to the service areas. The second floor holds three bedrooms and two full baths. A sitting area in the master suite separates it from family bedrooms. On the third floor is a guest bedroom with gracious bath and large walk-in closet.

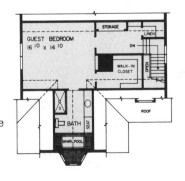

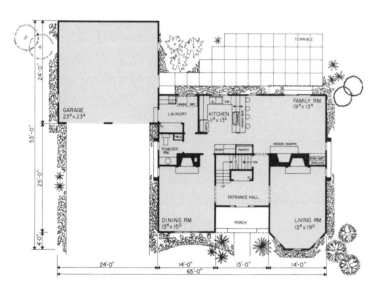

Design Y2646 First Floor: 1,274 square feet
Second Floor: 1,322 square feet; Total: 2,596 square feet

L **D**

● What a stylish departure from today's usual architecture. This refreshing exterior may be referred to as Neo-Victorian. Its vertical lines, steep roofs and variety of gables remind one of the old Victorian houses of yesteryear. Inside, there is an efficiently working floor plan that is delightfully spacious.

Design Y2645

First Floor: 1,600 square feet
Second Floor: 1,095 square feet
Third Floor: 911 square feet
Total: 3,606 square feet

L

Design Y2647 First Floor: 2,104 square feet; Second Floor: 1,230 square feet; Total: 3,334 square feet

L

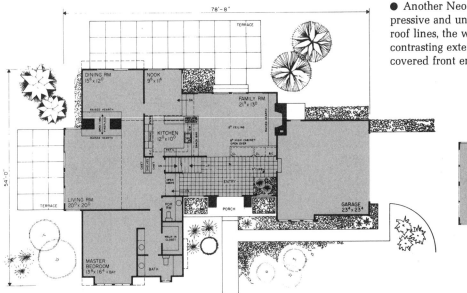

● Another Neo-Victorian, and what an impressive and unique design it is. Observe the roof lines, the window treatment, the use of contrasting exterior materials and the arched, covered front entrance.

● Reminiscent of the Gothic Victorian style of the mid-19th Century, this delightfully detailed, three-story house has a wraparound veranda for summertime relaxing. The parlor and family room, each with fireplaces, provide excellent formal and informal living facilities. The third floor houses two more great areas plus bath.

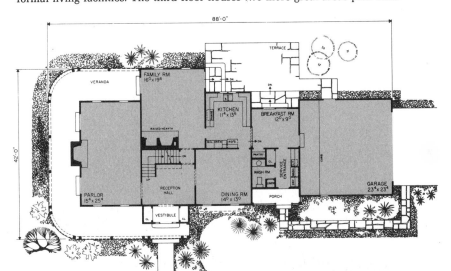

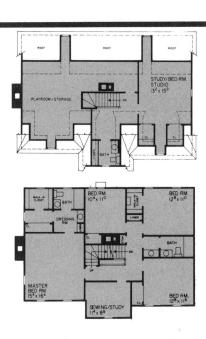

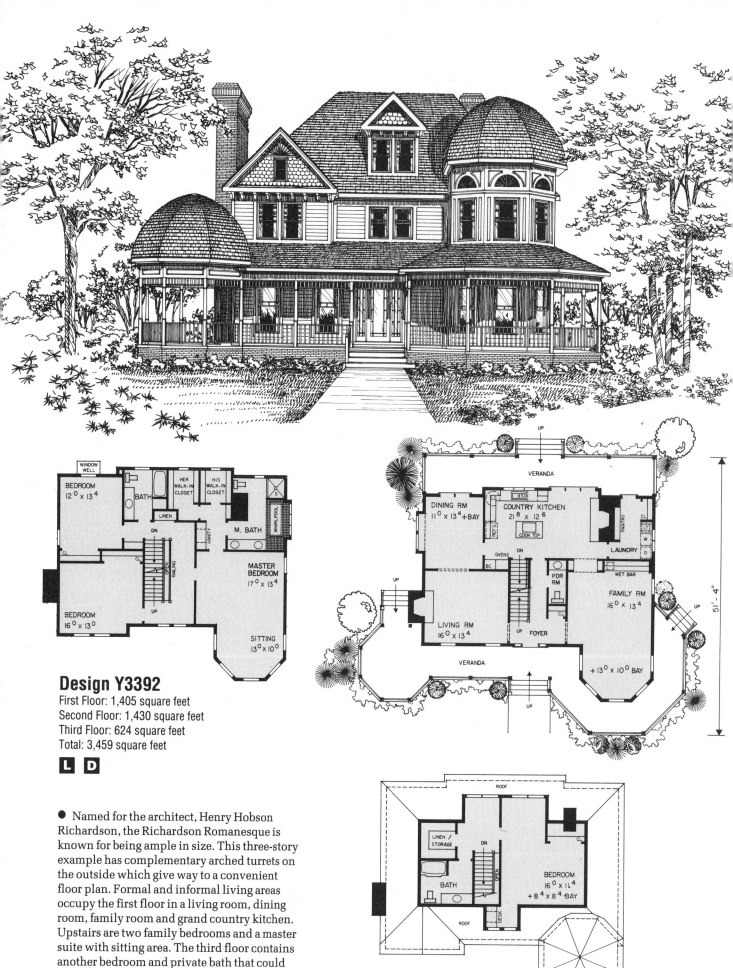

Design Y3392

First Floor: 1,405 square feet
Second Floor: 1,430 square feet
Third Floor: 624 square feet
Total: 3,459 square feet

L **D**

● Named for the architect, Henry Hobson Richardson, the Richardson Romanesque is known for being ample in size. This three-story example has complementary arched turrets on the outside which give way to a convenient floor plan. Formal and informal living areas occupy the first floor in a living room, dining room, family room and grand country kitchen. Upstairs are two family bedrooms and a master suite with sitting area. The third floor contains another bedroom and private bath that could serve guests.

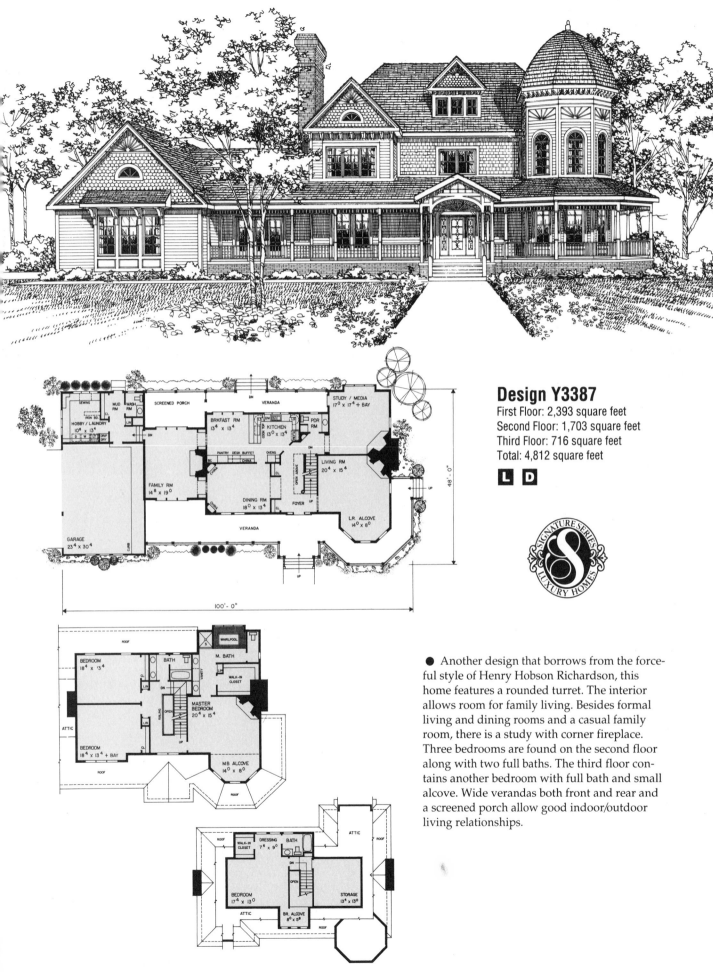

Design Y3387

First Floor: 2,393 square feet
Second Floor: 1,703 square feet
Third Floor: 716 square feet
Total: 4,812 square feet

L **D**

● Another design that borrows from the force-ful style of Henry Hobson Richardson, this home features a rounded turret. The interior allows room for family living. Besides formal living and dining rooms and a casual family room, there is a study with corner fireplace. Three bedrooms are found on the second floor along with two full baths. The third floor contains another bedroom with full bath and small alcove. Wide verandas both front and rear and a screened porch allow good indoor/outdoor living relationships.

● A magnificent, finely wrought covered porch wraps around this impressive Victorian estate home. The gracious two-story foyer provides a direct view past the stylish bannister and into the great room with large central fireplace. To the left of the foyer is a bookshelf-lined library and to the right is a dramatic, octagonal-shaped dining room. The island cooktop completes a convenient work triangle in the kitchen, and a pass-through connects this room with the Victorian-style morning room. A butler's pantry, walk-in closet, and broom closet offer plenty of storage space. A luxurious master suite is located on the first floor and opens to the rear covered porch. A through-fireplace warms the bedroom, sitting room, and dressing room, which includes His and Hers walk-in closets. The step-up whirlpool tub is an elegant focal point to the master bath. Four uniquely designed bedrooms, three full baths, and a restful lounge with fireplace are located on the second floor. Who says you can't combine the absolute best of today's amenities with the quaint styling and comfortable warmth of the Victorian past!

Design Y2953

First Floor: 2,991 square feet
Second Floor: 1,802 square feet
Total: 4,793 square feet

L D

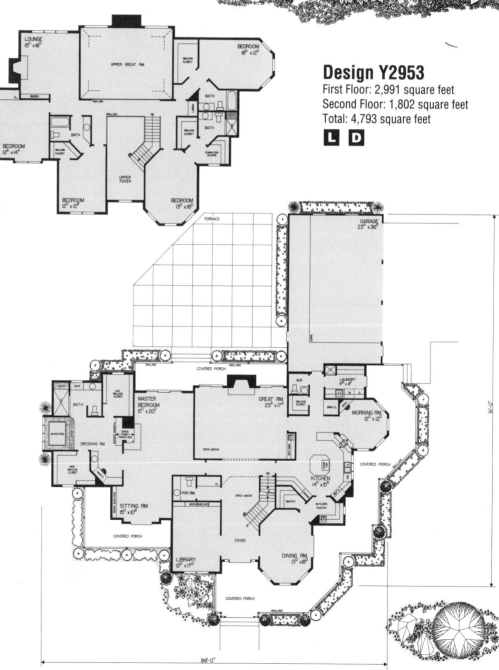

Design Y3304

First Floor: 2,102 square feet
Second Floor: 1,971 square feet
Total: 4,073 square feet

● Victorian style is displayed in most exquisite proportions in this three-bedroom, four-bath home. From verandas, both front and rear, to the stately turrets and impressive chimney stack, this is a beauty. Inside is a great lay-out with many thoughtful amenities. Besides the large living room, formal dining room, and two-story family room, there is a cozy study for private time. A gourmet kitchen with built-ins has a pass-through counter to the breakfast room. The master suite on the second floor includes many special features: whirlpool spa, His and Hers walk-in closets, exercise room, and fireplace. There are two more bedrooms, each with a full bath, on the second floor.

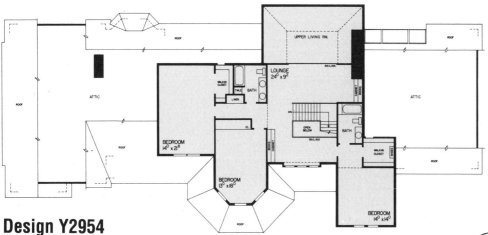

Design Y2954

First Floor: 3,079 square feet
Second Floor: 1,461 square feet
Total: 4,540 square feet

L

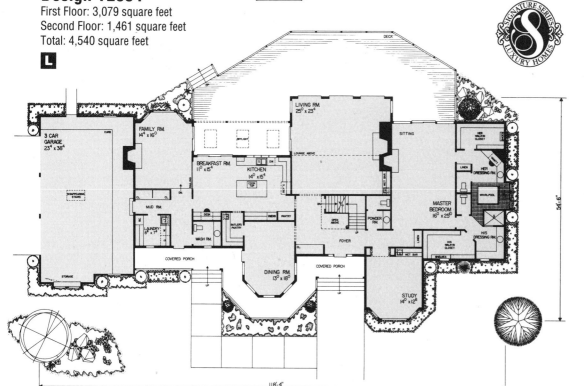

● This enchanting manor displays architectural elements typical of the Victorian Style: asymmetrical facade, decorative shingles and gables, and a covered porch. The two-story living room with fireplace and wet bar opens to the glass-enclosed rear porch with skylights. A spacious kitchen is filled with amenities, including an island cooktop, built-in desk, and butler's pantry connecting to the dining room. The master suite, adjacent to the study, opens to the rear deck. A cozy fireplace keeps the room warm on chilly evenings.

Separate His and Hers dressing rooms are outfitted with vanities and walk-in closets, and a luxurious whirlpool tub connects the baths. The second floor opens to a large lounge with built-in cabinets and bookshelves. Three bedrooms and two full baths complete the second-floor livability. The three-car garage contains disappearing stairs to an attic storage area.

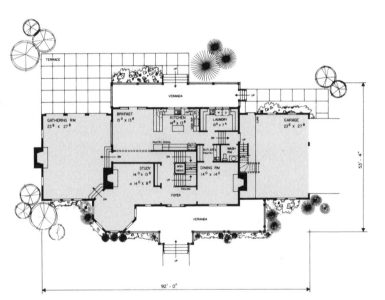

Design Y3395

First Floor: 2,248 square feet
Second Floor: 2,020 square feet
Third Floor: 1,117 square feet
Total: 5,385 square feet

L **D**

● This home is a lovely example of classic Queen Anne architecture. Its floor plan offers: a gathering room with fireplace, a study with an octagonal window area, a formal dining room and a kitchen with attached breakfast room. Bedrooms on the second floor include three family bedrooms and a grand master suite. On the third floor are a guest room with private bath and sitting room and a game room with attached library.

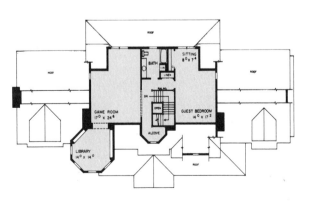

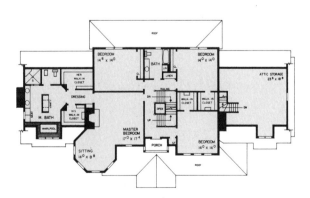

Design Y3386

First Floor: 1,683 square feet
Second Floor: 1,388 square feet
Third Floor: 808 square feet
Total: 3,879 square feet

● This beautiful Folk Victorian has all the properties of others in its class. Living areas include a formal Victorian parlor, a private study and large gathering room. The formal dining room has its more casual counterpart in a bay-windowed breakfast room. Both are near the well-appointed kitchen. Five bedrooms serve family and guest needs handily. Three bedrooms on the second floor include a luxurious master suite. For outdoor entertaining, there is a covered rear porch leading to a terrace.

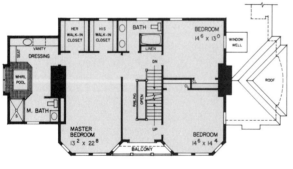

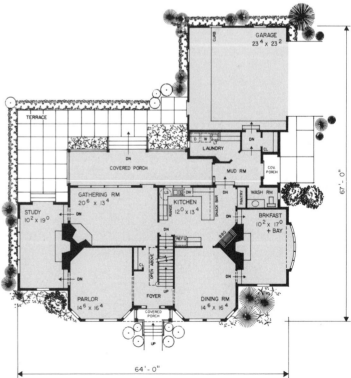

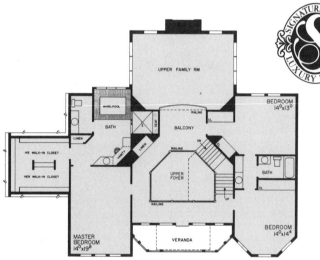

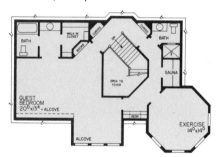

Design Y3308

First Floor: 2,515 square feet
Second Floor: 1,708 square feet
Third Floor: 1,001 square feet
Total: 5,224 square feet

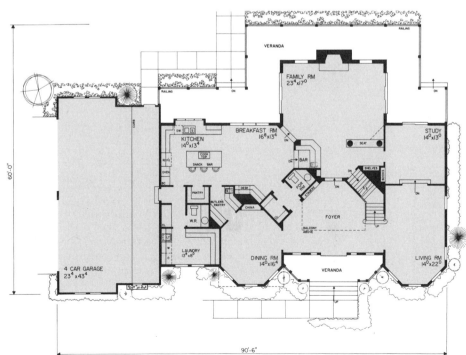

● Uniquely shaped rooms and a cache of amenities highlight this three-story beauty. Downstairs rooms accommodate both formal and informal entertaining and also provide a liberal share of work space in the kitchen and laundry. The second floor has two bedrooms and a full bath plus a master suite with His and Hers closets and whirlpool bath. An exercise room on the third floor has its own sauna and bath, while a guest room on this floor is complemented by a charming alcove and another full bath.

The Bungalow

An eclectic form of architecture that can be seen today throughout the nation is the bungalow, also referred to as Craftsman. The height of its popularity was reached during the first two decades of the 20th Century. The bungalow is easily identified by its low-pitched roof with wide, overhanging, unenclosed eaves; exposed rafter tails; and covered porches with roofs supported by square columns or pedestals often extending to ground level. Side- and cross-gabled roofs are most frequently observed, although hipped roofs are not unusual.

Design Y3313

First Floor: 1,482 square feet
Second Floor: 885 square feet
Total: 2,367 square feet

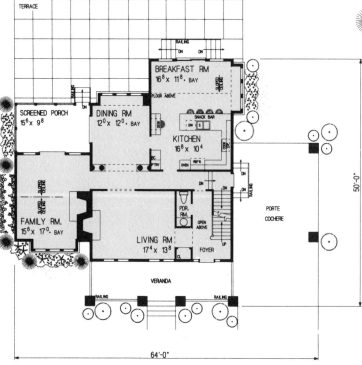

● Stone columns support the low-pitched roof of this shingle-sided bungalow. The resulting wide veranda provides sheltered passage to the front door as well as a pleasant outdoor spot for a couple of rocking chairs. The well-functioning kitchen area has a built-in planning desk, pantry, broom closet and snack bar adjoining the breakfast room with sloped ceiling. The formal dining room with a delightful columned opening is but a step away. At the end of the plan is the family room, featuring a sloped ceiling, a fireplace and direct access to the covered rear porch. Upstairs are three bedrooms and two baths.

Design Y3316 First Floor: 1,111 square feet
Second Floor: 886 square feet; Total: 1,997 square feet

● This charming clapboard-sided bungalow will provide a heap of living for the restricted budget. First of all, its narrow width will not require a costly building site. In addition, the rectangular shape leads to economical construction. The open planning between the formal living and dining rooms is highlighted by two delightful columns. The screened porch leads to a rear terrace with access to the breakfast room. Three bedrooms and two baths are located on the second floor.

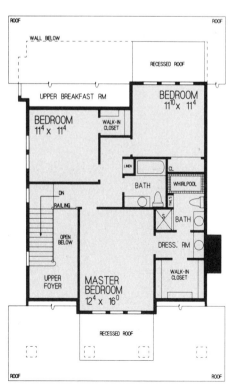

Design Y3315

First Floor: 2,918 square feet
Second Floor: 330 square feet
Total: 3,248 square feet

● Besides the covered front veranda, look for another full-width veranda to the rear of this charming home. The master bedroom, breakfast room, and gathering room all have French doors to this outdoor space. A handy wet bar/tavern enhances entertainment options. The upper lounge could be a welcome haven.

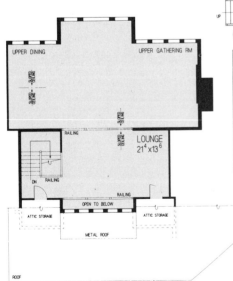

Design Y3314
Square Footage: 1,951

● This one-story bungalow
with wood shingles and accents
of brick and stucco has all the
charm of an upscale lodge, yet a
look at its floor plan reveals all
of the elements to assure full-
time livability. The deep veranda shelters the front door with
flanking sidelights. A step
inside reveals fine traffic patterns. From the foyer it is possible to look through the open
railing down to the bonus livability of the basement. To the
left is the living room with
sloped ceiling which flows into
the formal dining room. To the
rear are the interior kitchen and
cheerful breakfast room. Note
the planning desk and walk-in
pantry. To the right off the foyer
is the three-bedroom sleeping
area. Don't miss the screened
porch and the veranda to the
rear.

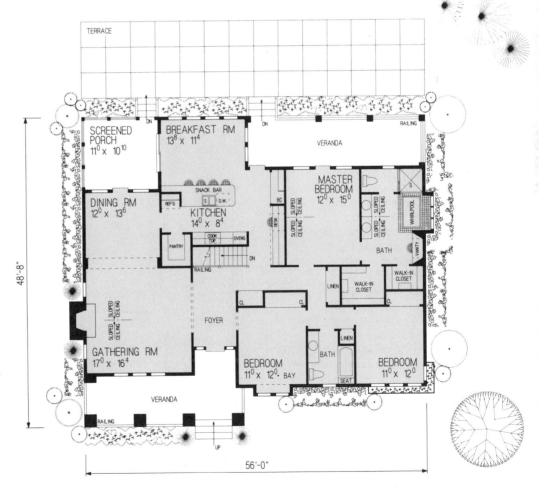

Design Y3319

Square Footage: 2,274

L **D**

● This hipped-roof bungalow has
interesting varying roof planes.
The high-ceilinged, covered front
entranceway shelters recessed
double doors topped by an appealing fanlight. The symmetry of the
exterior catches the eye. It is
enhanced by the balanced window
locations, flower boxes and stone
columns. The interior is well-
planned for active family living.
Noteworthy is the separation of
the master suite from the family
bedrooms. Nearby is a study or
home office. A feeling of spaciousness highlights the gathering,
dining and family room areas. The
efficient corner kitchen looks over
the snack bar into the family room.
Sliding glass doors from the master
bedroom and the gathering room
provide access to the terrace.

CUSTOMIZABLE

Custom Alterations? See page 381
for customizing this plan to your
specifications.

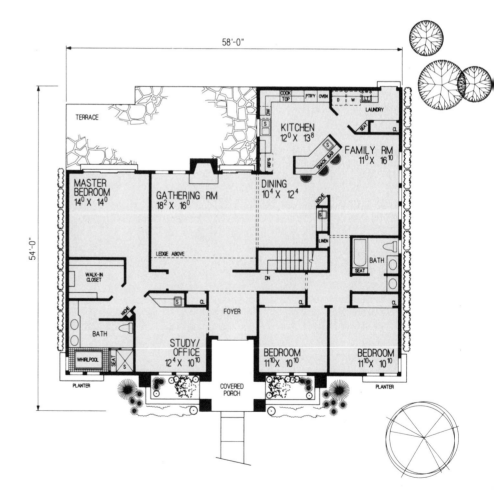

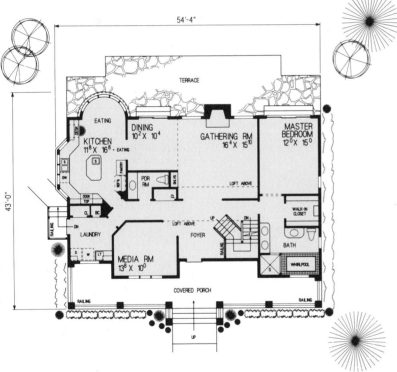

54'-4"

43'-0"

TERRACE

EATING
KITCHEN
11⁸ X 16⁸ EATING

DINING
10² X 10⁴

GATHERING RM
16⁴ X 15¹⁰

MASTER BEDROOM
12⁰ X 15⁰

LOFT ABOVE

PDR RM

COOK TOP

CL BC

LAUNDRY

DN

RAILING

LOFT ABOVE

FOYER

UP DN

WALK-IN CLOSET

BATH

WHIRLPOOL

MEDIA RM
13⁸ X 10⁰

COVERED PORCH

RAILING

RAILING

UP

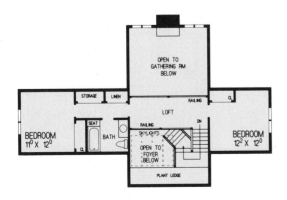

OPEN TO GATHERING RM BELOW

STORAGE LINEN

RAILING

LOFT

SEAT

BATH

RAILING
SKYLIGHTS

DN

OPEN TO FOYER BELOW

BEDROOM
11⁰ X 12⁰

BEDROOM
12² X 12⁰

PLANT LEDGE

Design Y3321

First Floor: 1,636 square feet
Second Floor: 572 square feet
Total: 2,208 square feet

L **D**

● Cozy and completely functional, this 1½-story bungalow has many amenities not often found in homes its size. The covered porch at the front opens at the entry to a foyer with angled staircase. To the left is a media room, to the rear the gathering room with fireplace. Attached to the gathering room is a formal dining room with rear terrace access. The kitchen features a curved casual eating area and island work station. The right side of the first floor is dominated by the master suite. It has access to the rear terrace and a luxurious bath. Upstairs are two family bedrooms connected by a loft area overlooking the gathering room and foyer. The dramatic open stairwell also has stairs to the lower-level basement where family recreational and hobby facilities can be developed.

CUSTOMIZABLE
Custom Alterations? See page 381 for customizing this plan to your specifications.

Design Y3318

First Floor: 1,557 square feet
Second Floor: 540 square feet
Total: 2,097 square feet

L **D**

● Details make the difference in this
darling two-bedroom (or three-bedroom if you choose) bungalow. From
covered front porch to covered rear
porch, there's a fine floor plan. Living
areas are to the rear: a gathering room
with through-fireplace and pass-
through counter to the kitchen and a
formal dining room with porch access.
To the front of the plan are a family
bedroom and bath and a study. The
study can also be planned as a guest
bedroom with bath. Upstairs is the master bedroom with through-fireplace to
the bath and a gigantic walk-in closet.
Other details include a generous
kitchen eating space, an island cooking
surface and cabinet, three linen closets
and a basement to accommodate the
laundry should the guest bedroom
option be exercised.

CUSTOMIZABLE

Custom Alterations? See page 381
for customizing this plan to your
specifications.

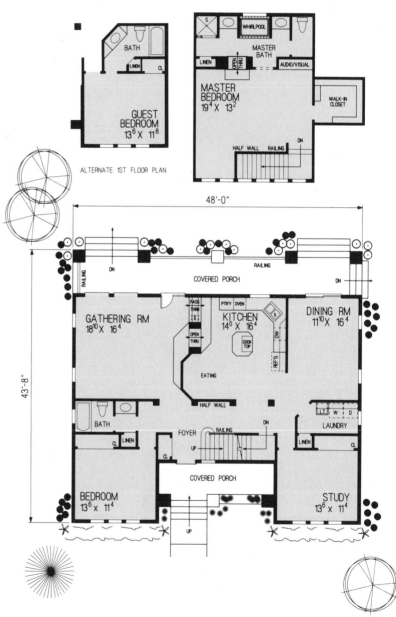

Traditional Adaptations

One-Story Houses, or ranch houses, are no recent phenomena. Early frontier dwellings, as well as those of the Dutch, French and Spanish colonies, were of one story. Today's technology and sophistication have made the one-story house a favorite. Here is a selection whose exteriors reflect a charming array of architectural details from the past. These houses are delightfully proportioned and offer all the convenience of one-story livability.

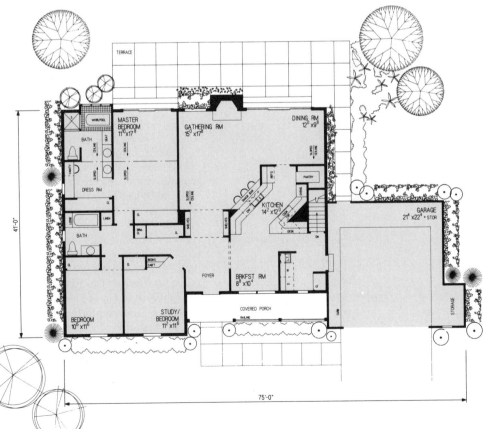

Design Y2947
Square Footage: 1,830

L D

● This charming one-story Traditional home greets visitors with a covered porch. A galley-style kitchen shares a snack bar with the spacious gathering room where a fireplace is the focal point. An ample master suite includes a luxury bath with whirlpool tub and separate dressing room. Two additional bedrooms, one that could double as a study, are located at the front of the home.

CUSTOMIZABLE
Custom Alterations? See page 381 for customizing this plan to your specifications.

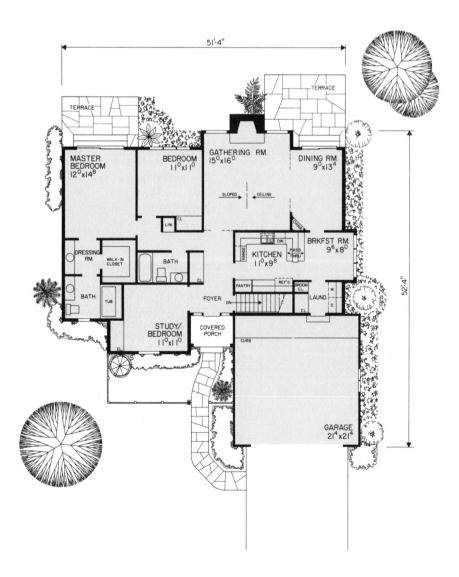

51'-4"

TERRACE

TERRACE

MASTER
BEDROOM
12⁰x14⁸

BEDROOM
11⁰x11⁰

GATHERING RM.
15⁰x16⁰

DINING RM.
9⁰x13⁴

SLOPED ⇨ ⇦ CEILING

LIN.

CL.

CHINA

DRESSING
RM.

WALK-IN
CLOSET

BATH

CL.

RANGE

KITCHEN
11⁰x9⁸

PASS
THRU

BRKFST RM.
9⁶x8⁰

BATH

TUB

PANTRY

REF'G.

BROOM
CL.

W.

LAUND

52'-4"

FOYER

DN

CL.

D.

STUDY/
BEDROOM
11⁰x11⁰

COVERED
PORCH

CURB

CL.

GARAGE
21⁴x21⁴

Design Y2878

Square Footage: 1,521

L **D**

● This charming one-story Traditional design offers plenty of livability in a compact size. Thoughtful zoning puts all bedroom sleeping areas to one side of the house apart from household activity in the living and service areas. The home includes a spacious gathering room with sloped ceiling, in addition to formal dining room and separate breakfast room. There's also a handy pass-thru between the breakfast room and an efficient, large kitchen. The laundry is strategically located adjacent to garage and breakfast/kitchen areas for handy access. A master bedroom enjoys its own suite with private bath and walk-in closet. A third bedroom can double as a sizable study just off the central foyer. This design offers the elegance of Traditional styling with the comforts of modern lifestyle.

CUSTOMIZABLE

Custom Alterations? See page 381 for customizing this plan to your specifications.

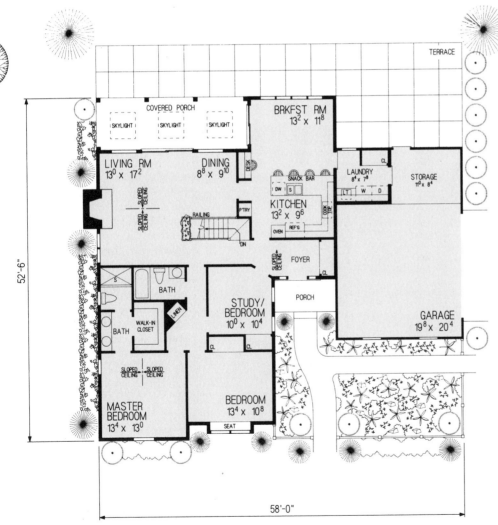

TERRACE

COVERED PORCH

SKYLIGHT | SKYLIGHT | SKYLIGHT

BRKFST RM
13² x 11⁸

LIVING RM
13⁰ x 17²

DINING
8⁸ x 9¹⁰

SLOPED CEILING | SLOPED CEILING

SNACK BAR

DW | S

LAUNDRY
8⁴ x 7⁸

LT | W | D

CL

STORAGE
11⁰ x 8⁴

RAILING

P'TRY

KITCHEN
13² x 9⁶

COOK TOP

OVEN | REF'G

DN

SLOPED CEILING

FOYER

CL

BATH

S

PORCH

STUDY/ BEDROOM
10⁰ x 10⁴

WALK-IN CLOSET

LINEN

BATH

CL | CL

GARAGE
19⁸ x 20⁴

SLOPED CEILING | SLOPED CEILING

MASTER BEDROOM
13⁴ x 13⁰

BEDROOM
13⁴ x 10⁸

SEAT

52'-6"

58'-0"

Design Y3340

Square Footage: 1,611

● You may not decide to build this design simply because of its delightful covered porch. But it certainly will provide its share of enjoyment if this plan is your choice. Notice also how effectively the bedrooms are arranged out of the traffic flow of the house. One bedroom could double nicely as a TV room or study. The living room/dining area is highlighted by a fireplace, sliding glass doors to the porch, and an open staircase with built-in planter to the basement.

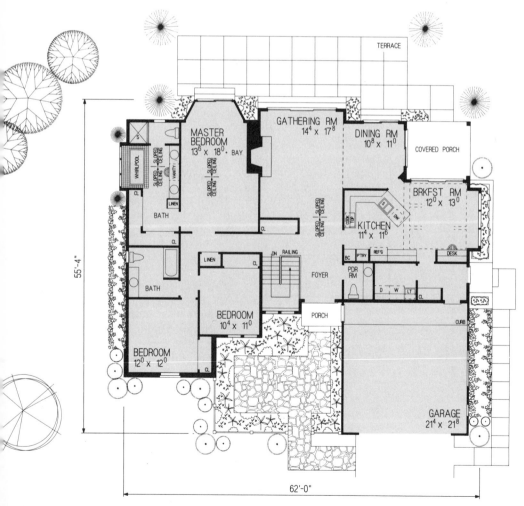

Design Y3336
Square Footage: 2,022

● Compact and comfortable! This three-bedroom home is a good consideration for a small family or empty-nester retirees. Of special note are the covered eating porch and sloped ceilings in the gathering room and master bedroom. The master bath accommodates every need with a whirlpool tub and shower, closet space, vanity and dual sinks. Stairs to the basement and a well-placed powder room are found at the front entry.

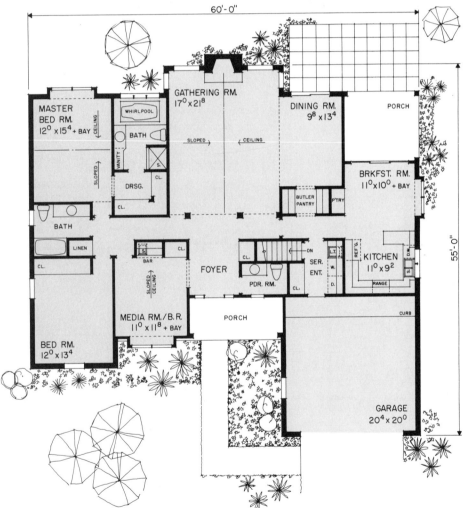

Design Y3376

Square Footage: 1,999

L **D**

● Small families or empty nesters will appreciate the layout of this traditional ranch. The foyer opens to the gathering room with fireplace and sloped ceiling. The dining room is open to the gathering room for entertaining ease and contains sliding doors to a rear terrace. The breakfast room also provides access to a covered porch for dining outdoors. The media room to the left of the home offers a bay window and a wet bar, or it can double as a third bedroom.

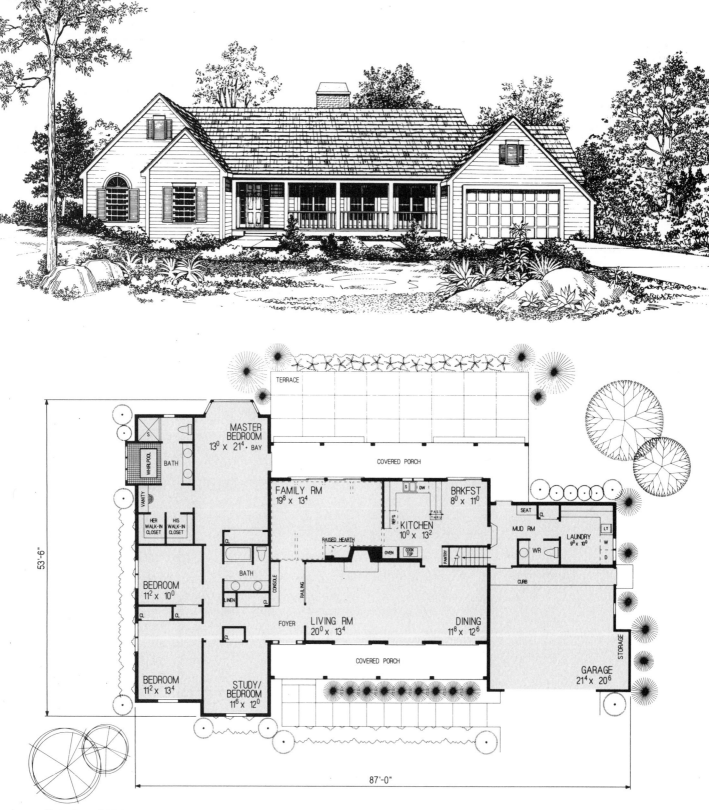

Design Y3348 Square Footage: 2,549

● Covered porches front and rear will be the envy of the neighborhood when this house is built. The interior plan meets family needs perfectly in well-zoned areas: a sleeping wing with four bedrooms and two baths, a living zone with formal and informal gathering space, and a work zone with U-shaped kitchen and laundry with washroom. The master bedroom with deluxe bath, including His and Hers walk-in closets, is noteworthy. Open planning and fireplaces enhance the living areas. Extra storage space is provided in the two-car garage.

Design Y3332

Square Footage: 2,168

● Nothing completes a traditional-style home quite as well as a country kitchen with fireplace. Notice also the sloped-ceiling living room and well-appointed master suite. A handy washroom is near the laundry, just off the garage.

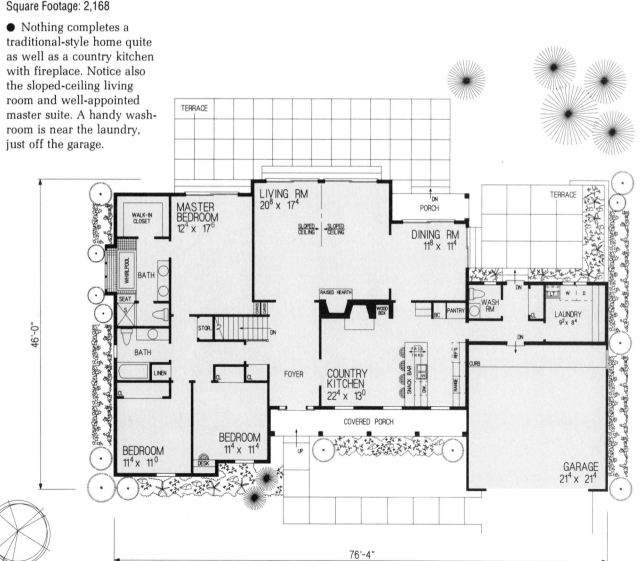

TERRACE

MASTER BEDROOM 12⁴ x 17⁶

WALK-IN CLOSET

LIVING RM 20⁸ x 17⁴

SLOPED CEILING   SLOPED CEILING

DN
PORCH

DINING RM 11⁸ x 11⁴

TERRACE

WHIRLPOOL

BATH

SEAT

RAISED HEARTH

WOOD BOX

PANTRY

BC

WASH RM

DN

W D

CL

LAUNDRY 9² x 8⁴

46'-0"

BATH

LINEN

CL

CL   CL

STOR.

DN

FOYER

COUNTRY KITCHEN 22⁴ x 13⁰

SNACK BAR

PASS THRU

DW

S

RANGE

REFG

DN

CURB

BEDROOM 11⁴ x 11⁰

DESK

BEDROOM 11⁴ x 11⁴

UP

COVERED PORCH

GARAGE 21⁴ x 21⁴

76'-4"

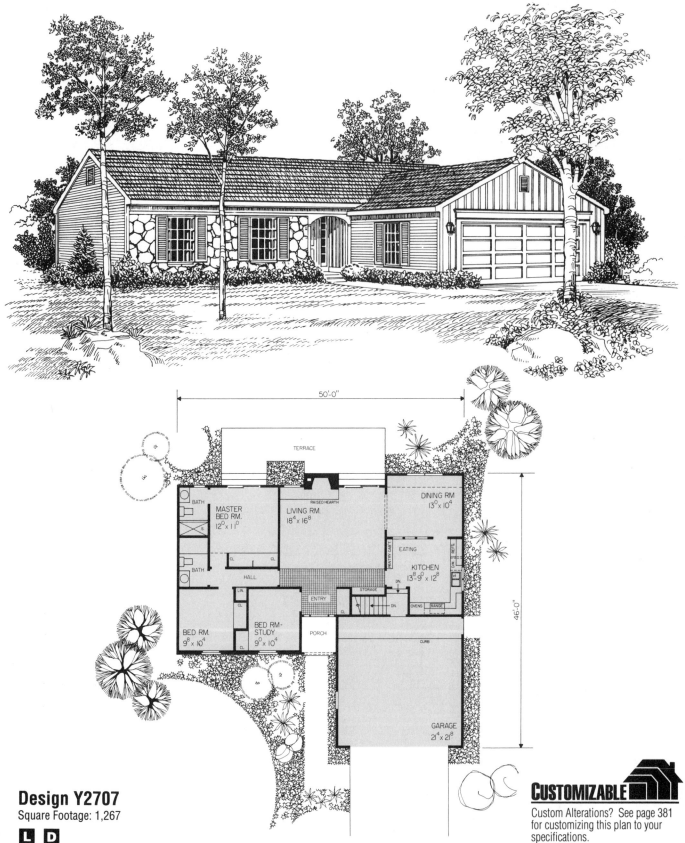

Design Y2707
Square Footage: 1,267

L **D**

● Here is a charming Early American adaptation that will serve as a picturesque and practical retirement home. Also, it will serve admirably those with a small family in search of an efficient, economically built home. The living area, highlighted by the raised hearth fireplace, is spacious. The kitchen features eating space and easy access to the garage and basement. The dining room is adjacent to the kitchen and views the rear yard. Then, there is the basement for recreation and hobby pursuits. The bedroom wing offers three bedrooms and two full baths. Don't miss the sliding doors to the terrace from the living room and the master bedroom. Storage units are plentiful including a pantry cabinet in the eating area of the kitchen. This plan will be efficient and livable.

CUSTOMIZABLE
Custom Alterations? See page 381 for customizing this plan to your specifications.

Design Y3355
Square Footage: 1,387

● Though it's only just under 1,400 total square feet, this plan offers three bedrooms (or two with study) and a sizable gathering room with fireplace and sloped ceiling. The galley kitchen provides a pass-through snack bar and has a planning desk and attached breakfast room. Besides two smaller bedrooms with a full bath, there's an extravagant master suite with large dressing area, double vanity and raised whirlpool tub. The full-length terrace to the rear of the house extends the living potential to the outdoors.

CUSTOMIZABLE

Custom Alterations? See page 381 for customizing this plan to your specifications.

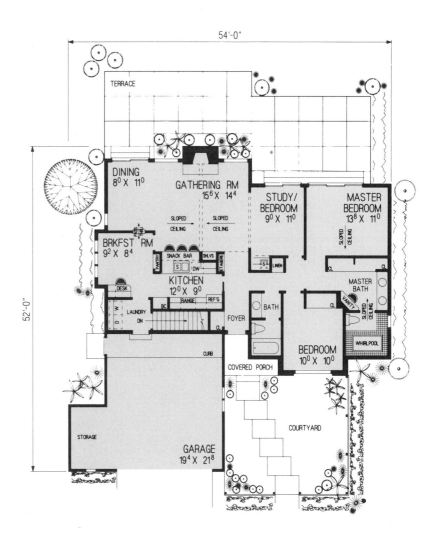

Design Y3373
Square Footage: 1,376

L **D**

● This charming Greek Revival plan packs a lot of livability into a compact frame. The interior contains a large living room/dining room combination with a fireplace, a media room, a U-shaped kitchen with breakfast room and two bedrooms accompanied by two full baths. If the extra space is needed, the media room could serve as a third bedroom. Note the terrace off the dining room and the sloped ceilings throughout.

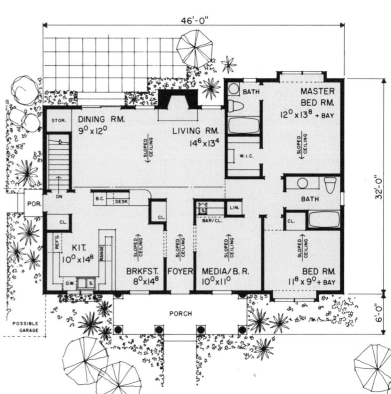

Design Y2565
Square Footage: 1,540

L **D**

● This modest-sized floor plan has much to offer in the way of livability. It may function as either a two- or three-bedroom home. The living room is huge and features a beamed ceiling and a raised-hearth fireplace. The open stairway to the basement is handy and will lead to what may be developed as the recreation area. In addition to the two full baths, there is an extra wash room. Adjacent is the laundry room and service entrance from the garage.

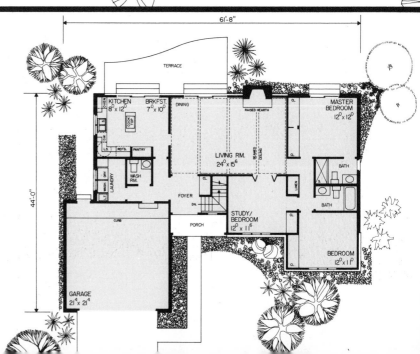

Design Y2505
Square Footage: 1,366

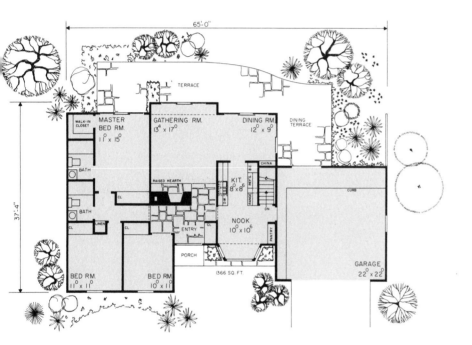

● This traditional home offers a wealth of features in less than 1,400 square feet—an excellent return on your construction dollar. A galley kitchen is accompanied by two eating areas, one for formal occasions, the other for sunny breakfasts. The gathering room features a raised-hearth fireplace. Make a note of the storage potential, particularly the linen closet, pantry, china cabinet and broom closet. The basement may be developed for recreational activities.

CUSTOMIZABLE

Custom Alterations? See page 381 for customizing this plan to your specifications.

Design Y3350
Square Footage: 1,777

L **D**

● Though smaller in size, this traditional one-story provides a family-oriented floor plan that leaves nothing out. Besides the formal living room (or study if you prefer) and dining room, there's a gathering room with fireplace, snack bar, and sliding glass doors to the rear terrace. The U-shaped kitchen is in close proximity to the handy utility area just off the garage. Of particular note is the grand master bedroom with garden whirlpool tub, walk-in closet and private terrace. The sleeping area is completed with two family bedrooms to the front.

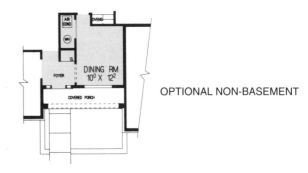

OPTIONAL NON-BASEMENT

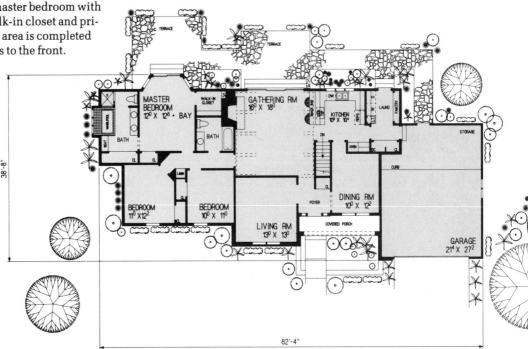

Traditional Adaptations

1½-Story Houses in America date back to the 17th-Century dwellings of Cape Cod. The houses on the following pages offer much variety in size, shape and functionality. Their facades reflect a wide and interesting use of varying exterior materials. Compare, for instance, both the exterior and interior features of Designs Y3372 and Y3378. Each has much to recommend it to the growing active family.

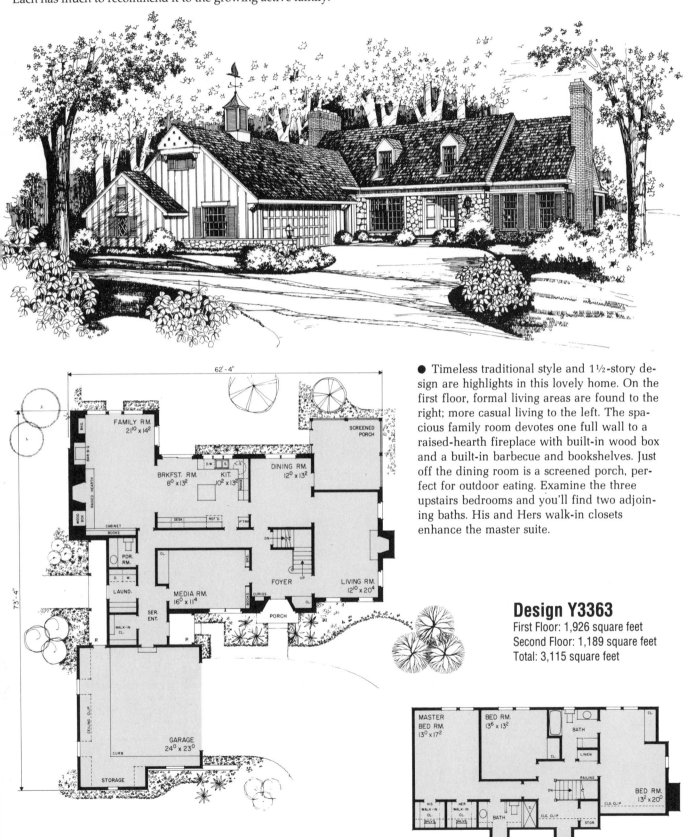

● Timeless traditional style and 1½-story design are highlights in this lovely home. On the first floor, formal living areas are found to the right; more casual living to the left. The spacious family room devotes one full wall to a raised-hearth fireplace with built-in wood box and a built-in barbecue and bookshelves. Just off the dining room is a screened porch, perfect for outdoor eating. Examine the three upstairs bedrooms and you'll find two adjoining baths. His and Hers walk-in closets enhance the master suite.

Design Y3363

First Floor: 1,926 square feet
Second Floor: 1,189 square feet
Total: 3,115 square feet

Design Y3353

First Floor: 2,191 square feet
Second Floor: 874 square feet
Total: 3,065 square feet

L **D**

● The facade of this 1½-story Southern Colonial with its clapboards, pediment and covered portico propped up by four columns recalls the 1820s. A bay window protrudes from the country kitchen to the front of the home. Modern window treatment enhances the rear elevation and provides the home with natural light. A wide rear terrace provides room for entertaining out-of-doors. Two chimneys rise impressively above the varying roof planes.

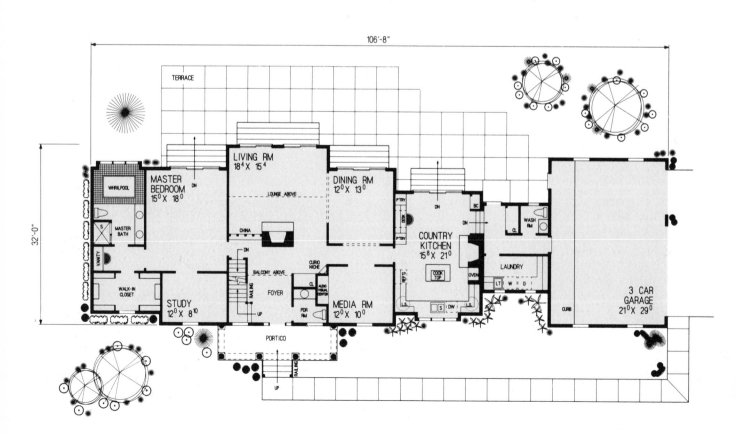

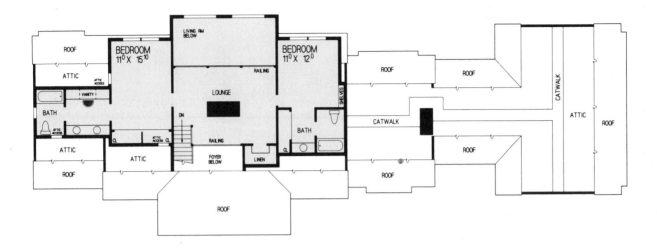

The central foyer ascends to the second story. A convenient powder room, closet, curio niche and stairwells to the second floor and basement are located here. Straight ahead, the large living room includes a central fireplace and a china cabinet. Open to the living room is the formal dining room. Notice the five sets of sliding glass doors that lead from each rear room to the terrace—a great place for entertaining on cool evenings or dining al fresco. The modern media room features a built-in audio/visual center. A country kitchen with fireplace, two Lazy Susans and an island cooktop offers casual living or dining space and a helpful planning desk. Two steps down from the kitchen is the utility area with closet, wash room and laundry area. The entrance to the attached three-car garage is located here. The master suite is also conveniently located on the first floor and has a lavish master bath with whirlpool spa, shower, dual lavatories, a separate vanity area and a gigantic walk-in closet. A private study or exercise room adjoins the master bedroom. Upstairs are two large family bedrooms, each with its own full bath, dressing area and a central lounge overlooking the living room and foyer. Note the linen closet and attic access.

Design Y3343 First Floor: 1,953 square feet
Second Floor: 895 square feet; Total: 2,848 square feet

● Beyond the simple traditional styling of this home's exterior are many of the amenities required by today's lifestyles. Among them: a huge country kitchen with fireplace, an attached greenhouse/dining area, a media room off the two-story foyer, split-bedroom planning, and a second-floor lounge. There are three bedrooms upstairs, which share a full bath.

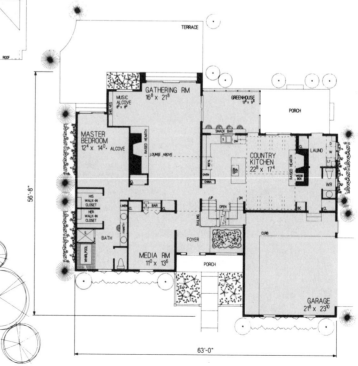

Design Y3372

First Floor: 1,259 square feet
Second Floor: 942 square feet
Total: 2,201 square feet

L **D**

● Charm is the key word for this delightful plan's exterior, but don't miss the great floor plan inside. The formal living room with its sloped ceiling and bay window and the formal dining room flank the entry foyer to the front. The large family room with fireplace and the breakfast room with sunlit bay both feature beamed ceilings. Sliding glass doors in the family room lead to a rear terrace. The kitchen and service areas function well together and are near the garage and service entrance for convenience. Upstairs are the sleeping accommodations: two family bedrooms and a master suite of nice proportion with a pampering bath.

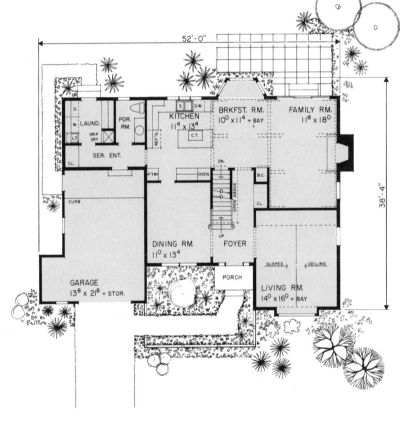

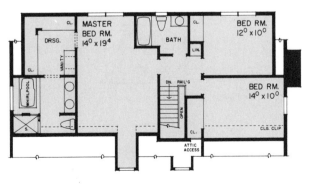

Design Y3351

First Floor: 1,794 square feet
Second Floor: 887 square feet
Total: 2,681 square feet

L D

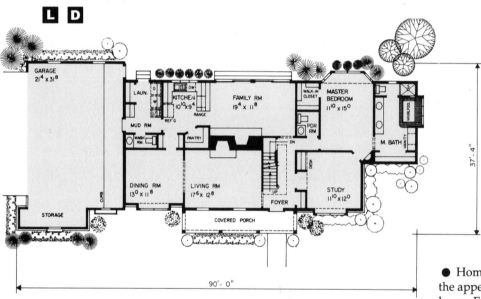

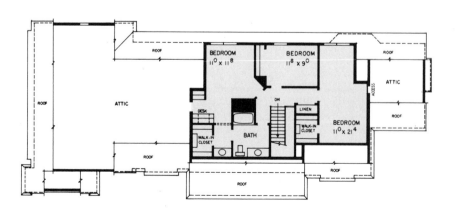

● Home-grown comfort is the key to the appeal of this traditionally styled home. From the kitchen with attached family room to the living room with fireplace and attached formal dining room, this plan has it all. Notice the first-floor master bedroom with whirlpool tub and adjacent study. A nearby powder room turns the study into a convenient guest room. On the second floor are three more bedrooms with ample closet space and a full bath. The two-car garage has a large storage area.

Design Y3334

First Floor: 2,193 square feet
Second Floor: 831 square feet
Total: 3,024 square feet

● A traditional favorite, this home combines classic style with progressive floor planning. Four bedrooms are split — master suite and one bedroom on the first floor, two more bedrooms upstairs. The second-floor lounge overlooks a large, sunken gathering room near the formal dining area. A handy butler's pantry connects the dining room and kitchen.

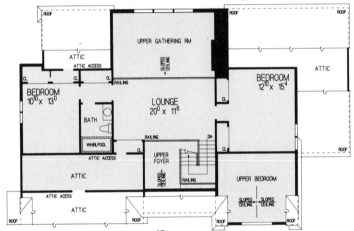

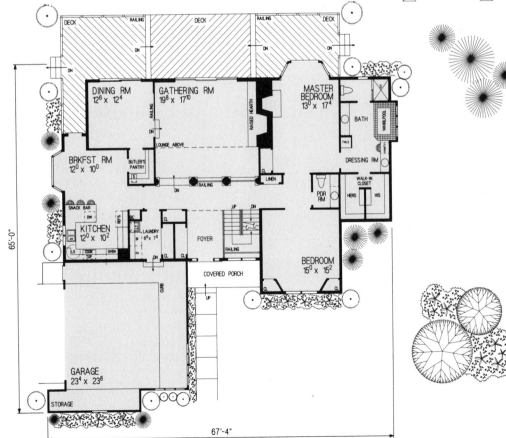

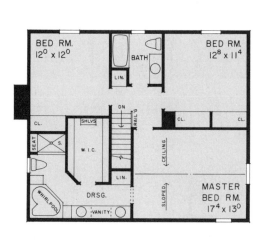

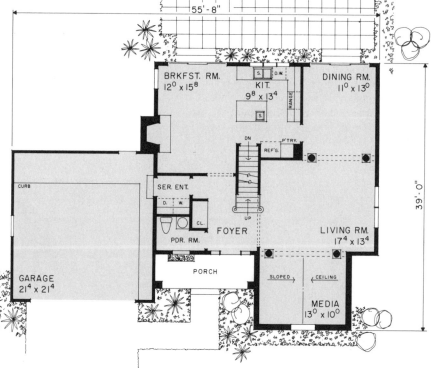

Design Y3564

First Floor: 1,113 square feet
Second Floor: 928 square feet
Total: 2,041 square feet

L **D**

● A quaint traditional exterior conceals a modern and elegantly designed floor plan. As you enter through the foyer, formal living areas to the right of the home include a media room with sloped ceiling, an expansive living room and a dining room with outdoor access. These formal areas maintain an open feeling yet are distinctly separated by columns. The rear kitchen is open to a large breakfast room with a fireplace and sliding glass doors to a terrace. Note the first-floor laundry area and convenient powder room. On the second floor, a generous-sized master bedroom with sloped ceiling comes complete with a well-planned bath featuring a whirlpool tub, dual lavatories, linen storage and a walk-in closet. Two family bedrooms share a full bath. The basement provides room for expansion.

Design Y3550 First Floor: 2,328 square feet
Second Floor: 712 square feet; Total: 3,040 square feet

L

● A transitional 1½-story home combines the best of contemporary and traditional elements. This one uses vertical wood siding, stone and multi-lite windows to beautiful advantage. The floor plan makes great use of space with elegant first-floor living and dining areas and a luxurious first-floor master suite. Socializing with the cook is easily accomplished with a 20-foot conversation area adjoining the kitchen. A media room to the front of the home features a built-in cabinet for audio and video equipment. Two secondary bedrooms, a full bath and an open lounge area are found on the second floor. The garage is accessed from the island kitchen through the laundry area.

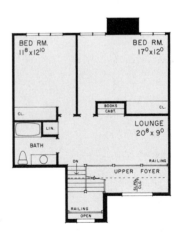

Design Y3378

First Floor: 2,997 square feet
Second Floor: 1,415 square feet
Total: 4,412 square feet

L **D**

● This large traditional home fits right in whether built in the busy city or a secluded rural area. Living areas on the first floor include a media room with bay window, gathering room with raised-hearth fireplace and a formal dining room. The kitchen area supplies room enough for a crowd with a snack bar and a 17-foot breakfast room with terrace access. A convenient first-floor master suite also includes terrace access, along with a sitting room and a dressing and bath area fit for a king. Two bedrooms and two full baths on the second floor are joined by a lounge and spacious bonus room. Note the three-car garage.

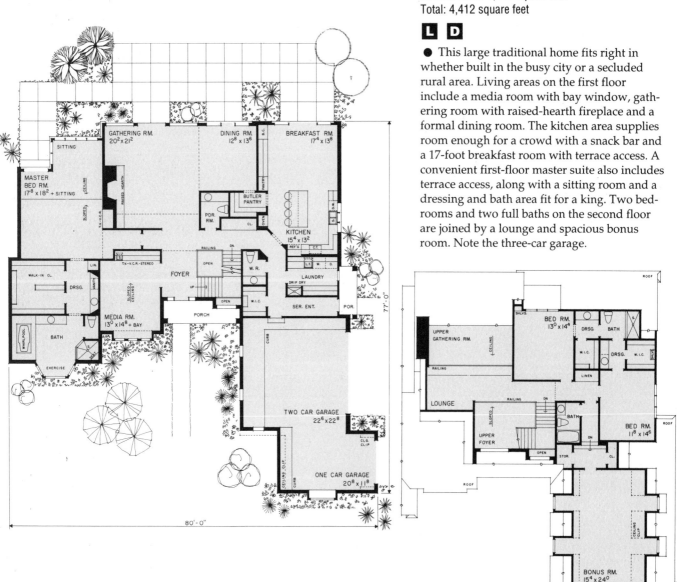

Traditional Adaptations

Two-Story Houses were the predominant structures of Colonial America. While the addition of various dependencies was common, the main portion of the house was rectangular. The 20th Century has seen the proliferation of houses whose style may be characterized as Colonial Revival. Unlike their forebears, they are asymmetrical. However, when one considers the various elements of their architectural detailing, there can be little doubt about their origins. Here is a selection of traditional adaptations reflecting today's tastes and livability.

Design Y3365 First Floor: 1,731 square feet
Second Floor: 1,248 square feet; Total: 2,979 square feet

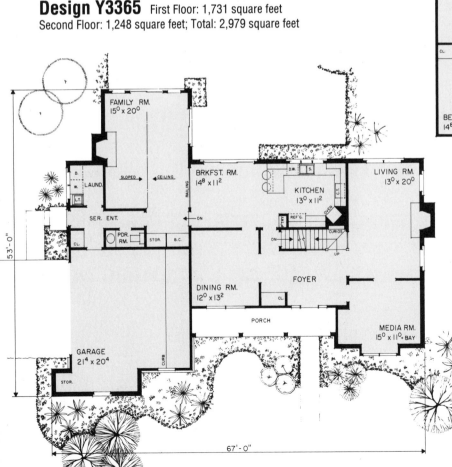

● One of the most popular home renditions is the two-story four-bedroom, and few designs of this type offer as much as the one shown here. The gracious entry opens to the right to a media room and to a living room with fireplace. On the left is a formal dining room. At the back, find the kitchen with attached breakfast room and just a step down is everyone's favorite family room. All four bedrooms are located on the second floor. The master suite features a double-size walk-in closet and bumped-out window in the bath. Three family bedrooms share a full bath.

Design Y3381

First Floor: 2,485 square feet
Second Floor: 1,864 square feet
Total: 4,349 square feet

L **D**

● A place for everything and everything in its place. If that's your motto, this is your house. A central foyer allows access to every part of the home. To the left sits the spacious gathering room with fireplace and music alcove. Straight ahead, the open living and dining rooms offer sweeping views of the back yard. The modern kitchen and conversation area are situated to the right of the home. Near the entrance, a library with bay window and built-in bookcase is found. Look for extra amenities throughout the home: curio cabinets in the foyer, stairwell, conversation area and hall; built-in desk; walk-in closet and a second fireplace. Upstairs, the master suite features an enormous walk-in closet and a pampering bath. Another bedroom has a private bath, while the remaining two bedrooms share a bath with dual lavs.

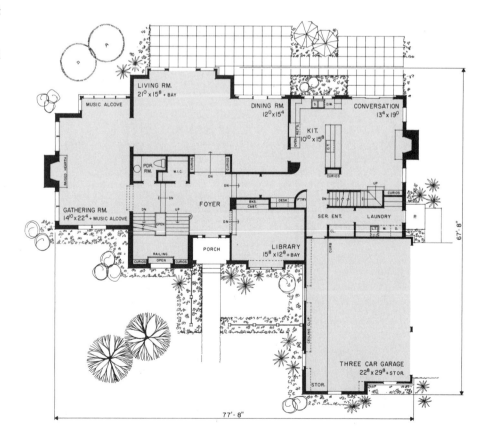

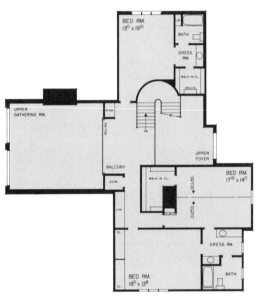

Design Y3367

First Floor: 3,634 square feet
Second Floor: 1,450 square feet
Total: 5,084 square feet

● This may be the perfect plan for you if your proposed building site is narrow but quite deep. Notice that the entire width of the home is only 64', while the depth is over 100'. The floor plan loses nothing to this unusual scheme. First-floor living areas include a two-story gathering room, more casual keeping room (note fireplaces in both rooms), media room (another fireplace!), dining room with bow window, and kitchen with butler's pantry. The handy service entrance off the garage has a huge walk-in closet, washroom, and laundry area. The master bedroom on this level has a sloped ceiling and His and Hers walk-ins. Three family bedrooms are upstairs. One of these has its own private bath; the other two share a full bath.

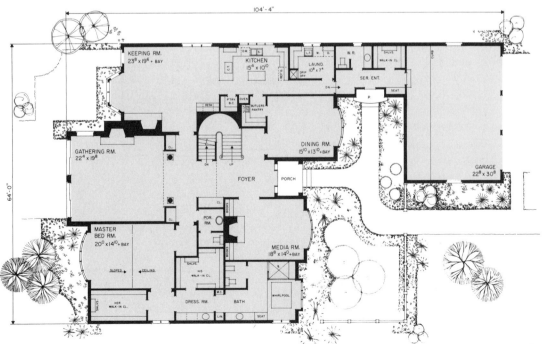

Design Y3552

First Floor: 1,784 square feet
Second Floor: 1,192 square feet
Total: 2,976 square feet

L **D**

● Smart exterior features mark this home as a classic: second-story pop-outs with half-round windows above multi-lite windows, charming lintels and a combination of horizontal wood siding and brick. Inside are living areas designed on a grand scale. The foyer is flanked by the formal dining room and the living room with breathtaking central fireplace and outdoor access. An informal breakfast room with snack bar provides access to a solarium. To the rear is the large family room with bay window, built-in bookshelves with cabinets below and a second fireplace. Sleeping areas on the second floor include a master suite, two family bedrooms and a sitting room or nursery. A three-car garage provides all the space necessary for the family vehicles and additional paraphernalia.

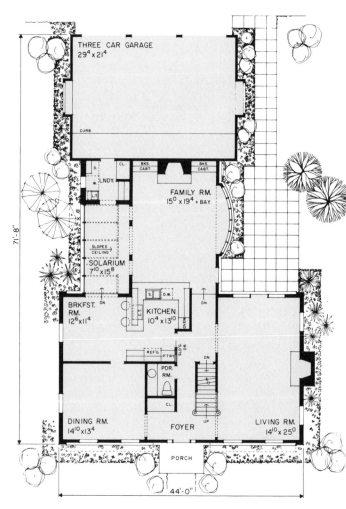

Design Y3356

First Floor: 1,610 square feet
Second Floor: 1,200 square feet
Total: 2,810 square feet

L **D**

● Traditionally speaking, this home takes first place. Its sunken family room has a raised-hearth fireplace and sliding glass doors to a covered porch for outdoor dining. The living room also has a fireplace and is open to the boxed-windowed dining room. The kitchen features an island cooktop and a breakfast area with a pantry and outdoor access. A large clutter room off the garage could be turned into a hobby or sewing room. Note the two first-floor powder rooms. Four bedrooms on the second floor include a master suite with His and Hers walk-in closets and three family bedrooms.

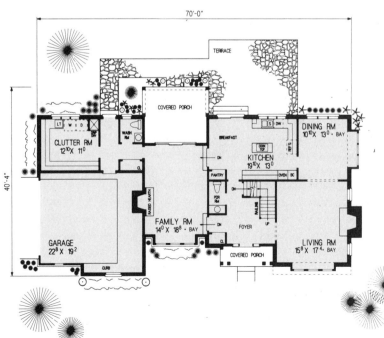

Design Y3555

First Floor: 1,930 square feet
Second Floor: 1,676 square feet
Total: 3,606 square feet

L **D**

● Round-top windows add elegance to the interior and exterior of this traditional home. Large gathering areas on the first floor flow together for ease in entertaining. The sunken gathering room stretches from the front of the house to the back, with a terrace at each end and a fireplace in the middle. Another fireplace is found in the conversation area adjoining the kitchen. The formal dining room features a bay window and elegant columns. A media room is located at the front of the house with the kitchen with snack bar and the convenient powder room close by. Sleeping areas upstairs include a master bedroom with spacious bath and walk-in closet, three family bedrooms and two full baths. The garage has space for three cars.

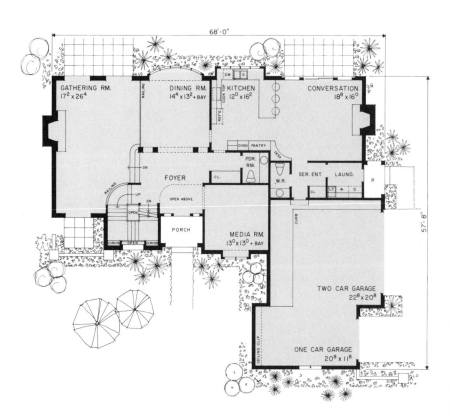

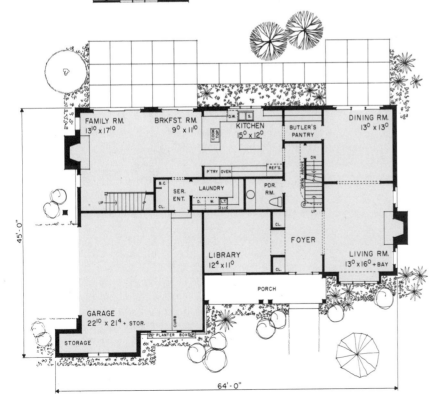

Design Y3551

First Floor: 1,575 square feet
Second Floor: 1,501 square feet
Total: 3,076 square feet

L **D**

● Efficient floor planning provides a spacious, yet economical home. The large kitchen adjoins a two-story breakfast/family room combination with fireplace. A butler's pantry connects the kitchen to the formal dining room with terrace access. A second fireplace is found in the formal living room. Also on the first floor: a library and convenient powder room. The master bedroom with sloped ceiling includes His and Hers walk-in closets and a grand bath with whirlpool tub. The bedroom next door would make a fine nursery or office. Two additional bedrooms share a full bath. A large bonus room over the garage offers many optional uses.

Design Y3553

First Floor: 2,471 square feet
Second Floor: 1,071 square feet
Total: 3,542 square feet

BED RM.
18⁴ x 12⁰

CL.

BED RM.
15⁰ x 12⁰

CL.

BATH

DN.

UPPER FOYER

BATH

W.I.C.

SHLVS.

LIN.

LINEN

SLOPED CEILING

LEDGE

CL.

BED RM.
18⁴ x 12⁰

CL.

● Delightful Colonial design makes a fine statement for two-story living. The bay windows, columned front porch and charming dormers are big attractions on the exterior. Inside, a wide entry foyer directs traffic to the left to living areas and to the right to a cozy study and the master bedroom suite. Highlights in the master suite include the bay window, sloped ceiling, humongous His

and Hers walk-in closets, dual lavatories and a well-planned bath with whirlpool tub and shower. The family room and living room to either side of the formal dining room both have fireplaces. The L-shaped kitchen is enhanced by an island cooktop, a walk-in pantry and a breakfast room with sliding glass doors to the rear porch. Upstairs are three spacious bedrooms and two full baths.

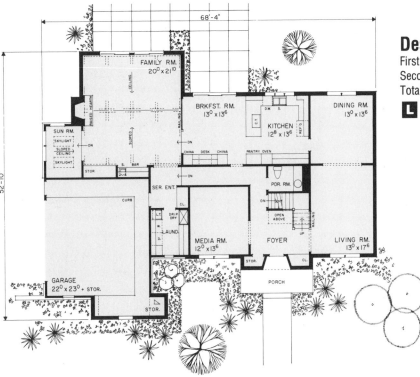

68'-4"

52'-10"

FAMILY RM.
20⁰ x 21¹⁰

SUN RM.

BRKFST. RM.
13⁰ x 13⁶

KITCHEN
12⁸ x 13⁶

DINING RM.
13⁰ x 13⁶

CHINA DESK CHINA

PANTRY OVEN

PDR. RM.

SER. ENT.

MEDIA RM.
12⁰ x 13⁶

FOYER

LIVING RM.
13⁰ x 17⁶

LAUND.

OPEN ABOVE

UP

GARAGE
22⁰ x 23⁰ + STOR.

STOR.

PORCH

Design Y3370

First Floor: 2,055 square feet
Second Floor: 1,288 square feet
Total: 3,343 square feet

BED RM.
12⁰ x 13⁶

BED RM.
12⁰ x 11⁴

WHIRLPOOL

BATH

WALK-IN CL.

LINEN

RAILING

BED RM.
12⁰ x 13⁶

OPEN

BATH

MASTER
BED RM.
13⁴ x 17⁴

● The combination of stone and brick creates an impressive facade on this traditional two-story. The symmetrically designed interior will provide efficient traffic patterns. Note the formal living and dining areas to the right. To the left of the foyer is a media room. A huge family room to the rear features a raised-hearth fireplace, an attached sun room, storage, a wet bar and terrace access. The U-shaped kitchen has an attached breakfast room and several built-ins. The second floor offers four bedrooms including a master suite with walk-in closet, double vanity and whirlpool tub.

Design Y3567

First floor: 1,778 square feet
Second floor: 1,663 square feet
Bonus room: 442 square feet
Total: 3,883 square feet

L **D**

● Spring breezes and summer nights will be a joy to take in on the verandas and balcony of this gorgeous Southern Colonial. Or, if you prefer, sit back and enjoy a good book in the library, or invite an old friend over for a chat in the conversation room. The first floor also includes formal dining and living rooms, a service entry with laundry and a three-car garage. You'll find a bonus room over the garage; you may decide to turn it into a media room or an exercise room. The master bedroom sports a fireplace, two walk-in closets, a double-bowl vanity, a shower and a whirlpool tub. Three other bedrooms occupy the second floor; one has its own full bath. Of course, the balcony is just a step away.

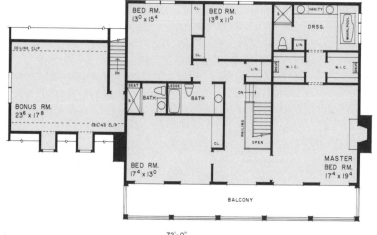

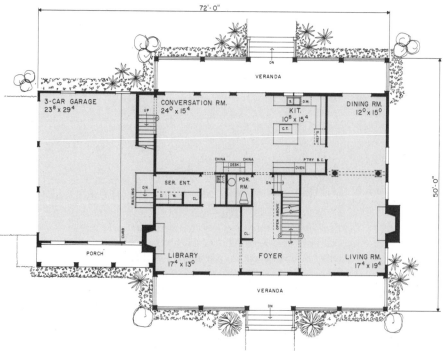

Design Y3558 First Floor: 2,328 square feet; Second Floor: 603 square feet; Total: 2,931 square feet

L **D**

● This home will keep even the most active family from feeling cramped. A broad foyer opens to a living room that measures 24 feet across and features sliding glass doors to a rear terrace and a covered porch. Adjacent to the kitchen is a conversation area with additional access to the covered porch, a snack bar, fireplace and a window bay. A butler's pantry leads to the formal dining room. Placed conveniently on the first floor, the master suite features a roomy bath with a huge walk-in closet and dual vanities. Two large bedrooms are found on the second floor.

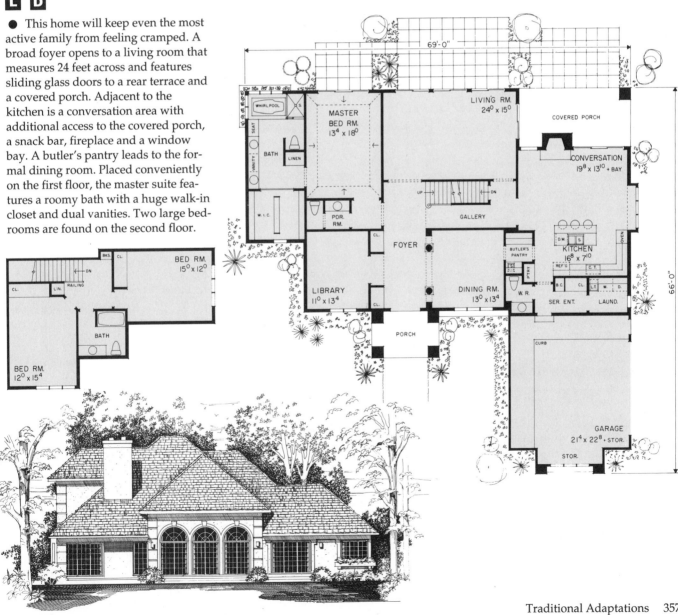

Design Y3366

Main Level: 1,638 square feet; Upper Level: 650 square feet
Lower Level: 934 square feet; Total: 3,222 square feet

L

● There is much more to this design than
meets the eye. While it may look like a 1½-story
plan, bonus recreation and hobby space in the
walk-out basement adds almost 1,000 square
feet. The first floor holds living and dining
areas as well as the master bedroom suite. Two
family bedrooms on the second floor are connected by a balcony area that overlooks the
gathering room below. Notice the covered
porch beyond the breakfast and dining rooms.

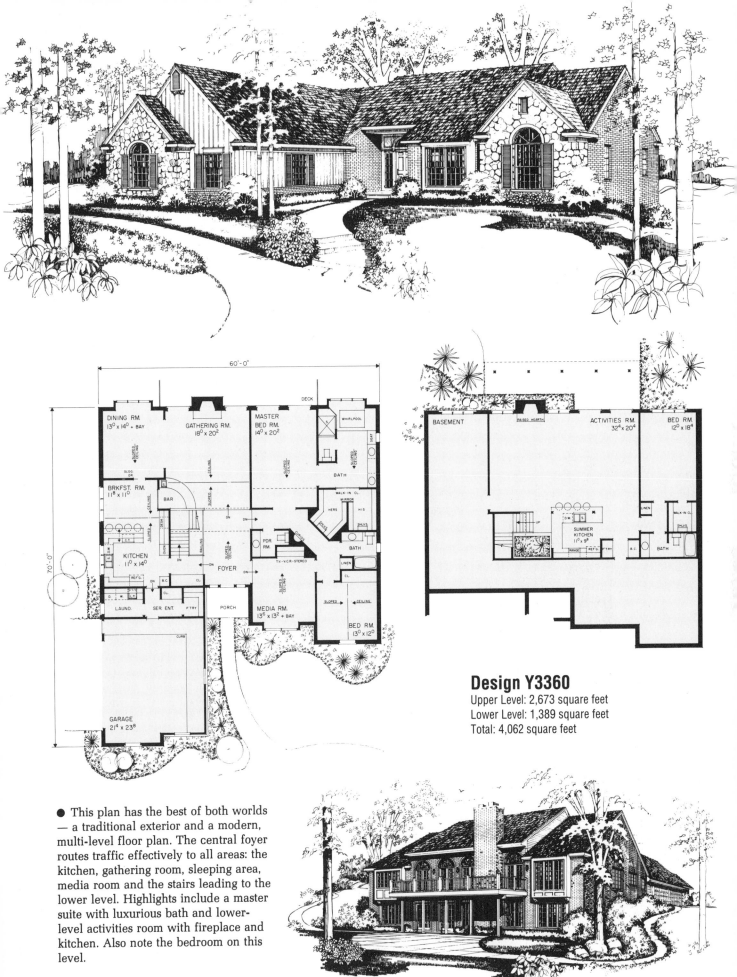

DINING RM.
13⁰ x 14⁰ + BAY

GATHERING RM.
18⁰ x 20²

MASTER BED RM.
14⁰ x 20²

DECK

WHIRLPOOL

60'-0"

SLOPED CEILING

SLOPED CEILING

BATH

BRKFST. RM.
11⁸ x 11⁰

BAR

CEILING

SLOPED

WALK-IN CL.

MIRROR

HERS   HIS

SHLVS.

BATH

70'-0"

OVEN

KITCHEN
11⁰ x 14⁰

DN   DN

SLOPED CEILING

FOYER

PDR. RM.

CLOSET

T.V.-V.C.R.-STEREO

LINEN

CL.

BATH

REF'G.   B.C.   CL.

CL.

D.   W.

LAUND.   SER. ENT.   P'TRY   PORCH

MEDIA RM.
13⁶ x 13² + BAY

SLOPED   CEILING

BED RM.
13⁰ x 12⁰

CURB

GARAGE
21⁴ x 23⁸

BASEMENT

RAISED HEARTH

ACTIVITIES RM.
32⁴ x 20⁴

BED RM.
12⁰ x 18⁴

LINEN

WALK-IN CL.

UP

SUMMER KITCHEN
11⁰ x 9⁸

SHLVS.

RANGE   REF'G.   P'TRY   B.C.   BATH

Design Y3360
Upper Level: 2,673 square feet
Lower Level: 1,389 square feet
Total: 4,062 square feet

● This plan has the best of both worlds — a traditional exterior and a modern, multi-level floor plan. The central foyer routes traffic effectively to all areas: the kitchen, gathering room, sleeping area, media room and the stairs leading to the lower level. Highlights include a master suite with luxurious bath and lower-level activities room with fireplace and kitchen. Also note the bedroom on this level.

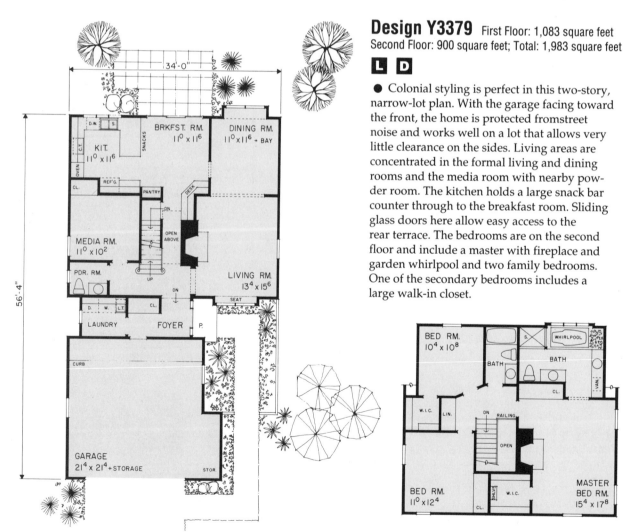

Design Y3379 First Floor: 1,083 square feet
Second Floor: 900 square feet; Total: 1,983 square feet

L **D**

● Colonial styling is perfect in this two-story, narrow-lot plan. With the garage facing toward the front, the home is protected from street noise and works well on a lot that allows very little clearance on the sides. Living areas are concentrated in the formal living and dining rooms and the media room with nearby powder room. The kitchen holds a large snack bar counter through to the breakfast room. Sliding glass doors here allow easy access to the rear terrace. The bedrooms are on the second floor and include a master with fireplace and garden whirlpool and two family bedrooms. One of the secondary bedrooms includes a large walk-in closet.

The Signature Series

The Signature Series is a unique series of designs that embodies an admirable assortment of amenities that signal luxury living at its finest. Appreciable features include interior balcony overlooks, unconventional shapes, dramatic styling and abundant space for elegant living and entertaining. Styles vary from Contemporary to the stately Tudor manor to the charming Victorian estate.

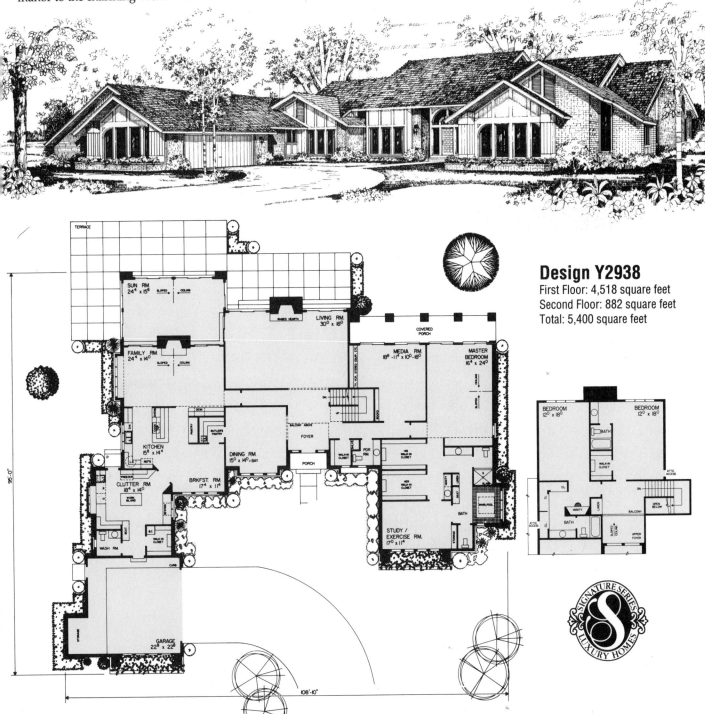

Design Y2938

First Floor: 4,518 square feet
Second Floor: 882 square feet
Total: 5,400 square feet

● A semi-circular fanlight and side-lights grace the entrance of this striking contemporary. The lofty foyer, with balcony above, leads to an elegant, two-story living room with fireplace. The family room, housing a second fireplace, leads to a glorious sunroom; both have dramatic sloped ceilings.

The kitchen and breakfast room are conveniently located for access to informal family room or to the formal dining room via the butler's pantry. The large adjoining clutter room with work island offers limitless possibilities for the seamstress, hobbyist, or indoor gardener. An executive-sized, first-

floor master suite offers privacy and relaxation; the bath with whirlpool tub and dressing area with twin walk-in closets open to a study that could double as an exercise room. Two second-floor bedrooms with private baths and walk-in closets round out the livability in this gracious home.

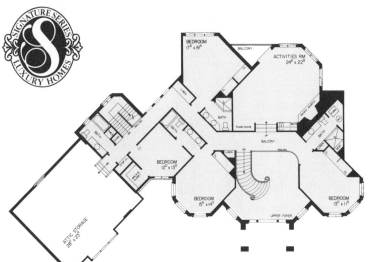

Design Y2968

First Floor: 3,736 square feet
Second Floor: 2,264 square feet
Total: 6,000 square feet

● The distinctive covered entry to this stunning manor, flanked by twin turrets, leads to a gracious foyer with impressive fan lights. The plan opens from the foyer to a formal dining room, master study and step-down gathering room. The spacious kitchen has numerous amenities including an island workstation and built-in desk. The adjacent morning room and gathering room with wet bar and raised-hearth fireplace are bathed in light and open to the terrace for outdoor entertaining. The luxurious master suite has a wealth of amenities as well. The second floor features four bedrooms and an oversized activities room with fireplace and balcony. Unfinished attic space can be completed to your specifications.

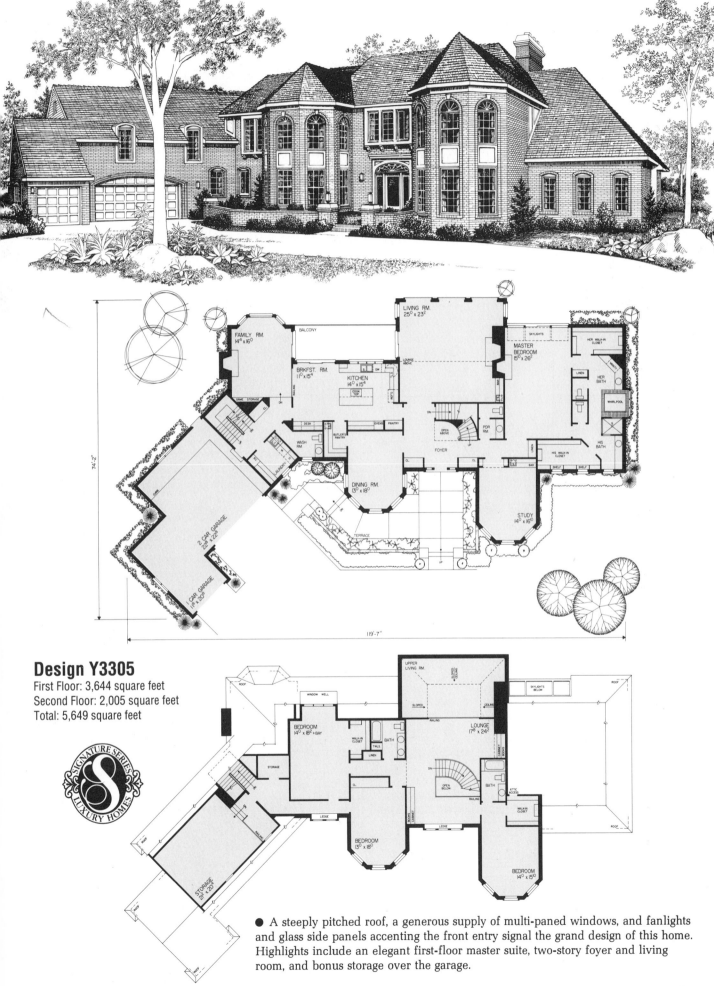

Design Y3305

First Floor: 3,644 square feet
Second Floor: 2,005 square feet
Total: 5,649 square feet

● A steeply pitched roof, a generous supply of multi-paned windows, and fanlights and glass side panels accenting the front entry signal the grand design of this home. Highlights include an elegant first-floor master suite, two-story foyer and living room, and bonus storage over the garage.

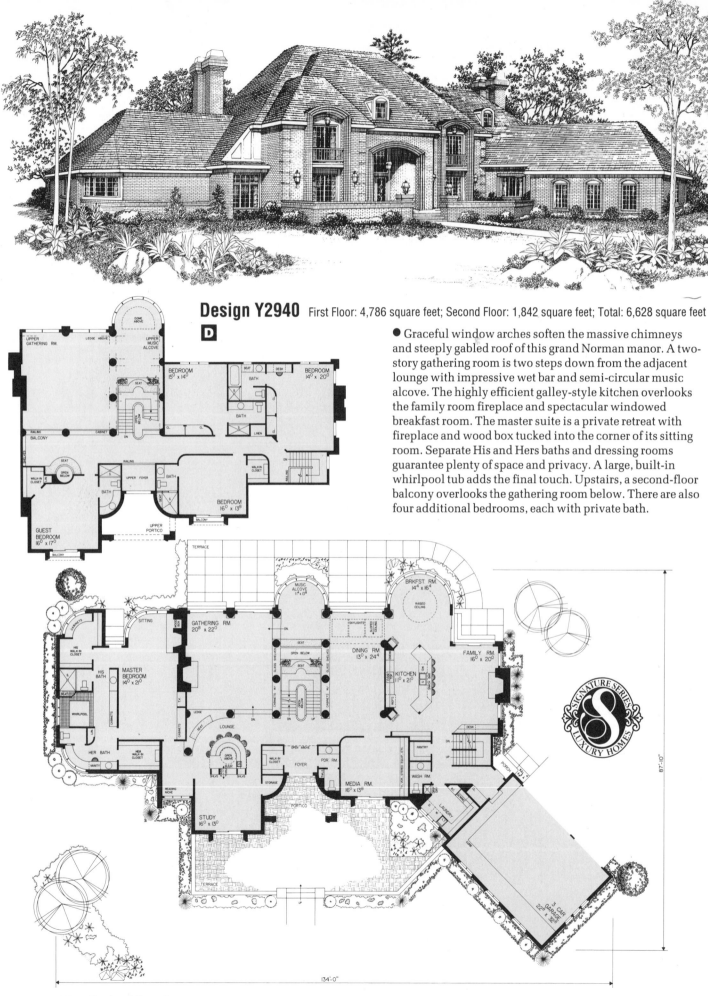

Design Y2940 First Floor: 4,786 square feet; Second Floor: 1,842 square feet; Total: 6,628 square feet

D

● Graceful window arches soften the massive chimneys and steeply gabled roof of this grand Norman manor. A two-story gathering room is two steps down from the adjacent lounge with impressive wet bar and semi-circular music alcove. The highly efficient galley-style kitchen overlooks the family room fireplace and spectacular windowed breakfast room. The master suite is a private retreat with fireplace and wood box tucked into the corner of its sitting room. Separate His and Hers baths and dressing rooms guarantee plenty of space and privacy. A large, built-in whirlpool tub adds the final touch. Upstairs, a second-floor balcony overlooks the gathering room below. There are also four additional bedrooms, each with private bath.

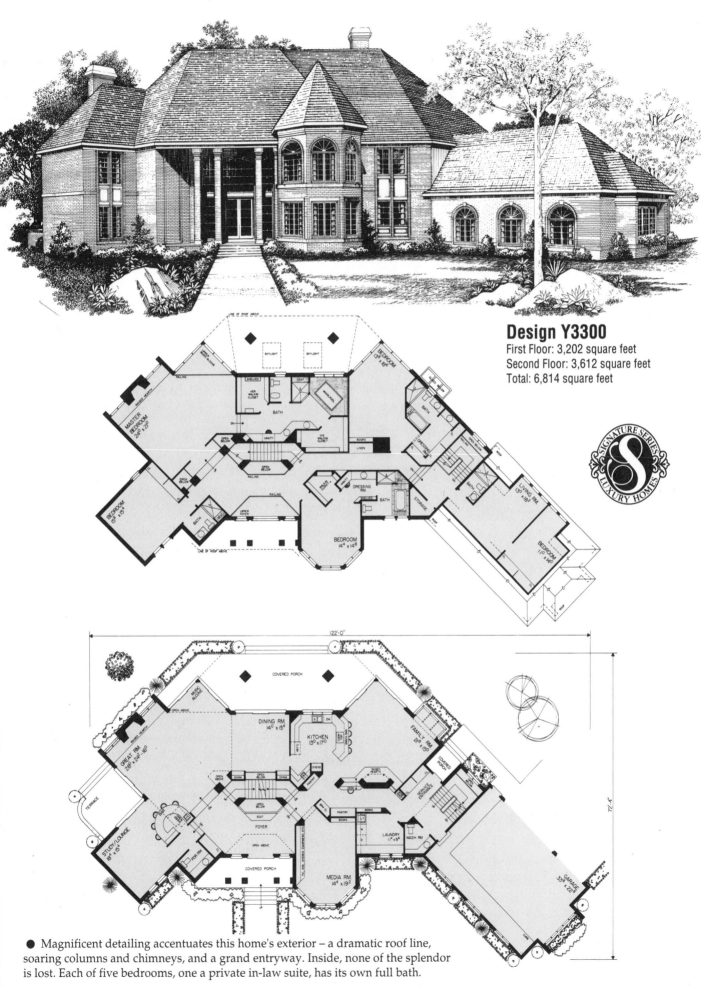

Design Y3300

First Floor: 3,202 square feet
Second Floor: 3,612 square feet
Total: 6,814 square feet

● Magnificent detailing accentuates this home's exterior – a dramatic roof line, soaring columns and chimneys, and a grand entryway. Inside, none of the splendor is lost. Each of five bedrooms, one a private in-law suite, has its own full bath.

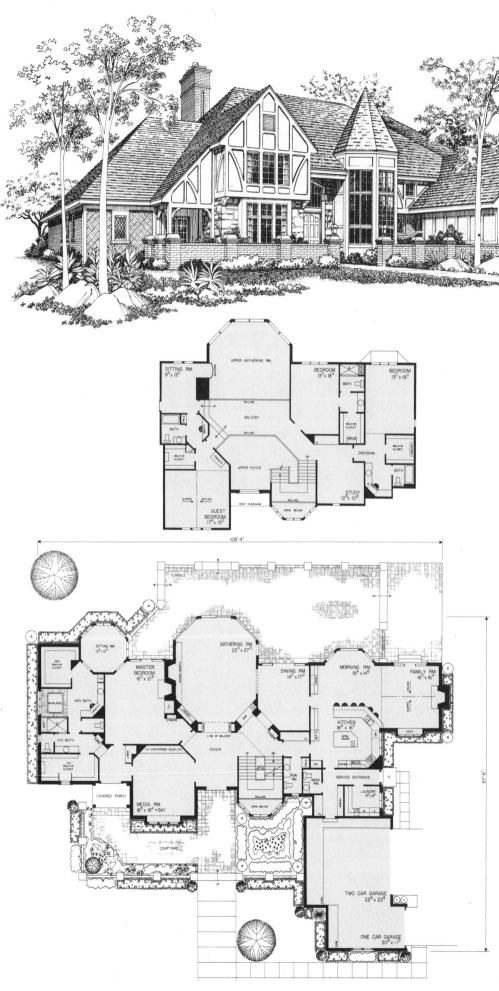

Design Y2951

First Floor: 4,195 square feet
Second Floor: 2,094 square feet
Total: 6,289 square feet

● A single prominent turret with two-story divided windows draws attention to this stately Tudor home. The open foyer allows an uninterrupted view into the impressive, two-story great room with wet bar, where a fireplace with raised hearth runs the entire length of one wall. The expansive kitchen, conveniently located near the service entrance, has a U-shaped work area and a snack bar that opens to the morning room. The adjacent sloped-ceiling family room has an additional fireplace and a comfortable window seat. A Victorian-inspired, octagon-shaped sitting room is tucked into the corner of the unique master bedroom. His and Hers baths and walk-in closets complete the impressive first-floor suite. Two bedrooms, a study, and a guest suite with private sitting room are located on the second floor. A magnificent second-floor bridge overlooks foyer and gathering room and provides extraordinary views to guests on the way to their bedroom.

Design Y2955 First Floor: 4,274 square feet
Second Floor: 3,008 square feet; Total: 7,282 square feet

● A circular staircase housed in the turret
makes an impressive opening statement
in the two-story foyer of this Tudor. Two
steps down lead to the elegant living room
with music alcove or the sumptuous
library with wet bar. The kitchen is a chef's
delight with work island, full cooking
counter and butler's pantry leading to a
formal dining room. The second floor features four bedrooms, two with fireplaces,
and each with private bath and abundant
closet space. The master has an additional
fireplace. Adjacent to the master bedroom
is a nursery that would make an ideal
exercise room.

Design Y3301

First Floor: 3,425 square feet
Second Floor: 2,501 square feet
Total: 5,926 square feet

● Masterful use of space with
a profusion of windows and
terrace access are all employed
in this Tudor treasure. A two-
story foyer points the way directly to the living room which
features a raised-hearth fireplace, huge bay window, and
curved bar. The angular
kitchen has a center island and
is strategically placed with relationship to the formal dining
room, the family room and its
gracious fireplace, and a captivating breakfast room. A media
room to the left of the foyer
provides built-in space for an
entertainment system. The
sloped-ceiling master bedroom
contains a third fireplace and
another gigantic bay window.
Its adjoining bath is divided
into His and Hers dressing
areas and closets, and centers
around a relaxing whirlpool
spa. Guests are easily accommodated in a full suite with its
own living room and bath on
the second floor. Three other
bedrooms and a lounge on this
floor share a balcony overlook
to the living room below.

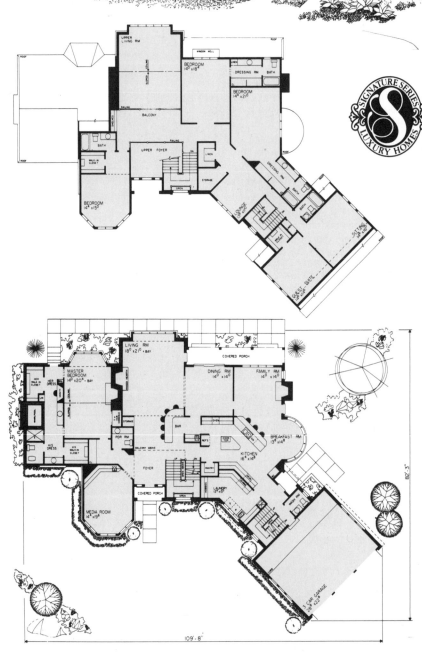

Design Y2957

First Floor: 2,557 square feet
Second Floor: 1,939 square feet
Total: 4,496 square feet

L **D**

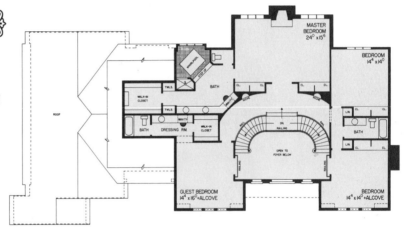

● The decorative half timbers and stone wall-cladding on this manor are stately examples of Tudor architecture. A grand double staircase is the highlight of the elegant, two-story foyer that opens to each of the main living areas. The living and gathering rooms are anchored by impressive central fireplaces. Handy built-ins, including a lazy susan and desk, and an island workstation with sink and cooktop, are convenient amenities in the kitchen. The adjacent breakfast room opens to the terrace for a sunny start to the day. Functioning with both the kitchen and the formal dining room is the butler's pantry. It has an abundance of cabinet and cupboard space and even a sink for a wet bar. Accessible from both the gathering and living rooms is the quiet study. If desired this could become a media center, sewing room or home office. The outstanding master suite features a cozy bedroom fireplace, picturesque whirlpool bath, and a convenient walk-in closet. Three additional second-floor bedrooms include a guest suite with dressing room and walk-in closet. Every part of this house speaks elegance, formality and the time-honored values for which Tudor is renowned.

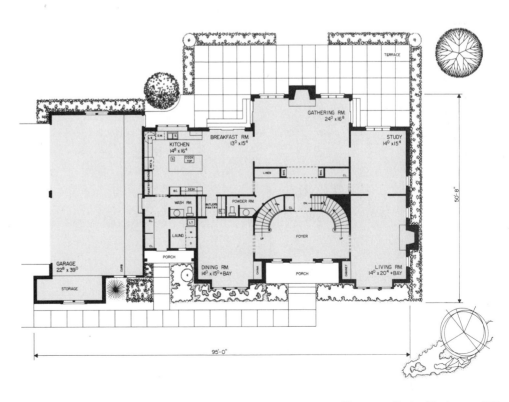

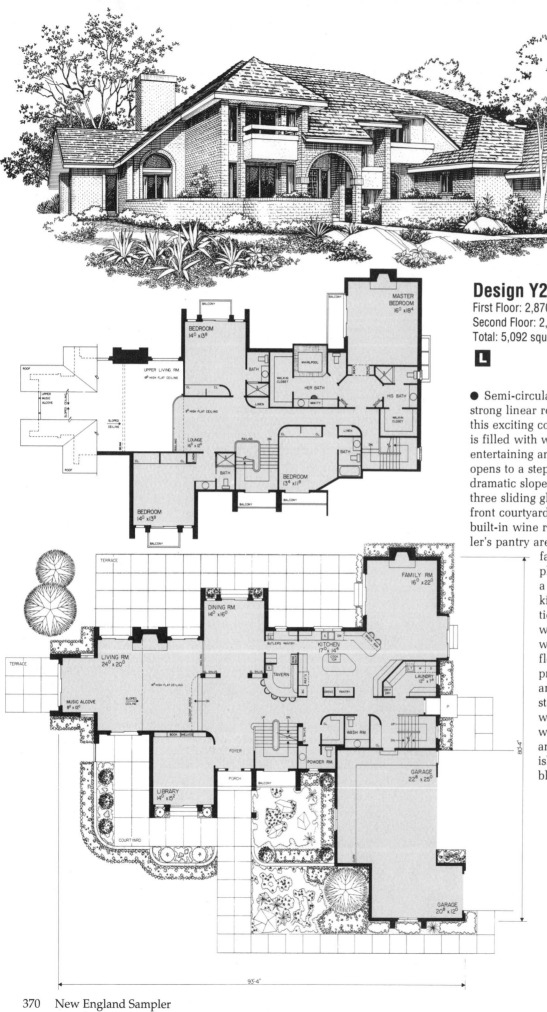

Design Y2952

First Floor: 2,870 square feet
Second Floor: 2,222 square feet
Total: 5,092 square feet

L

● Semi-circular arches complement the strong linear roof lines and balconies of this exciting contemporary. The first floor is filled with well-planned amenities for entertaining and relaxing. The foyer opens to a step-down living room with a dramatic sloped ceiling, fireplace, and three sliding glass doors that access the front courtyard and terrace. A tavern with built-in wine rack and an adjacent butler's pantry are ideal for entertaining. The family room features a fireplace, sliding glass door, and a handy snack bar. The kitchen allows meal preparation, cooking and storage within a step of the central work island. Three second-floor bedrooms, each with a private bath and balcony, are reached by either of two staircases. The master suite, with His and Hers baths and walk-in closets, whirlpool, and fireplace, adds the finishing touch to this memorable home.

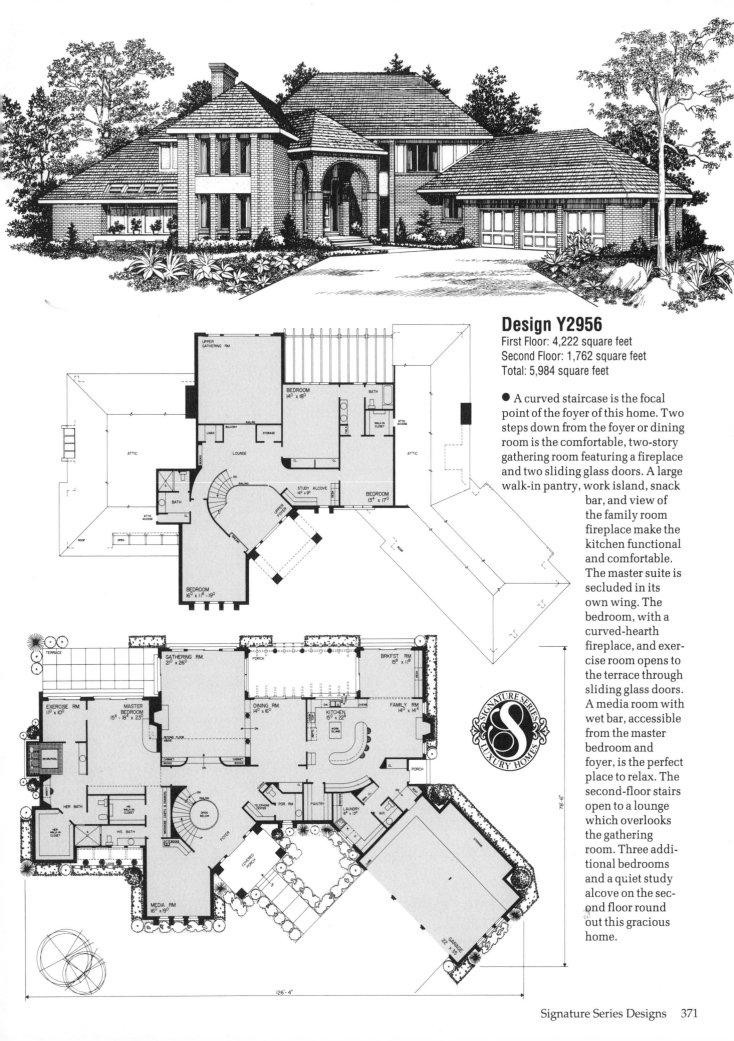

Design Y2956

First Floor: 4,222 square feet
Second Floor: 1,762 square feet
Total: 5,984 square feet

● A curved staircase is the focal point of the foyer of this home. Two steps down from the foyer or dining room is the comfortable, two-story gathering room featuring a fireplace and two sliding glass doors. A large walk-in pantry, work island, snack bar, and view of the family room fireplace make the kitchen functional and comfortable. The master suite is secluded in its own wing. The bedroom, with a curved-hearth fireplace, and exercise room opens to the terrace through sliding glass doors. A media room with wet bar, accessible from the master bedroom and foyer, is the perfect place to relax. The second-floor stairs open to a lounge which overlooks the gathering room. Three additional bedrooms and a quiet study alcove on the second floor round out this gracious home.

When You're Ready To Order . . .

Let Us Show You Our Home Blueprint Package.

Building a home? Planning a home? Our Blueprint Package contains nearly everything you need to get the job done right, whether you're working on your own or with help from an architect, designer, builder or subcontractors. Each Blueprint Package is the result of many hours of work by licensed architects or professional designers.

QUALITY

Hundreds of hours of painstaking effort have gone into the development of your blueprint set. Each home has been quality-checked by professionals to insure accuracy and buildability.

VALUE

Because we sell in volume, you can buy professional-quality blueprints at a fraction of their development cost. With our plans, your dream home design costs only a few hundred dollars, not the thousands of dollars that custom architects charge.

SERVICE

Once you've chosen your favorite home plan, you'll receive fast efficient service whether you choose to mail your order to us or call us toll free at 1-800-521-6797.

SATISFACTION

Our years of service to satisfied home plan buyers provide us the experience and knowledge that guarantee your satisfaction with our product and performance.

ORDER TOLL FREE 1-800-521-6797

After you've studied our Blueprint Package and Important Extras on the following pages, simply mail the accompanying order form on page 381 or call toll free on our Blueprint Hotline: 1-800-521-6797. We're ready and eager to serve you.

Each set of blueprints is an interrelated collection of floor plans, interior and exterior elevations, dimensions, cross-sections, diagrams and notations showing precisely how your house is to be constructed.

Here's what you get:

Frontal Sheet
This artist's sketch of the exterior of the house, done in realistic perspective, gives you an idea of how the house will look when built and landscaped. Large ink-line floor plans show all levels of the house and provide a quick overview of your new home's livability, as well as a handy reference for studying furniture placement.

Foundation Plan
Drawn to 1/4-inch scale, this sheet shows the complete foundation layout including support

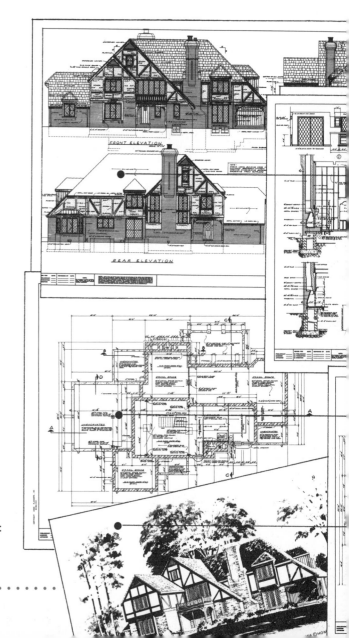

walls, excavated and unexcavated areas, if any, and foundation notes. If slab construction rather than basement, the plan shows footings and details for a monolithic slab. This page, or another in the set, also includes a sample plot plan for locating your house on a building site.

Detailed Floor Plans
Complete in 1/4-inch scale, these plans show the layout of each floor of the house. All rooms and interior spaces are carefully dimensioned and keys are provided for cross-section details given later in the plans. The positions of all electrical outlets and switches are clearly shown.

House Cross-Sections
Large-scale views, normally drawn at 3/8-inch equals 1 foot, show sections or cut-aways of the foundation, interior walls, exterior walls,

floors, stairways and roof details. Additional cross-sections are given to show important changes in floor, ceiling or roof heights or the relationship of one level to another. Extremely valuable for construction, these sections show exactly how the various parts of the house fit together.

Interior Elevations
These large-scale drawings show the design and placement of kitchen and bathroom cabinets, laundry areas, fireplaces, bookcases and other built-ins. Little "extras," such as mantelpiece and wainscoting drawings, plus moulding sections, provide details that give your home that custom touch.

Exterior Elevations
Drawings in 1/4-inch scale show the front, rear and sides of your house and give necessary notes on exterior materials and finishes. Particular attention is given to cornice detail, brick and stone accents or other finish items that make your home distinctive.

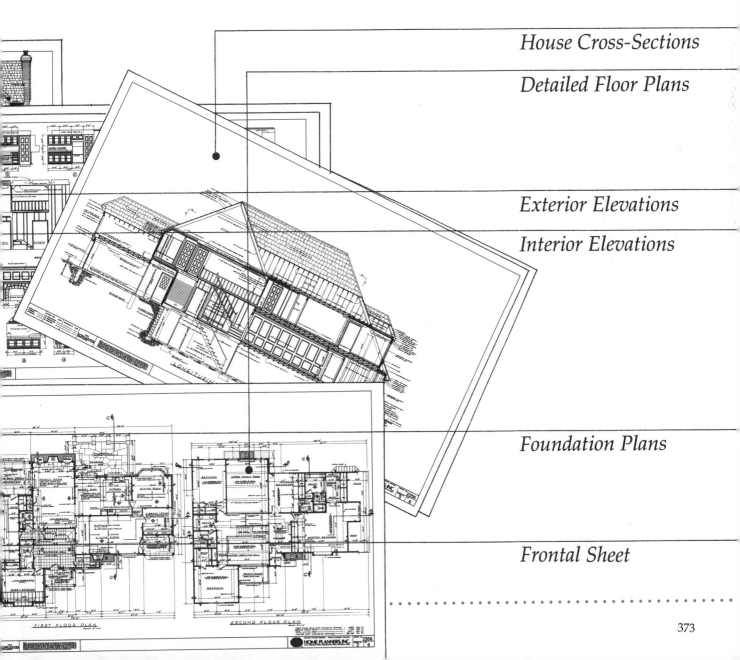

House Cross-Sections

Detailed Floor Plans

Exterior Elevations

Interior Elevations

Foundation Plans

Frontal Sheet

373

Important Extras To Do The Job Right!

Introducing seven important planning and construction aids developed by our professionals to help you succeed in your home-building project.

To Order, Call Toll Free 1-800-521-6797

To add these important extras to your Blueprint Package, simply indicate your choices on the order form on page 381 or call us Toll Free 1-800-521-6797 and we'll tell you more about these exciting products.

MATERIALS LIST

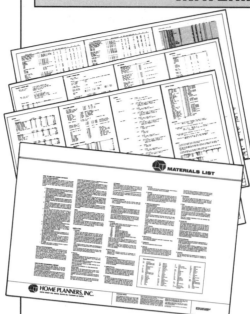

For many of the designs in our portfolio, we offer a customized materials take-off that is invaluable in planning and estimating the cost of your new home. This comprehensive list outlines the quantity, type and size of material needed to build your house (with the exception of mechanical system items). Included are:

- framing lumber
- roofing and sheet metal
- windows and doors
- exterior sheathing material and trim
- masonry, veneer and fireplace materials
- tile and flooring materials
- kitchen and bath cabinetry
- interior drywall and trim
- rough and finish hardware
- many more items

(Note: Because of differing local codes, building methods, and availability of materials, our Materials Lists do not include mechanical materials. To obtain necessary take-offs and recommendations, consult heating, plumbing and electrical contractors. Materials Lists are not sold separately from the Blueprint Package.)

This handy list helps you or your builder cost out materials and serves as a ready reference sheet when you're compiling bids. It also provides a cross-check against the materials specified by your builder and helps coordinate the substitution of items you may need to meet local codes.

SPECIFICATION OUTLINE

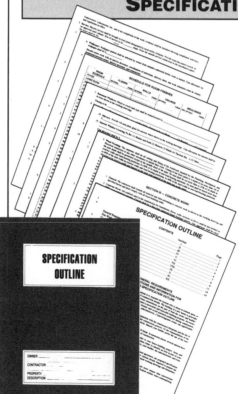

This valuable 16-page document is critical to building your house correctly. Designed to be filled in by you or your builder, this booklet lists 166 stages or items crucial to the building process.

For the layman, it provides a comprehensive review of the construction process and helps in making the specific choices of materials, models and processes. For the builder, it serves as a guide to preparing a building quotation and forms the basis for the construction program.

Designed primarily as a reference for the homeowner, this Specification Outline can become a legally binding document. Once it is filled out and agreed upon by owner and builder, it becomes a complete Project Specification.

When combined with the blueprints, a signed contract and schedule, the Specification Outline becomes a legal document and record for the building of your home. Many home builders find it useful to order two of these outlines—one as a worksheet in formulating the specifications and another to be carefully completed as a legal document.

DETAIL SHEETS

If you want to know more about techniques—and deal more confidently with subcontractors—we offer these remarkably useful detail sheets. Each is an excellent tool that will enhance your understanding of these technical subjects.

Plan-A-Home®

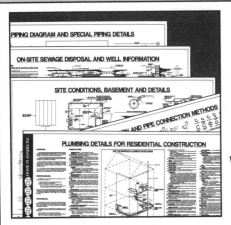

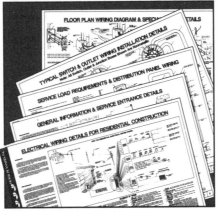

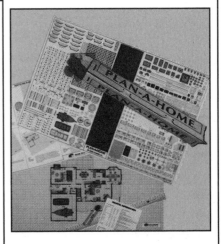

PLUMBING

The Blueprint Package includes locations for all the plumbing fixtures in your new house, including sinks, lavatories, tubs, showers, toilets, laundry trays and water heaters. However, if you want to know more about the complete plumbing system, these 24x36-inch detail sheets will prove very useful. Prepared to meet requirements of the National Plumbing Code, these six fact-filled sheets give general information on pipe schedules, fittings, sump-pump details, water-softener hookups, septic system details and much more. Color-coded sheets include a glossary of terms.

ELECTRICAL

The locations for every electrical switch, plug and outlet are shown in your Blueprint Package. However, these Electrical Details go further to take the mystery out of household electrical systems. Prepared to meet requirements of the National Electrical Code, these comprehensive 24x36-inch drawings come packed with helpful information, including wire sizing, switch-installation schematics, cable-routing details, appliance wattage, door-bell hookups, typical service panel circuitry and much more. Six sheets are bound together and color-coded for easy reference. A glossary of terms is also included.

Plan-A-Home® is an easy-to-use tool that helps you design a new home, arrange furniture in a new or existing home, or plan a remodeling project. Each package contains:

- More than *700 peel-off planning symbols* on a self-stick vinyl sheet, including walls, windows, doors, all types of furniture, kitchen components, bath fixtures and many more. All are made of durable, peel-and-stick vinyl you can use over and over.

- A reusable, transparent, *1/4-inch scale planning grid* made of tough mylar that matches the scale of actual working drawings (1/4 -inch equals 1 foot). This grid provides the basis for house layouts of up to 140x92 feet.

- *Tracing paper* and a protective sheet for copying or transferring your completed plan.

- A *felt-tip pen*, with water-soluble ink that wipes away quickly.

CONSTRUCTION

The Blueprint Package contains everything an experienced builder needs to construct a particular house. However, it doesn't show all the ways that houses can be built, nor does it explain alternate construction methods. To help you understand how your house will be built—and offer additional techniques—this set of drawings depicts the materials and methods used to build foundations, fireplaces, walls, floors and roofs. Where appropriate, the drawings show acceptable alternatives. These six sheets will answer questions for the advanced do-it-yourselfer or home planner.

MECHANICAL

This package contains fundamental principles and useful data that will help you make informed decisions and communicate with subcontractors about heating and cooling systems. The 24 x 36-inch drawings contain instructions and samples that allow you to make simple load calculations and preliminary sizing and costing analysis. Covered are today's most commonly used systems from heat pumps to solar fuel systems. The package is packed full of illustrations and diagrams to help you visualize components and how they relate to one another.

With Plan-A-Home®, you can make basic planning decisions for a new house or make modifications to an existing house. Use with your Blueprint Package to test modifications to rooms or to plan furniture arrangements before you build. Plan-A-Home® lets you lay out areas as large as a 7,500 square foot, six-bedroom, seven-bath house.

D *The Deck Blueprint Package*

Many of the homes in this book can be enhanced with a professionally designed Deck Plan. Those home plans highlighted with a **D** have a matching or corresponding deck plan available which includes a Deck Plan Frontal Sheet, Deck Framing and Floor Plans, Deck Elevations and a Deck Materials List. A Standard Deck Details Package, also available, provides all the how-to information necessary for building *any* deck. Our Complete Deck Building Package contains 1 set of Custom Deck Plans of your choice, plus 1 set of Standard Deck Building Details all for one low price. Our plans and details are carefully prepared in an easy-to-understand format that will guide you through every stage of your deck-building project. Twelve of our 25 different Deck layouts to match your favorite house are illustrated below.

SPLIT–LEVEL SUN DECK
Deck Plan D100

BI–LEVEL DECK WITH COVERED DINING
Deck Plan D101

FRESH–AIR CORNER DECK
Deck Plan D102

BACK–YARD EXTENDER DECK
Deck Plan D103

WRAP–AROUND FAMILY DECK
Deck Plan D104

DRAMATIC DECK WITH BARBECUE
Deck Plan D105

SPLIT–PLAN COUNTRY DECK
Deck Plan D106

OUTDOOR LIFESTYLE DECK
Deck Plan D118

CONTEMPORARY LEISURE DECK
Deck Plan D120

WEEKEND ENTERTAINER DECK
Deck Plan D112

TREND–SETTER DECK
Deck Plan D110

TURN–OF–THE–CENTURY DECK
Deck Plan D111

⬛ *The Landscape Blueprint Package*

For the homes marked with an ⬛ in this book, Home Planners has created a front-yard landscape plan that matches or is complementary in design to the house plan. These comprehensive blueprint packages include a Frontal Sheet, Plan View, Regionalized Plant & Materials List, a sheet on Planting and Maintaining Your Landscape, Zone Maps and Plant Size and Description Guide. These plans will help you achieve professional results, adding value and enjoyment to your property for years to come. Each set of blueprints is a full 18" x 24" in size with clear, complete instructions and easy-to-read type. See below for six of our 25 different front-yard Landscape Plans to match your favorite house.

Regional Order Map

Most of the Landscape Plans shown on these pages are available with a Plant & Materials List adapted by horticultural experts to 8 different regions of the country. Please specify Geographic Region when ordering your plan. See pages 378-380 for prices, ordering information and regional availability.

Region	1	Northeast
Region	2	Mid-Atlantic
Region	3	Deep South
Region	4	Florida & Gulf Coast
Region	5	Midwest
Region	6	Rocky Mountains
Region	7	Southern California & Desert Southwest
Region	8	Northern California & Pacific Northwest

CAPE COD TRADITIONAL
Landscape Plan L200

RAISED–PORCH FARMHOUSE
Landscape Plan L209

GEORGIAN MANOR
Landscape Plan L214

SPRAWLING RANCH
Landscape Plan L227

CALIFORNIA STUCCO
Landscape Plan L233

LOW–GABLE CONTEMPORARY
Landscape Plan L234

Price Schedule & Plans Index

House Blueprint Price Schedule
(Prices guaranteed through December 31, 1993)

	1-set Study Package	4-set Building Package	8-set Building Package	1-set Reproducible Sepias
Schedule A	$210	$270	$330	$420
Schedule B	$240	$300	$360	$480
Schedule C	$270	$330	$390	$540
Schedule D	$300	$360	$420	$600
Schedule E	$390	$450	$510	$660

Additional Identical Blueprints in same order...............$50 per set
Reverse Blueprints (mirror image)..................................$50 per set
Specification Outlines ....$7 each
Materials Lists (for Home Planners', Design Basics', Alan Mascord's, and Donald Gardner's Plans only):
- ▲ Home Planners' Designs
  - Schedule A-D $40
  - Schedule E $50
- † Design Basics' Designs.............................$75
- ✳ Alan Mascord's Designs $40
- ◆ Donald Gardner's Designs......................$40

Deck Plans Price Schedule

CUSTOM DECK PLANS

Price Group	Q	R	S
1 Set Custom Plans	$25	$30	$35

Additional identical sets..$10 each
Reverse sets (mirror image)...$10 each

STANDARD DECK DETAILS
1 Set Generic Construction Details..................................$14.95 each

COMPLETE DECK BUILDING PACKAGE

Price Group	Q	R	S
1 Set Custom Plans, plus 1 Set Standard Deck Details	$35	$40	$45

Landscape Plans Price Schedule

Price Group	X	Y	Z
1 set	$35	$45	$55
3 sets	$50	$60	$70
6 sets	$65	$75	$85

Additional Identical Sets ....$10 each
Reverse Sets (mirror image)..$10 each

These pages contain all the information you need to price your blueprints. In general, the larger and more complicated the house, the more it costs to design and thus the higher the price we must charge for the blueprints. Remember, however, that these prices are far less than you would normally pay for the services of a licensed architect or professional designer.

Custom home designs and related architectural services often cost thousands of dollars, ranging from 5% to 15% of the cost of construction. By ordering our blueprints you are potentially saving enough money to afford a larger house, or to add those "extra" amenities such as a patio, deck, swimming pool or even an upgraded kitchen or luxurious master suite.

Index

To use the Index below, refer to the design number listed in numerical order (a helpful page reference is also given). Note the price index letter and refer to the House Blueprint Price Schedule above for the cost of one, four or eight sets of blueprints or the cost of a reproducible sepia. Additional prices are shown for identical and reverse blueprint sets, as well as a very useful Materials List for some of the plans. Also note in the Index below those plans that have matching or complementary Deck Plans or Landscape Plans. Refer to the schedules above for prices of these plans. Some of our plans can be customized through Home Planners ' Home Customizer® Service. These plans are indicated below with this symbol: 🏠 See page 381 for more information.

To Order: Fill in and send the order form on page 381—or call toll free 1-800-521-6797.

DESIGN	PRICE	PAGE	CUSTOMIZABLE	DECK	DECK PRICE	LANDSCAPE	LANDSCAPE PRICE	REGIONS
Y1700	C	100						
Y1701	B	58		D117	S			
Y1718	B	54		D114	R	L210	Y	1-3,5,6,8
Y1719	A	96		D105	R	L203	Y	1-3,5,6,8
Y1787	C	49		D117	S			
Y1791	B	57		D114	R	L205	Y	1-3,5,6,8
Y1849	B	97						
Y1856	A	104		D117	S			
Y1858	C	228		D101	R			
Y1870	B	59						
Y1887	B	94						
Y1900	C	78						
Y1956	A	148	🏠	D117	S			
Y1970	C	51		D100	Q			
Y1987	B	56		D101	R	L203	Y	1-3,5,6,8
Y2100	C	197						
Y2101	B	84						
Y2102	C	196						
Y2103	B	100		D124	S			
Y2131	B	58		D117	S	L203	Y	1-3,5,6,8
Y2132	C	233				L201	Y	1-3,5,6,8
Y2139	B	237						
Y2145	A	38				L209	Y	1-6,8
Y2146	A	39		D114	R	L203	Y	1-3,5,6,8
Y2157	C	137						
Y2174	B	153		D117	S	L220	Y	1-3,5,6,8
Y2176	B	237		D112	R	L206	Z	1-6,8
Y2184	C	258						
Y2185	C	259						
Y2188	C	195						
Y2191	C	85				L222	Y	1-3,5,6,8
Y2192	D	217		D117	S	L218	Z	1-6,8
Y2211	B	105		D117	S	L201	Y	1-3,5,6,8
Y2221	C	194						
Y2223	B	151		D112	R	L205	Y	1-3,5,6,8
Y2225	D	41						
Y2230	D	246						
Y2250	C	236						
Y2253	C	101						
Y2283	C	256		D114	R	L206	Z	1-6,8
Y2301	D	238						
Y2320	D	127						
Y2395	B	60						
Y2396	B	59		D100	Q			

DESIGN	PRICE	PAGE	CUSTOMIZABLE	DECK	DECK PRICE	LANDSCAPE	LANDSCAPE PRICE	REGIONS
Y2398	B	86						
Y2399	B	90						
Y2500	B	152		D100	Q	L204	Y	1-3,5,6,8
Y2505	A	335	🏠	D113	R	L226	X	1-8
Y2520	B	231		D105	R	L201	Y	1-3,5,6,8
Y2521	B	47						
Y2522	C	189						
Y2538	B	99		D113	R	L201	Y	1-3,5,6,8
Y2539	B	98						
Y2540	B	105		D113	R	L205	Y	1-3,5,6,8
Y2542	D	140				L208	Z	1,2,5,6,8
Y2556	C	181		D103	R			
Y2559	B	61	🏠	D112	R			
Y2563	B	55		D114	R	L201	Y	1-3,5,6,8
Y2565	B	334		D101	R	L225	X	1-3,5,6,8
Y2569	A	60		D112	R	L200	X	1-3,5,6,8
Y2571	A	62		D114	R	L202	X	1-3,5,6,8
Y2596	B	61		D114	R	L201	Y	1-3,5,6,8
Y2599	C	151		D100	Q			
Y2600	C	193						
Y2610	C	102		D114	R	L204	Y	1-3,5,6,8
Y2614	C	152		D114	R			
Y2615	D	37		D106	S	L211	Y	1-8
Y2616	B	91	🏠					
Y2622	A	103		D103	R	L200	X	1-3,5,6,8
Y2623	B	102		D100	Q	L205	Y	1-3,5,6,8
Y2631	B	57		D112	R	L201	Y	1-3,5,6,8
Y2632	B	144						
Y2633	C	124						
Y2635	A	42						
Y2636	A	43						
Y2638	C	234						
Y2639	C	190		D114	R	L215	Z	1-3,5,6,8
Y2640	B	177		D1214	R			
Y2641	C	186						
Y2642	B	87						
Y2644	B	52						
Y2645	C	309				L224	Y	1-3,5,6,8
Y2646	B	308		D114	R	L224	Y	1-3,5,6,8
Y2647	D	309				L224	Y	1-3,5,6,8
Y2649	C	93						
Y2650	B	128		D117	S	L201	Y	1-3,5,6,8
Y2651	C	88						
Y2652	C	44						
Y2653	C	192						
Y2654	A	92						
Y2655	A	28				L200	X	1-3,5,6,8
Y2656	B	53		D105	R	L203	Y	1-3,5,6,8
Y2657	B	32				L200	X	1-3,5,6,8
Y2658	A	50						
Y2659	B	178		L113	R	L202	X	1-3,5,6,8
Y2660	D	261	🏠					
Y2661	A	24		D113	R	L202	X	1-3,5,6,8
Y2662	C	222				L216	Y	1-3,5,6,8
Y2663	B	268						
Y2664	B	122		D113	R			
Y2665	D	240						
Y2666	B	80						
Y2667	B	221				L216	Y	1-3,5,6,8
Y2668	B	244				L214	Z	1-3,5,6,8
Y2680	C	132		D114	R			
Y2681	B	145	🏠					
Y2682	A	30		D115	Q	L200	X	1-3,5,6,8
Y2683	D	214		D101	R	L214	Z	1-3,5,6,8
Y2684	C	235		D114	R	L204	Y	1-3,5,6,8
Y2685	C	142						
Y2686	C	269		D112	R	L209	Y	1-6,8
Y2687	C	174		D117	S	L204	Y	1-3,5,6,8
Y2688	B	271						
Y2689	B	45						
Y2690	C	191						
Y2691	B	232						
Y2692	C	89						

DESIGN	PRICE	PAGE	CUSTOMIZABLE	DECK	DECK PRICE	LANDSCAPE	LANDSCAPE PRICE	REGIONS
Y2693	D	249						
Y2694	C	120				L209	Y	1-6,8
Y2695	C	230						
Y2696	D	243						
Y2697	C	130						
Y2698	B	274						
Y2699	C	36	🏠			L211	Y	1-8
Y2707	A	332		D117	S	L226	X	1-8
Y2731	B	99		D114	R	L205	Y	1-3,5,6,8
Y2733	B	104	🏠	D100	Q	L205	Y	1-3,5,6,8
Y2774	B	147		D100	Q	L207	Z	1-6,8
Y2775	B	150	🏠			L207	Z	1-6,8
Y2776	B	138		D113	R	L207	Z	1-6,8
Y2786	B	149						
Y2799	A	96						
Y2840	C	194						
Y2852	A	62		D105	R	L202	X	1-3,5,6,8
Y2865	C	153		D114	R			
Y2870	A	197	🏠					
Y2878	B	326		D112	R	L200	X	1-3,5,6,8
Y2888	D	40				L211	Y	1-8
Y2889	D	239		D107	S	L215	Z	1-6,8
Y2890	C	139		D114	R			
Y2897	C	95						
Y2898	C	272		D118	R			
Y2899	C	236						
Y2907	B	146	🏠					
Y2908	B	148	🏠	D117	S	L205	Y	1-3,5,6,8
Y2921	D	26		D104	S	L212	Z	1-8
Y2938	E	361						
Y2940	E	364	🏠	D114	R			
Y2946	E	147		D114	R	L207	Z	1-6,8
Y2947	B	325		D112	R	L200	X	1-3,5,6,8
Y2951	E	366						
Y2952	E	370				L235	Z	1-3,5,6,8
Y2953	E	312		D111	S	L223	Z	1-3,5,6,8
Y2954	E	314				L223	Z	1-3,5,6,8
Y2955	E	367						
Y2956	E	371						
Y2957	D	369		D107	S	L218	Z	1-6,8
Y2963	D	154						
Y2968	E	362						
Y2969	C	296		D110	R	L223	Z	1-3,5,6,8
Y2970	D	299				L223	Z	1-3,5,6,8
Y2971	C	297				L223	Z	1-3,5,6,8
Y2972	B	306	🏠			L223	Z	1-3,5,6,8
Y2973	B	306				L223	Z	1-3,5,6,8
Y2974	A	301				L223	Z	1-3,5,6,8
Y2975	D	226						
Y2976	C	143						
Y2977	D	251				L214	Z	1-3,5,6,8
Y2978	C	82						
Y2979	C	198						
Y2980	C	183						
Y2981	D	135						
Y2982	C	229						
Y2983	A	34						
Y2984	E	257						
Y2986	B	46						
Y2987	D	254						
Y2988	B	136		D120	R	L201	Y	1-3,5,6,8
Y2989	D	188				L215	Z	1-6,8
Y2990	D	218						
Y2991	D	262		D111	S	L215	Z	1-6,8
Y2992	E	184		D103	R	L203	Y	1-3,5,6,8
Y2993	D	260		D115	Q	L214	Z	1-3,5,6,8
Y2994	E	187		D105	R	L216	Y	1-3,5,6,8
Y2995	D	48		D106	S	L217	Y	1-8
Y2996	E	134		D111	S	L235	Z	1-3,5,6,8
Y2997	D	270		D106	S	L214	Z	1-3,5,6,8
Y2998	D	185		D103	R	L210	Y	1-3,5,6,8
Y2999	N	224		D105	R	L218	Z	1-6,8
Y3300	E	365						

Before You Order . . .

Before completing the coupon at right or calling us on our toll-free Blueprint Hotline, you may be interested to learn more about our services and products. Here's some information you will find helpful.

Quick turnaround

We process and ship every blueprint order from our office within 48 hours. On most orders, we do even better. Normally, if we receive your order by 5 p.m. Eastern time, we'll process it the same day and ship it the following day. Because of this quick turnaround, we won't send a formal notice acknowledging receipt of your order.

Our exchange policy

Since blueprints are printed in response to your order, we cannot honor requests for refunds. However, we will exchange your entire first order for an equal number of blueprints at a price of $40 for the first set and $10 for each additional set; $60 total exchange fee for 4 sets; $90 total exchange fee for 8 sets . . . *plus* the difference in cost if exchanging for a design in a higher price bracket or *less* the difference in cost if exchanging for a design in a lower price bracket. (Sepias are not exchangeable.) All sets from the first order must be returned before the exchange can take place. Please add $8 for postage and handling via ground service; $20 via 2nd Day Air.

About reverse blueprints (mirror image)

If you want to build in reverse of the plan as shown, we will include an extra set of reversed blueprints (mirror image) for an additional fee of $50. Although lettering and dimensions appear backward, reverses will be a useful visual aid if you decide to flop the plan.

Modifying or customizing our plans

With such a great selection of homes, you are bound to find the one that suits you. However, alterations can be made to many of the plans—call our Customizer Specialist at 800/322-6797, ext 800 to see if the plan you would like to build can be customized. The Home Customizer® Kit (for customizing many of Home Planners' designs) may be purchased by using the order form at right.

Architectural and engineering seals

Some cities and states are now requiring that a licensed architect or engineer review and "seal" your blueprints prior to construction. This is often due to local or regional concerns over energy consumption, safety codes, seismic ratings, etc. For this reason, you may find it necessary to consult with a local professional to have your plans reviewed. This can normally be accomplished with minimum delays and for a nominal fee.

Compliance with local codes and regulations

At the time of creation, our plans are drawn to specifications published by Building Officials Code Administrators (BOCA), the Southern Standard Building Code, or the Uniform Building Code, and are designed to meet or exceed national building standards.

Some states, counties, and municipalities have their own codes, zoning requirements, and building regulations. Before starting construction, consult with local building authorities and make sure you comply with local ordinances and codes, including obtaining any necessary permits or inspections as building progresses. In some cases, minor modifications to your plans by your builder, local architect, or designer may be required to meet local conditions and requirements. We may be able to make these changes to customizable plans providing you supply all pertinent information from your local building authorities.

Foundation and exterior wall changes

Most of our plans are drawn with either a full or partial basement foundation. Depending upon your specific climate or regional building practices, you may wish to convert this basement to a slab or crawl space. If your plan can be customized, we'll be happy to make this change for you. If not, most professional contractors and builders can easily adapt your plans to alternate foundation types. Likewise, most can easily convert 2 x 4 wall construction to 2 x 6, or vice versa.

How many blueprints do you need?

A single set of blueprints is sufficient to study a home in greater detail. However, if you are planning to obtain cost estimates from a contractor or subcontractors—or if you are planning to build immediately—you will need more sets. Because additional sets are cheaper when ordered in quantity with the original order, make sure you order enough blueprints to satisfy all requirements. The following checklist will help you determine how many you need:

_____ Owner

_____ Builder (generally requires at least three sets; one as a legal document, one to use during inspections, and at least one to give to subcontractors)

_____ Local Building Department (often requires two sets)

_____ Mortgage lender (usually one set for a conventional loan; three sets for FHA or VA loans)

_____ TOTAL NUMBER OF SETS

The Home Customizer®

Many of the plans in this book are customizable through our Home Customizer® service. Look for this symbol 🏠 on the pages of home designs. It indicates that the plan on that page is part of The Home Customizer® service.

Some changes to customizable plans that can be made include:

- exterior elevation changes
- kitchen and bath modifications
- roof, wall and foundation changes
- room additions
- and much more!

If the plan you have chosen to build is one of our customizable homes, you can easily order the Home Customizer® kit to start on the path to making your alterations. The kit, priced at only $19.95, may be ordered at the same time you order your blueprint package by calling on our toll-free number or using the order blank at right. Or you can wait until you receive your blueprints, spend some time studying them and then order the kit by phone, FAX or mail. If you then decide to proceed with the customizing service, the $19.95 price of the kit will be refunded to you after your customization order is received. The Home Customizer® kit includes:

- instruction book with examples
- architectural scale
- clear acetate work film
- erasable red marker
- removable correction tape
- ¼" scale furniture cutouts
- 1 set of Customizable Drawings with floor plans and elevations

The service is easy, fast and *affordable*. Because we know and work with our plans and have them available on state-of-the-art computer systems, we can make the changes efficiently at prices much lower than those charged by normal architectural or drafting services. In addition, you'll be getting custom changes directly from Home Planners—the company whose dedication to excellence and long-standing professional experience are well recognized in the industry.

Call now to learn more about how simple it can be to have the *custom home* you've always wanted.

☎ Toll Free
1-800-322-6797, Ext. 800

Toll Free 1-800-521-6797

Normal Office Hours:
8:00 a.m. to 8:00 p.m. Eastern Time
Monday through Friday
Our staff will gladly answer any questions during normal office hours. Our answering service can place orders after hours or on weekends.

If we receive your order by 5:00 p.m. Eastern Time, Monday through Friday, we'll process it the same day and ship it the following business day. When ordering by phone, please have your charge card ready. We'll also ask you for the Order Form Key Number at the bottom of the coupon. Please use our Toll-Free number for blueprint and book orders only.
For Customization orders call 1-800-322-6797, ext. 800.

By FAX: Copy the Order Form on the next page and send it on our International FAX line: 1-602-297-6219.

Canadian Customers
Order Toll-Free 1-800-848-2550
For faster, more economical service, Canadian customers may now call in orders on our Toll-Free line. Or, complete the order form at right adding 30% to all prices and mail in Canadian funds to:

Home Planners, Inc.
3275 W. Ina Road, Suite 110
Tucson, AZ 85741

By FAX: Copy the Order Form at right and send it on our International FAX line: 1-602-297-6219.

ORDER FORM

HOME PLANNERS, INC., 3275 WEST INA ROAD
SUITE 110, TUCSON, ARIZONA 85741

THE BASIC BLUEPRINT PACKAGE
Rush me the following (please refer to the Plans Index and Price Schedule in this section):

_____ Set(s) of blueprints for plan number(s) _____.		$_____
_____ Set(s) of sepias for plan number(s) _____.		$_____
_____ Additional identical blueprints in same order @ $50.00 per set.		$_____
_____ Reverse blueprints @ $50.00 per set.		$_____
_____ Home Customizer® Kit(s) for Plan(s)_____ @ $19.95 per kit.		$_____

IMPORTANT EXTRAS
Rush me the following:

_____ Materials List: Home Planners' Designs @ $40 Schedule A-D; $50 Schedule E; $75 Design Basics' Designs; $40 Alan Mascord's Designs; $40 Donald Gardner's Designs. $_____

_____ Specification Outlines @ $7.00 each. $_____

_____ Detail Sets @ $14.95 each; any two for $22.95; any three for $29.95; all four for $39.95 (save $19.85). $_____
❏ Plumbing ❏ Electrical ❏ Construction ❏ Mechanical (These helpful details provide general construction advice and are not specific to any single plan.)

_____ Plan-A-Home® @ $29.95 each. $_____

DECK BLUEPRINTS
_____ Set(s) of Deck Plan _____. $_____
_____ Additional identical blueprints in same order @ $10 per set. $_____
_____ Reverse blueprints @ $10 per set. $_____
_____ Set of Standard Deck Details @ $14.95 per set. $_____
_____ Set of Complete Building Package (Best Buy!) Includes Custom Deck Plan _____ (See Index and Price Schedule) Plus Standard Deck Details $_____

LANDSCAPE BLUEPRINTS
_____ Set(s) of Landscape Plan _____. $_____
_____ Additional identical blueprints in same order @ $10.00 per set. $_____
_____ Reverse blueprints @ $10.00 per set. $_____

Please indicate the appropriate region of the country for Plant & Material List. (See Map on page 377): Region _____

SUB-TOTAL $_____

SALES TAX (Arizona residents add 5% sales tax; Michigan residents add 4% sales tax.) $_____

POSTAGE AND HANDLING	1-3 sets	4 or more sets	
DELIVERY (Requires street address - No P.O. Boxes)			
•Regular Service Allow 4-6 days delivery	❏ $6.00	❏ $8.00	$_____
•2nd Day Air Allow 2-3 days delivery	❏ $12.00	❏ $20.00	$_____
•Next Day Air Allow 1 day delivery	❏ $22.00	❏ $30.00	$_____
POST OFFICE DELIVERY If no street address available. Allow 4-6 days delivery	❏ $8.00	❏ $12.00	$_____
OVERSEAS AIR MAIL DELIVERY Note: All delivery times are from date Blueprint Package is shipped.	❏ $30.00	❏ $50.00	$_____
	❏ Send COD		

TOTAL (Sub-total, tax, and postage) $_____

YOUR ADDRESS (please print)

Name _____

Street _____

City _____ State _____ Zip _____

Daytime telephone number (_____) _____

FOR CREDIT CARD ORDERS ONLY
Please fill in the information below:
Credit card number _____
Exp. Date: Month/Year _____
Check one ❏ Visa ❏ MasterCard ❏ Discover Card

Signature _____

Order Form Key   Please check appropriate box:
┌─────────┐   ❏ Licensed Builder-Contractor
│ TB30   │   ❏ Home Owner
└─────────┘

☎ **ORDER TOLL FREE**
1-800-521-6797

Additional Plans Books

THE DESIGN CATEGORY SERIES

1.

2.

3.

4.

ONE-STORY HOMES
A collection of 470 homes to suit a range of budgets in one-story living. All popular styles, including Cape Cod, Southwestern, Tudor and French. **384 pages. $8.95 ($11.95 Canada)**

TWO-STORY HOMES
478 plans for all budgets in a wealth of styles: Tudors, Saltboxes, Farmhouses, Victorians, Georgians, Contemporaries and more. **416 pages. $8.95 ($11.95 Canada)**

MULTI-LEVEL AND HILL-SIDE HOMES 312 distinctive styles for both flat and sloping sites. Includes exposed lower levels, open staircases, balconies, decks and terraces. **320 pages. $6.95 ($9.95 Canada)**

VACATION AND SECOND HOMES 258 ideal plans for a favorite vacation spot or perfect retirement or starter home. Includes cottages, chalets, and 1-, 1½-, 2-, and multi-levels. **256 pages. $5.95 ($7.95 Canada)**

THE EXTERIOR STYLE SERIES

9.

10.

11.

12.

THE ESSENTIAL GUIDE TO TRADITIONAL HOMES
Over 400 traditional homes in one special volume. American and European styles from Farmhouses to Norman French. "Readers' Choice" highlights best sellers in four-color photographs and renderings. **304 pages. $9.95 U.S. ($12.95 Canada)**

THE ESSENTIAL GUIDE TO CONTEMPORARY HOMES More than 340 contemporary designs from Northwest Contemporary to Post-Modern Victorian. Four-color section of best sellers; two-color illustrations and line drawings throughout the remainder. **304 pages. $9.95 U.S. ($12.95 Canada)**

VICTORIAN DREAM HOMES 160 Victorian and Farmhouse designs by three master designers. Victorian style from Second Empire homes through the Queen Anne and Folk Victorian era. Beautifully drawn renderings accompany the modern floor plans. **192 pages. $12.95 ($16.95 Canada)**

WESTERN HOME PLANS
Over 215 home plans from Spanish Mission and Monterey to Northwest Chateau and San Francisco Victorian. Historical notes trace the background and geographical incidence of each style. **208 pages. $8.95 ($11.95 Canada)**

OUR BEST PLAN PORTFOLIOS

NEW ENCYCLOPEDIA OF HOME DESIGNS
Our best collection of plans is now bigger and better than ever! Over 500 plans organized by architectural category including all types and styles and 269 brand-new plans. The most comprehensive plan book ever.

AFFORDABLE HOME PLANS For the prospective home builder with a modest or medium budget. Features 430 one-, 1½-, two-story and multi-level homes in a wealth of styles. Included are cost saving ideas for the budget-conscious.

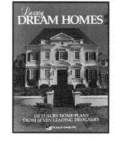

LUXURY DREAM HOMES At last, the home you've waited for! A collection of 150 of the best luxury home plans from seven of the most highly regarded designers and architects in the United States. A dream come true for anyone interested in designing, building or remodeling a luxury home.

15. **352 pages. $9.95 ($12.95 Canada)**

16. **320 pages. $8.95 ($11.95 Canada)**

17. **192 pages. $14.95 ($17.95 Canada)**

HOME IMPROVEMENT AND LANDSCAPE BOOKS

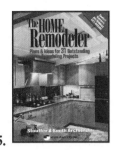

5.

THE HOME REMODELER
A revolutionary book of 31 remodeling plans backed by complete construction-ready blueprints and materials lists. Sections on kitchens, baths, master bedrooms and much more. Ideas galore; helpful advice and valuable suggestions. **112 pages. $7.95 U.S. ($10.95 Canada)**

6.

DECK PLANNER 25 practical plans and details for decks the do-it-yourselfer can actually build. How-to data and project starters for a variety of decks. Construction details available separately. **112 pages. $7.95 ($10.95 Canada)**

7.

THE HOME LANDSCAPER
55 fabulous front and back-yard plans that even the do-it-youselfer can master. Complete construction blueprints and regionalized plant lists available for each design. **208 pages. $12.95 ($16.95 Canada)**

8.

BACKYARD LANDSCAPER Sequel to the popular *Home Landscaper*, contains 40 professionally designed plans for backyards to do yourself or contract out. Complete construction blueprints and regionalized plant lists available. **160 pages. $12.95 ($16.95 Canada)**

INTRODUCING THE NEW BLUE RIBBON DESIGNER SERIES

13.

200 FARMHOUSES & COUNTRY HOME PLANS Styles and sizes to match every taste and budget. Grouped by type, the homes represent a variety from Classic Farmhouses to Country Capes & Cottages. Introductions and expertly drawn floor plans and renderings enhance the sections. **224 pages. $6.95 ($9.95 Canada)**

14.

200 BUDGET-SMART HOME PLANS The definitive source for the home builder with a limited budget, this volume shows that you can have your home and enjoy it, too! Amenity-laden homes, in many sizes and styles, can all be built from our plans. **224 pages. $6.95 ($9.95 Canada)**

Please fill out the coupon below. We will process your order and ship it from our office within 48 hours. Send coupon and check for the total to:

HOME PLANNERS, INC.
3275 West Ina Road, Suite 110, Dept. BK
Tucson, Arizona 85741

THE DESIGN CATEGORY SERIES—A great series of books edited by design type. Complete collection features 1376 pages and 1273 home plans.

1. ____One-Story Homes @ $8.95 ($11.95 Canada)	$ _____
2. ____Two-Story Homes @ $8.95 ($11.95 Canada)	$ _____
3. ____Multi-Level & Hillside Homes @ $6.95 ($9.95 Canada)	$ _____
4. ____Vacation & Second Homes @ $5.95 ($7.95 Canada)	$ _____

HOME IMPROVEMENT AND LANDSCAPE BOOKS

5. ____The Home Remodeler @ $7.95 ($10.95 Canada)	$ _____
6. ____Deck Planner @ $7.95 ($10.95 Canada)	$ _____
7. ____The Home Landscaper @ $12.95 ($16.95 Canada)	$ _____
8. ____The Backyard Landscaper @ $12.95 ($16.95 Canada)	$ _____

THE EXTERIOR STYLE SERIES

9. ____Traditional Homes Plans @ $9.95 ($12.95 Canada)	$ _____
10. ____Contemporary Homes Plans @ $9.95 ($12.95 Canada)	$ _____
11. ____Victorian Dream Homes @ $12.95 ($16.95 Canada)	$ _____
12. ____Western Home Plans @ $8.95 ($11.95 Canada)	$ _____

THE BLUE RIBBON DESIGNER SERIES

13. ____200 Farmhouse & Country Home Plans @ $6.95 ($9.95 Canada)	$ _____
14. ____200 Budget-Smart Home Plans @ $6.95 ($9.95 Canada)	$ _____

OUR BEST PLAN PORTFOLIOS

15. ____New Encyclopedia of Home Designs @ $9.95 ($12.95 Canada)	$ _____
16. ____Affordable Home Plans @ $8.95 ($11.95 Canada)	$ _____
17. ____Luxury Dream Homes @ $14.95 ($17.95 Canada)	$ _____
Sub-Total	$ _____
Arizona residents add 5% sales tax; Michigan residents add 4% sales tax	$ _____
ADD Postage and Handling	$ _____
TOTAL (Please enclose check)	$ 3.00

Name (please print) _____

Address _____

City _____ State _____ Zip _____

CANADIAN CUSTOMERS: Order books Toll-Free 1-800-848-2550. Or, complete the order form above, using Canadian prices, and mail with your check in Canadian funds to: Home Planners, Inc. 3275 W. Ina Road, Suite 110, Tucson, AZ 85741.

 TO ORDER BOOKS BY PHONE CALL TOLL FREE 1-800-322-6797

TB30BK

INDEX

SEE WAINSCOT DETAIL - SHEET #13

DOOR TO
LINEN CL.

DOOR TO
BEDROOM

ENTRANCE
DOOR

7'-0"

3'-0"

1'-2"

2x8 STUDS @ 16" O.C.

12" HIGH CORNICE - SEE DETAIL SHEET #

4 - 2x12 HEADER

5'-0"

19'-2" PLATE HEIGHT

16 RISERS @ 7.56" = 10'-1"

STAIRS BY:
PRAIRE STAR
PRODUCTS INC.
P.O. BOX 544
#2 SERVICE RD. EAST
WHITE CITY, SASK.
CANADA   SOG 580

2 - 2'-0" x 7'
TO KITCHEN

4" CONCRETE SLAB

3'-0"

DR CORNICE DETAIL

DOOR TO
POWDER ROOM

FRONT ENT.
DOOR

4/8

3/4 x 1 1/4" CAP

3/4 x 2 1/2" CASING

1/2" DRYWALL

SEE WAINSCOT DETAIL SHEET #13

WITHDRAWN

JUN 0 3 2024

DAVID O. McKAY LIBRARY
BYU-IDAHO

BIFOLD
CLOSET DOOR

DOOR TO
KITCHEN

DOOR TO
POWDER ROOM

4'-0" x 7'-5" ELIPTICAL
HEAD ARCH OPENING
TO COUNTRY KITCHEN

3'-0"

5"   5"